Illustrations by Edward Shenton

New York ∾ London ∾ Toronto ∾ Sydney

Cross Creek

by Marjorie Kinnan Rawlings

A TOUCHSTONE BOOK

Published by Simon & Schuster

TOUCHSTONE
Rockefeller Center
1230 Avenue of the Americas
New York, NY 10020

First Touchstone Edition 1996

Designed by Elina D. Nudelman
Manufactured in the United States of America

21

Library of Congress Cataloging-in-Publication Data
Rawlings, Marjorie Kinnan, 1896–1953.
   Cross Creek / by Marjorie Kinnan Rawlings—1st Touchstone ed.
     p.   cm.
   "A Touchstone book."
     1. Rawlings, Marjorie Kinnan, 1896–1953—Homes and haunts—
Florida—Cross Creek. 2. Women authors, American—20th century—
Biography. 3. Women authors, American—Florida—Biography.
4. Cross Creek (Fla.)—Social life and customs. 5. Farm life—
Florida—Cross Creek. I. Title.
PS3535.A845Z467   1996
813'.52—dc20
[B]   95-51012
                                                            CIP

ISBN 978-0-684-81879-5

Contents

Cross Creek 9

1. For This Is an Enchanted Land 15
2. Taking Up the Slack 26
3. The Magnolia Tree 36
4. The Pound Party 48
5. The Census 56
6. The Evolution of Comfort 64
7. Antses in Tim's Breakfast 72
8. The Widow Slater 77
9. Catching One Young 85
10. 'Geechee 90
11. A Pig Is Paid For 105
12. My Friend Moe 116
13. Residue 130
14. Toady-frogs, Lizards, Antses, and Varmints 152
15. The Ancient Enmity 175
16. Black Shadows 189
17. Our Daily Bread 215
18. Spring at the Creek 254
19. Summer 279
20. Fall 309
21. Winter 322
22. Hyacinth Drift 354
23. Who Owns Cross Creek? 371

Cross Creek

*C*ross Creek is a bend in a country road, by land, and the flowing of Lochloosa Lake into Orange Lake, by water. We are four miles west of the small village of Island Grove, nine miles east of a turpentine still and on the other sides we do not count distance at all, for the two lakes and the broad marshes create an infinite space between us and the horizon. We are five white families; "Old Boss" Brice, the Glissons, the Mackays and the Bernie Basses; and two colored families, Henry Woodward and the Mickenses. People in Island Grove consider us just a little biggety and more than a little queer. Black Kate and I between us once misplaced some household object, quite unreasonably.

I said, "Kate, am I crazy, or are you?"

She gave me her quick sideways glance that was never entirely impudent.

"Likely all two of us. Don't you reckon it take somebody a little bit crazy to live out here at the Creek?

At one time or another most of us at the Creek have been suspected of a degree of madness. Madness is only a variety of mental nonconformity and we are all individualists here. I am reminded of Miss Malin and the Cardinal in the Gothic tale, "The Deluge at Norderney."

"But are you not," said the Cardinal, "a little—"

"Mad?" asked the old lady. "I thought that you were aware of that, My Lord."

The Creek folk of color are less suspect than the rest of us. Yet there is something a little different about them from blacks who live gregariously in Quarters, so that even if they did not live at the Creek, they would stay, I think, somehow aloof from the layer-cake life of the average Negro. Tom Glisson and Old Boss and I think anybody is crazy not to live here, but I know what Kate meant. We have chosen a deliberate isolation, and are enamored of it, so that to the sociable we give the feeling that St. Simeon Stylites on top of his desert pillar must have given the folk who begged him to come down and live among them. He liked the pillar or he would not have been there. Something about it suited his nature. And something about Cross Creek suits us—or something about us makes us cling to it contentedly, lovingly and often in exasperation, through the vicissitudes that have driven others away.

"I wouldn't live any place else," Tom said, "if I had gold buried in Georgia. I tell you, so much happens at Cross Creek."

There is of course an affinity between people and places. "And God called the dry land Earth; and the gathering together of waters called He Seas; and God saw that it was good." This was before man, and if there be such a thing as racial memory, the consciousness of land and water must lie deeper in the core of us than any knowledge of our fellow beings. We were bred of earth before we were born of our mothers. Once born, we can live without mother or father, or any other kin, or any friend, or any human love. We cannot live without the earth or apart from it, and something is shrivelled in a man's heart when he turns away from it and concerns himself only with the affairs of men.

And along with our deep knowledge of the earth is a preference of each of us for certain different kinds of it, for the earth is various as we are various. One man longs for the mountains, and does not even need to have been a child of the mountains to have this longing; and another man yearns for the valleys or the plains. A seaman I know said that he was making a great effort to assure himself of going to Hell, for the Bible says that in Heaven "there shall be no more sea," and Heaven for him is a place of great waters.

We at the Creek need and have found only very simple things. We must need flowering and fruiting trees, for all of us have citrus groves of one size or another. We must need a certain blandness of season, with a longer and more beneficent heat than many require, for there is never too much sun for us, and through the long summers we do not complain. We need the song of birds, and there is none finer than the red-bird. We need the sound of rain coming across the *hamaca*, and the sound of wind in trees—and there is no more sensitive Aeolian harp than the palm. The pine is good, for the needles brushing one another have a great softness, and we have the wind in the pines, too.

We need above all, I think, a certain remoteness from urban confusion, and while this can be found in other places, Cross Creek offers it with such beauty and grace that once entangled with it, no other place seems possible to us, just as when truly in love none other offers the comfort of the beloved. We are not even offended when others do not share our delight. Tom Glisson and I often laugh together at the people who consider the Creek dull, or, in the precise sense, outlandish.

"There was a fellow woke me up," he said, "was lost. I'd heard his car go by and hit the Creek bridge like cattle stompeding. I wondered if ary one in that big of a hurry knowed where he was going. Directly he come back and stopped and I heard him holler from the gate. I pulled on my breeches and went out to him. I said, 'Reckon you're lost.' 'Lost ain't the word for it,' he said. 'Is this the end of the world? Where in God's name am I?' I said. 'Mister, you're at Cross Creek.' 'That don't tell me a thing,' he said. 'I still ain't anywhere.'"

"People in town sometimes say to me when I start home at night," I said, "'We hate to see you drive off alone to that awful place.'"

"Well," he said comfortably, "they just don't know the Creek."

We do. We know one another. Our knowledge is a strange kind, totally without intimacy, for we go our separate ways and meet only when new fences are strung, or some one's stock intrudes on another, or when one of us is ill or in trouble, or when woods fires come too close, or when a shooting occurs and we must agree who is right and who must go to jail, or when the weather is so preposterous, either as to heat or cold, or rain or drought, that we seek out excuses to be together, to talk together about the common menace. We get into violent arguments and violent quarrels, sometimes about stock, sometimes because we take sides with our favorites when the dark Mickens family goes on the warpath. The village exaggerates our differences and claims that something in the Creek water makes people quarrelsome. Our amenities pass unnoticed. We do injustices among ourselves, and another of us, not directly involved, usually manages to put in a judicious word on the side of right. The one who is wrong usually ends by admitting it, and all is well again, and I have done my share of the eating of humble pie. And when the great enemies of Old Starvation and Old Death come skulking down on us, we put up a united front and fight them side by side, as we fight the woods fires.

Each of us knows the foibles of the others and the strength and the weaknesses, and who can be counted on for what. Old Aunt Martha Mickens, with her deceptive humility and her face like poured chocolate, is perhaps the shuttle that has woven our knowledge, carrying back and forth, with the apparent innocence of a nest-building bird, the most revealing bits of gossip; the sort of gossip that tells, not trivial facts, but human motives and the secrets of human hearts. Each of us pretends that she carries these threads only about others and never about us, but we all know better, and that none of us is spared.

A dozen other whites, and a baker's dozen of other blacks have lived at one time or another among us, or in the immediate vicinity of the Creek, coming and going like the robins. We are clannish and do not feel the same about them as we feel about ourselves. It was believed in the beginning that I was one of these. Surely the Creek would drive me away. When it was clear that a freezing of the orange crop was as great a catastrophe to me as to the others, surely I would not be here long. It was when old Martha, who had set up the Brices as Old Boss and Old Miss, referred to me one day as Young Miss, that it was understood by all of us that I was here to stay.

For myself, the Creek satisfies a thing that had gone hungry and unfed since childhood days. I am often lonely. Who is not? But I should be lonelier in the heart of a city. And as Tom says, "So much happens here." I walk at sunset, east along the road. There are no houses in that direction, except the abandoned one where the wild plums grow, white with bloom in springtime. I usually walk halfway to the village and back again. No one goes, like myself, on foot, except Bernie Bass perhaps, striding firmly in rubber boots with his wet sack of fish over his shoulder. Sometimes black Henry passes with a mule and wagon, taking a load of lighter'd home to Old Boss; sometimes a neighbor's car, or the wagon that turns off toward the turpentine woods to collect the resin, or the timber truck coming out from the pine woods. The white folks call "Hey!" and children wave gustily and with pleasure. A stranger driving by usually slows down and asks whether I want a lift. The Negroes touch a finger to their ragged caps or pretend courteously not to see me. Evening after evening I walk as far as the magnolias near Big Hammock, and home, and see no one.

Folk call the road lonely, because there is not human traffic and human stirring. Because I have walked it so many times and seen such a tumult of life there, it seems to me one of the most populous highways of my acquaintance. I have walked it in ecstasy, and in joy it is beloved. Every pine tree, every gallberry bush, every passion vine, every joree rustling in the underbrush, is vibrant. I have walked it in trouble, and the wind in the trees beside me is easing. I have walked it in despair, and the red of the sunset is my own blood dissolving into the night's darkness. For all such things were on earth before us, and will survive after us, and it is given to us to join ourselves with them and to be comforted.

1. For this is an enchanted land

The road goes west out of the village, past open pine woods and gallberry flats. An eagle's nest is a ragged cluster of sticks in a tall tree, and one of the eagles is usually black and silver against the sky. The other perches near the nest, hunched and proud, like a griffon. There is no magic here except the eagles. Yet the four miles to the Creek are stirring, like the bleak, portentous beginning of a good tale. The road curves sharply, the vegetation thickens, and around the bend masses into dense hammock. The hammock breaks, is pushed back on either side of the road, and set down in its brooding heart is the orange grove.

Any grove or any wood is a fine thing to see. But the magic here, strangely, is not apparent from the road. It is necessary to leave the impersonal highway, to step inside the rusty gate and close it behind. By this, an act of faith is committed, through which one accepts blindly the communion cup of beauty. One is now inside the grove, out of one world and in the mysterious heart of another. Enchantment lies in different things for each of us. For me, it is in this: to step out of the bright sunlight into the shade of orange trees; to walk under the arched canopy of their jadelike leaves; to see the long aisles of lichened trunks stretch ahead in a geometric rhythm; to feel the mystery of a seclusion that yet has shafts of light striking through it. This is the essence of an ancient and secret magic. It goes back, perhaps, to the fairy tales of childhood, to Hansel and Gretel, to Babes in the Wood, to Alice in Wonderland, to all half-luminous places that pleased the imagination as a child. It may go back still farther, to racial Druid memories, to an atavistic sense of safety and delight in an open forest. And after long years of spiritual homelessness, of nostalgia, here is that mystic loveliness of childhood again. Here is home. An old thread, long tangled, comes straight again.

I think that the shabbiness of the Creek is a part of its endearing quality. I for one might admire, but never truly love, an affluent perfection. The Williamsburg restoration, for instance, is fine and proud, but it is something only to be stared at. Old Williamsburg lived in a genteel poverty that was more elegant than the new shining Governor's mansion, for its gentility came not from superimposed wealth but from long years of gracious living. The restoration is a good thing, of course, and Time will make all come right again. The Creek shabbiness was never elegant and never will be. It is merely comfortable and weather-beaten, meeting Time halfway. I am sometimes tempted to put up a new fence across the house yard. I have always thought that a white picket fence must be a great comfort to a householder. I think of the pride I should take in seeing white paint gleaming from around the bend in the road. Then Snow the grove man becomes quietly tired of waiting for me to do something, and comes driving the farm truck into the yard over the cattle-gap with a load of fresh fatwood pine posts from the hammock.

He asks, "You aim just to use the old gate, don't you?"

I aim to use the old gate, and say so, and Snow goes ahead and replaces the rotten and sagging posts with new ones. He tightens the fence wire, "Hog and cattle 4-inch mesh," and the effect is trim and eminently suitable. I tell myself that a white picket fence would interfere with the feeling one has inside the house of being a part of the grove; that a new fence would mean tearing out the coral honeysuckle vines that cling passionately to the old wire. But the real objection is that an elegant fence would bring to the Creek a wanton orderliness that is out of place.

When I came to the Creek, and knew the old grove and farmhouse at once as home, there was some terror, such as one feels in the first recognition of a human love, for the joining of person to place, as of person to person, is a commitment to shared sorrow, even as to shared joy. The farmhouse was all dinginess. It sat snugly then as now under tall old orange trees, and had a simple grace of line, low, rambling and one-storied. But it was cracked and gray for lack of paint, there was a tin roof that would have ruined a mansion, and the porch was an excrescence, scarcely wide enough for one to pass in front of the chairs. The yard was bare sand spotted with sandspurs, with three lean Duchess rosebushes left behind to starve, like cats. Inside the house, all the delight of the Florida sunlight vanished. The walls were painted a battleship gray and the floors a muddy ochre. The brick fireplaces were walled over with tin and filled with a year's rubbish. It was four years before the gray of the last room was decently covered with white, money for paint being scarce, and time so filled with other work that an hour with the brush was a stolen pleasure. And even now, the house shining inside and out, roofed with good gray hand-hewn cypress shingles, the long wide screened veranda an invitation to step either inside or out, the yard in lush green grass, there is still a look of weather-worn shabbiness. It is a constant reminder that wind and rain and harsh sun and the encroaching jungle are ready at any moment to take over. I suppose that a millionaire, perhaps even just a New Englander, might stand off the elements and maintain a trim tidiness—and a picket fence. But the rest of the Creek would not know what to make of it, and would be made most unhappy.

The battle has not gone too well for all at the Creek. One or two have gone ahead, some hold precariously to the narrow ledge of existence, and others have slipped back, and back, until each day's subsistence has become a triumph. Their houses reflect their fortunes. Mine lies the farthest east in the small settlement. To the west are my neighbors, my friends. There have been enmities. At the moment, we are living in unparalleled amiability, a state at Cross Creek that, like a sinner's hope of Heaven, is never assured. But it makes a good moment in which to speak of other people.

I live within screaming distance of Tom Glisson and Old Boss Brice. This is literal. No ordinary sound carries from one place to the other. We hear faintly the barking of one another's dogs. We hear the far crowing at dawn of one another's roosters. Occasionally, when the wind is right, I hear the Brice or Glisson cows lowing at milking time, night or morning. No voice carries, ever. A determined scream is audible. This I proved, not in a time of fear, but a time of fury. I should be ashamed but am not. Of folk who would have been silent under the circumstances, there comes to mind only St. Francis, and I believe that he might have cast despairing eyes to Heaven.

I can bear much physical discomfort and a great deal of actual pain, but now and then one achieves a combination of bodily annoyances that makes Job's boils seem a luxury. I shall be brief and explicit. I was entirely alone on the grove. The summer was one of the two unbearable ones, as to heat, that I have known in my years here. Summer is our unproductive period for vegetables. I had been some time without them, and was afflicted with an itching rash that I recognized too late as nutritional. The Widow Slater and I had been repairing fences together, for I gave her pasture for her milch cow in return for milking my own. We had plowed through long vines of poison ivy along the decrepit fence. Her long black flowing skirts had evidently protected her. I had worked stockingless and in brief voile. The poison ivy had erupted from hips to ankle, from fingertips to throat, overlaying the rash.

Soothing ointments and a prone position might have brought some ease. I was far from ointments and too busy to lie down. My cow broke loose from the pasture and came into the grove, tearing at the low-hanging orange boughs. I drove her out and penned her properly, and returning to the house, found myself in the middle of a patch of sandspurs waist-high. These barbed instruments of torture are all the proof one needs that there is a devil as well as a God. I was enmeshed with sandspurs, they stuck to voile skirt and to petticoat, creeping up underneath and getting a firm hold with one or two barbs, leaving the others free to grate against my skin. On normal skin they are like arrows. On a skin covered with rash and poison ivy, they were shafts of fire. I plucked at them as I went and came to the house. There the dogs were waiting for me, shut on the back porch, since they had nothing but chaos to contribute in the matter of penning a cow.

I did not think they had been there very long. Even for puppies, it did not seem too much to ask of them that they wait like gentlemen for, say, half an hour. There were four, all told. There was my own puppy. There were two of his litter mates that the travelling owner had asked me to keep for him. There was old Sport, whose huntsman master, my friend Fred, had left with me while he fished on the east coast. I can only relate that time is relative, and that what seemed like a short period to me, was evidently a long, long time in the minds of three puppies. Old Sport had become excited at their incontinence and forgotten himself, too. The porch was a shambles. Water for cleansing had to be brought from the outside pump, a bucket at a time. It took twenty buckets, as I remember, and dusk was on me when I finished.

I went then, the porch well cleaned, wet and glistening in the fading light, to water my garden. There were a few carrots that I hoped to bring through the heat, a few zinnias, half a dozen desperate collard plants, poor things but mine own. I pulled away sandspurs abstractedly as I carried out the watering pot. The mosquitoes descended on me. One would think that exposed neck, arms and face would suffice the hungriest of insects. But a mosquito is Freudian, taking delight only in the hidden places. They wavered with their indecisive flight up under my skirts and stabbed me in the poison ivy, in the nutritional rash, around the sandspurs, and settled with hums of joy in all unoccupied small spaces. It was too much. I set down the watering pot, and with no thought of help for my distress, for I was past helping, let out shriek after shriek of sheer indulgent frustration. As I say, St. Francis might have blessed the puppies and old Sport and the mosquitoes, with a kind word thrown in for the sandspurs, but I am not of the stuff of saints. I screamed. The screaming satisfied me. I finished the watering, went into the house, fed the dogs, made myself a supper, and went to the veranda to meditate. As I sat, exhausted but content, two figures strolled cautiously up the road and paused in front of my gate. It was Tom Glisson and Old Boss.

Old Boss called, "Everything all right?"

"Why, yes," I said. "Yes, indeed."

Tom said, "Seemed to us like we heard somebody call for help. We just wondered, was everything all right."

I hesitated. After all, there was nothing to be done, and at the moment, it seemed, all was too embarrassing to be told.

"I was singing," I said. "Perhaps you heard me—singing."

"Oh," they said, and turned and walked home again.

So I say that I live within screaming distance of my nearest neighbors.

Old Boss' grove joins up with mine. We share an east-west fence line and a double row of spite trees. The spite is none of our doing, but an inheritance from earlier owners of the adjoining groves. There was a day, before the Big Freeze of '94–'95, when oranges were truly golden apples, bringing, in their rareness, incredible sums. Suitable orange land was considered worth its weight in gold. So the two unfriendly neighbors planted their orange trees, each as close to the joint fence as possible, to get all the good of the priceless soil. The result is that two lines of scrawny trees send out their roots futilely in search of sufficient nourishment. Among large trees, there are few of whom two can live as cheaply as one.

Old Boss wandered down to Florida from Georgia as a boy, nearly sixty years ago. He came down to die, he told me once, and wanted to die in the tropical sunshine. He is still a frail little man, but I think he drew sustenance from the sun and earth and the fruiting trees around him. He clerked in a country store in the village and became the owner. He yearned always for the Creek, he said. At last he took over the neglected grove on an unpaid mortgage and moved out. It means to him precisely what it means to me, and we sometimes sit together on his back porch and just look about us and say nothing. We seldom meet, but when we see each other down the road, we wave, and I know that the same warm feeling comes over the old man that comes to me. He has been father, arbiter, disciplinarian to all the Negroes who have ever lived or worked here. I challenged his authority on one occasion, but that is another story. His house is a rococo two-story affair, tall and gangling like an antique spinster. There is bamboo in the sandy yard, and hibiscus and allamanda, and a pittosporum that is so old it is not a shrub, but a great tree, covered in spring with minute flowers of a strange exotic scent. The house is on the opposite side of the road from mine, just out of sight.

Tom Glisson lives on the same side of the road as I do, and opposite Old Boss. Tom has prospered. He and his wife are Georgia folk, too, and as hard workers as I have ever known. I am not at all sure that Tom can read or write, but he talks well, with a flair for the picturesque and the dramatic. He was put to the plow when he was so small he could scarcely reach the plow handles, he told me. He was given no education.

"I made up my mind," he said, "my young uns would get a better chance than their daddy."

It has been good to see the three children grow tall and bright and handsome. The oldest boy even had a year at the University. The youngest, "J. T.," was a tragic little cripple when I first knew him. I would see him hobbling down the road on his crooked legs, with the luminous expression on his face that seems peculiar to those we call the "afflicted." Tom and his wife were not of the breed to accept an evil that could be changed, and they worked day and night to save money to send the boy away for braces and treatments. Now he too is tall and strong, and I saw him ride by yesterday on his own dwarf-mule, talking to himself and lifting his hand to an invisible audience. He was, I knew, the Lone Ranger or perhaps Buck Rogers, but he took time out courteously from his duties to call "Hey!" to me, then returned to his important and secret activities.

The Glisson house is small and brown, well kept, and the yard has been slowly given shrubs and even a bit of grass. Tom raises hogs and some cattle, has built up a little grove, and he and his wife do anything profitable they can turn their hands to. They have fought ill health as well as poverty, and it is sometimes hard to feel sympathy for what seem offhand less fortunate people, knowing what can be done with courage and hard work and thrift. Tom and I began with a strange mistrust of each other, and had some harsh encounters. I was in the wrong, and that is a story, too, and now I know him for a friend and would turn to him in any trouble.

There are no further houses until you take the sharp curve in the road that sweeps down to the Creek itself. There is a patch of thick hammock, an open field, and then, on the right, Old Joe's abandoned house. Old Joe Mackay is the last of a good farming family. The Mackay acres were well-tilled and profitable some fifty years ago. There has been no regular cultivation for years, though now and then lately some farmer from the village rents the largest cleared field to raise some special crop. Old Joe lived alone in the old Mackay house. He is ageless in appearance, small and stooped and wiry, with his thin face ruddy from being on Orange Lake in every sort of weather. He runs a catfish line for a living. The house is as silver gray as the speckled perch he sometimes catches. It is a tall box of a house and even in its desertion maintains a look of sturdy livability. It was a good house in its day. Something about it is beautiful, its color most of all, and tall palms bend over it, and there are live oaks and holly and a few orange trees around it, and the hammock is a soft curtain beyond it. It was because he had a house that he was able to get a wife. His good friend Tom Morrison found a very pretty widow. He married the pretty widow to Old Joe, and Tom and Old Joe and the widow and the widow's children lived happily in the house.

Tom said, "Somebody has to look out for Old Joe."

I suppose the roof leaked, as old roofs do. The cockroaches may have become too abundant in the walls and floors. At any rate, the contented family left the house a few years ago and moved a hundred yards closer to the Creek, into the abandoned church on the same side of the road. They put up partitions to make rooms, moved the old pews out into the yard and swept out the hymnbooks. The church has made a fine home. It sits under a magnificent live oak and is cozy in winter and cool in summer.

The old Mackay house was turned over for a time to Aunt Martha Mickens and her husband, Old Will. It was agreed that Martha and Will, progenitors of all the colored help that had ever been at the Creek, should be brought back home again. Old Joe's wife found Martha good company when she was alone. There was trouble, and Martha and Will were obliged to leave, and that again is a story. The old Mackay house is now tenantless. But it is still hospitable, and when some family in the environs finds itself temporarily roofless, it moves in for a time, and then moves on again. The house has sheltered a slow stream of deserted husbands and wives with large numbers of children, homeless for the moment.

At an angle from the bend in the road is a deep sand road that leads through hammock, and past the north edge of Old Boss' grove, to another house. The house is not the same one that was there when I first came to the Creek. It seems as though one house, one family, is all the dusky break in the forest will tolerate. The house I used to know belonged to Old Boss and was inhabited by the Widow Slater and her brood. The Slater house lived from rain to rain and the Slaters from hand to mouth. The widow moved back to Carolina with her "chappies," leaving Snow behind, and in time he became my grove-man and co-worrier over the hazardous fortunes of my grove. The Slater house, stricken of the moral support of human occupancy, fell promptly to the ground. Now there is another small house up the deep hammock road. The Bernie Basses live there.

This makes up the white population of the Creek. Across the lovely Creek itself, over the narrow bridge, are scattered in a migratory flux two or three other families. We do not say of them that they live "at" the Creek but that they live "beyond" it. Mr. Martin is a newcomer. He has prospered and I presume he is here to stay. It looked at one time as though the Creek area were too small to hold both me and Mr. Martin. If Mr. Martin had put me under the jail, as he threatened, or sent me to eternity by way of gunshot, as he wanted, I should have made an effort to take his big burly body along to either place with me. We have become good friends. I was never angry with Mr. Martin. He was only angry with me.

Past Mr. Martin's place have been Mr. Swilley and George Fairbanks and the Townsends and Mr. Marsh Turner. Mr. Swilley has gone of late to a widow and Mr. Marsh Turner has gone to Hell. I know he is in Hell by his own choice. And even if the Angel Gabriel forgave his sins, as his friends did, and called him to Heaven, that peaceful and virtuous stamping ground would above all be Hell to Marsh. George Fairbanks drifts from cabin to cabin and the Townsends drift from one new baby to another. They have a young un, as we say, every time the woods burn, and each one is welcome and a fresh surprise.

The colored population of the Creek has the solid base of the Mickens family, against which other transient Negroes surge and retreat. When old Martha Mickens shall march at last through the walls of Jericho, shouting her Primitive Baptist hymns, a dark rock at the core of the Creek life will have been shattered to bits. She is nurse to any of us, black or white, who fall ill. She is midwife and layer out of the dead. She is the only one who gives advice to all of us impartially. She is a dusky Fate, spinning away at the threads of our Creek existence.

2. Taking up the slack

*I*t is always bewildering to change one's complete way of life. I was fitted by temperament and by inheritance for farm and country living, yet to take it up after some thirty years of urban life was not too easy. I had known my maternal grandfather's Michigan farm, but there I was both guest and child, and the only duties were to gather the eggs from the sweet-smelling hayloft. I had known my father's Maryland farm, but that farm was his love, his escape from Washington governmental routine, and we lived there only in the too few summers. I had no duties there at all. There was only delight; the flowering locust grove; the gentle cows in pasture; Rock Creek, which ran, ten miles away from its Washington park, at the foot of the hill of the locusts, where my brother and I learned to swim and to fish for tiny and almost untakable fishes; long walks with my father through the woods where he hoped some day to build a home; jaunts with him behind Old Dan in the carriage, to the county seat of Rockville, or to buy mules at Frederick. These things got in the blood but were no preparation for running a farm oneself. When I bought the Florida orange grove with my inheritance that represented my share of the Maryland farm, my father's sister Madeline wrote me in lament.

"You have in you," she said, "that fatal drop of Pearce blood, clamoring for change and adventure, and above all, for a farm. I never knew a Pearce who didn't secretly long for a farm. Mother had one, Uncle Pierman was ruined by one, there was your father's tragic experience. I had one, once—."

I see no reason for denying so fundamental an urge, ruin or no. It is more important to live the life one wishes to live, and to go down with it if necessary, quite contentedly, than to live more profitably but less happily. Yet to achieve content under sometimes adverse circumstances, requires first an adjustment within oneself, and this I had already made, and after that, a recognition that one is not unique in being obliged to toil and struggle and suffer. This is the simplest of all facts and the most difficult for the individual ego to accept. As I look back on those first difficult times at the Creek, when it seemed as though the actual labor was more than I could bear, and the making of a living on the grove impossible, it was old black Martha who drew aside a curtain and led me in to the company of all those who had loved the Creek and been tormented by it.

Martha welcomed me with old-fashioned formality. She came walking toward me in the grove one bright sunny December day. I turned to watch her magnificent carriage. It was erect, with a long free graceful stride. It was impossible to tell her age. She walked like a very young woman and walks so to this day. She is getting on to seventy, yet glimpsing her down the road she might be a girl. She was dressed neatly in calico, with a handkerchief bound around her head, bandana fashion. She was a rich smooth brown. She came directly to me and inclined her head.

She said, "I come to pay my respecks. I be's Martha. Martha Mickens."

I said, "How do you do, Martha."

She said, "I wants to welcome you. Me and my man, Old Will, was the first hands on this place. Time the grove was planted, me and Will worked here. It's home to me."

"Where do you live now?"

"T' other side o' the Creek. We too old now to do steady work, but I just wants to tell you, any time you gets in a tight, us is here to do what we can."

"How long has it been since you worked here on the grove?"

"Sugar," she said, "I got no way o' tellin' the years. The years comes and the years goes. It's been a long time."

"Was it the Herberts you worked for?"

"Yessum. They was mighty fine folks. They's been fine folks here since and they's been trash. But Sugar, the grove ain't trash, and the Creek be's trashified here and there, but it's the Creek right on. I purely loves the Creek."

I said, "I love it, too."

"Does you? Then you'll make out. I reckon you know, you got to be satisfied with a place to make out. And is you satisfied, then it don't make too much difference does you make out or no."

We laughed together.

She said, "Heap o' folks has lived here. Ain't nobody has lived here since the Herberts but had to scratch and scramble. The ones loved it, stayed 'til death or sich takened 'em away. The ones ain't loved it, has moved on like the wind moves."

I said, "The grove hasn't always made a living, then."

"'Pends on what you calls a livin'. To get yo' grease an' grits in the place you enjoys gettin' 'em, ain't that makin' a livin'?"

"Yes."

"Then lemme tell you. Ain't nobody never gone cold-out hongry here. I'se seed the grove freeze to the ground. I'se seed it swivvel in a long drought. But Sugar, they was grove here before my folks crossed the big water. They was wild grove here as long back as tongue can tell. Durin' the war for freedom the white ladies used to drive out here in wagons and pick the wild oranges to squeeze out the juice and send it to the sojers. And they'll be grove here right on, after you and me is forgotten. They'll be good land to plow, and mast in the woods for hogs, and ain't no need to go hongry. All the folks here ahead o' you has fit cold and wind and dry weather, but ain't nary one of 'em has goed hongry."

Hunger at the moment was not immediate, but when it menaced later, I remembered the things the old black woman said, and I was comforted, sensing that one had only to hold tight to the earth itself and its abundance. And if others could fight adversity, so might I.

"I won't keep you," she said. "I jes' wanted to tell you I was here."

She bobbed her head and went away.

She lived at the time four miles away, across the Creek, in an old gray house immaculately kept, with oleanders and dogwood in the clean bare yard. She had always "porch plants" about, grown from slips, of geranium and aspidistra; fuchsia, "the Georgia flower," sansivaria and elephant-ear and impatient Sultana, all blooming lushly in containers of old tin. She walked the four miles back and forth to help in the bean field or the cucumber patch, to nurse the sick, to wash and clean for Old Boss or the Mackays or, as time went on, for me. About her, the nucleus, were her sons and daughters and their wives and husbands, who worked transiently for the rest of us. The best of her daughters, to my personal knowledge, is Estelle. There is a very elegant daughter who works for a wealthy family outside of

Baltimore, and of her I know nothing, except that she sends her mother good clothes not too much worn. Estelle and her husband Sam worked many years for Old Boss. They lived at the edge of the road and were patient and faithful, except that Sam had an unwonted impudence "under the influence." A son-in-law of Old Boss was somehow unable to deal with Sam, and in a huff he took Estelle and moved off to Hawthorn. Estelle is gentle and softspoken like her mother.

For a long time I knew of Zamilla only that she was "the one what got shot." I pictured a leaf-brown hussy subject to brawling, whose wild life finally caught up with her. I was never more mistaken. When Sam and Estelle cleared out in righteous indignation, Old Boss notified Martha that it was up to her to replace her delinquent offspring. Henry and Sissie appeared on the scene and took over the small cabin. Sissie, too, was gentle, bearing Henry's abuse when he was drunk and, absurdly, jealous. One day I discovered that Sissie was the wounded Zamilla, shot innocently in a jook from which she was trying to extricate her husband. The shot was probably intended for Henry, and much as I like him, sober, I know of no darky who more deserves shooting when drunk.

Adrenna is a daughter whose life became so involved with mine that I have wondered where one ended and the other began. She was a lean angular creature whom at first I took to be a girl, but found to be of my own age. She was shingle-butted, but what there was of butt stuck out sharply. She was a *femme fatale*, and I have never been able to identify any possible appeal she might have for the colored men, unless it be that little square boxlike rear. She was careless in her dress and cleanliness, to Martha's distress, and mine, and usually wore her hair in Topsy pigtails that stuck out around her face like a halo. She could seduce any man she wanted, for the moment, but she could not hold them, or, if they were faithful, she grew tired of them.

She did my work for several years and there was true love and exasperation between us. Our involvement came through her attempts to capture a husband. The husband must serve a dual purpose. He must provide her with whatever she wanted of a husband, and me with a good grove and yard man. Adrenna and I fell constantly between the upper and the nether millstone.

"Little Will" Mickens, her brother, is my grove man at this instant, and while all seems well, I can guarantee nothing by the time this chronicle goes to press. Other sons and daughters of Martha are scattered here and there through the state.

"I was a fast-breedin' woman," Martha says with dignity and without apology. Such things are elemental, a matter of fact. "I got sympathy for a woman is a fast-breeder."

When any of the daughters working at the Creek are ill or absent or brought to child-bed, or the sons or husbands are drunk and cannot do their work, Martha takes their places. Last winter a freeze menaced and Little Will was taken suddenly drunk. Martha came without notice to gather Spanish moss to cover the flower plants in my garden. I drove in from town and found her bending over the plants.

"I always likes to take up the slack," she said.

There have been occasions when her slack-taking has been so zealous as better to have gone untaken. I left the Creek for a vacation at a beach cottage seventy miles away. Adrenna left behind by accident six napkins that I had picked up at the dime store for twenty cents. The morning after our arrival at the cottage, my farm truck clattered up to the door. Little Will presented me breathlessly with a neatly wrapped package.

"Mama sont me to carry you these. She say she jes' know you wanted 'em. She say, tell you you don't never need worry when Adrenna forget things. She see you gets 'em."

The parcel contained the twenty cents' worth of napkins. The round trip for the truck stood me several dollars. Will had left the grove fertilizing in the very middle, while the extra hands must sit idle, waiting for the return of the truck to move the fertilizer. I accepted the napkins and sent him on his way. Two hours later he returned on foot. The truck had broken a spring on a rough back road. I was editing a story to meet a magazine deadline and was obliged to drop my work, arrange for a new spring and a repairman from the nearest city. The job cost fifteen dollars, the details filled my day, and it was night before Little Will reached the grove again. I take a rueful satisfaction in using the flimsy napkins, saying to friends, "Please be careful. These napkins are worth about six dollars apiece." My only dividend on the investment is their puzzled expression at my bad taste and the obvious worthlessness of the napkins. I take no more chances on Martha's slack-taking. Whenever I leave the Creek for the beach, I say, "If we leave anything behind, do not send the truck with it." I have probably deprived her of many triumphs in despatching a pound of butter or a magazine by farm express.

We call Martha "old-timey." That means specifically that to our white faces she presents a low-voiced deference, to our backs an acute criticism, and to the colored world a tongue before which it bows as before a flail. She has an inviolable sense of proportion. It comes of the gift, and I think it is a gift, that many of her alleged superiors do not possess, of seeing people as they are. Wealth does not impress her, on the rare occasions when she encounters it. "Fame" is a word without meaning. Those few of the worldly great who have paused briefly at the Creek have passed before her silent appraisal as they must pass that of St. Peter. On the other hand, the poorest tramp receives a kind word from her if she senses in him that integrity that even the most fortunate often possess. I fed one such one day, for at the Creek the hungry have a great claim on us. The ragged creature blessed me as he went away with his full stomach and small gifts.

"It will all come back to you," he said, "many times over."

It was of course the ancient response of the mendicant, through whom the charitable curry favor in the sight of the gods, but the man had something more.

Martha said, "That ain't no beggar. That's a person."

She has her own standards of payment for services rendered. She accepts nothing from those too poor to pay. When I came to my own lean period, and found that I could not carry all the manual labor alone, she washed and cleaned for me, at the current rate of ten cents an hour. She would not cheapen herself by loitering over her work, to draw a higher pay, and was always finished in a few hours. I paid her the small sums with guilt and necessity. She accepted with infinite politeness. Now, when accident has raised my fortunes, I pay her generously for the smallest labors, and she accepts the over-pay with equal understanding. Who knows better than she that one pays as one can, and that the Lord giveth and the Lord taketh away? Blessed be the name of the Lord.

None of her get is of the same stuff as her own. If she were white I should call her a natural aristocrat, and I see no reason to withhold the adjective because of color or race. She is illiterate, she can tell a judicious lie when necessary, she does not know sterling silver from aluminum, and scours old English Sheffield along with the cooking pots and pans. But she is well-bred. Breeding is after all a matter of manner, of social adjustment, of exquisite courtesy. Perhaps she is descended from old African kings and queens. At any rate, the hallmark is on her.

Old Will, her husband, some ten years older than she, is almost of her breed. He has the arrogance of the elite but not the graciousness. Many of the quarrels at the Creek have been of his instigating.

Perhaps he too came of a regal line but a more belligerent one. He looks for all the world like Uncle Tom, with grizzled hair and whiskers, and walks with a cane. The cane is a badge of his independence, indicating that he is frail and cannot or will not stoop to labor. But he was a hard worker in his day and made money on cotton and at sharecropping of all sorts. When I am his age, if I have no other subsistence, I think that I too shall walk with a cane and accept a livelihood as my right, after years of toiling.

Martha is a Primitive, or foot-washing, Baptist, militant and certain of her doctrines. She does not go often to church only because there is none nearby of her denomination. There was a Primitive Baptist church across the Creek when I first came, but the leader absconded with the hard-saved church funds, and his house, which was also the meeting-house, was quite properly struck by lightning and burned to the ground by the wrath of the Lord. Martha is an inexhaustible fount of old spirituals. When we get hungry for song, she gathers several of her family together, lines them up in a row and "leads off." Her voice is high and reedlike and utterly true. The other voices weave in and out of her melody, sometimes only humming, for some of the songs are so rare and old that only she is familiar with the words. Her favorite, and mine, is "Come, Mary, toll the bell." For this, she throws back her kerchiefed head, closes her eyes, pats her foot and accompanies herself with an intricate syncopation of hand clapping. Rhythm-minded friends attempt to follow her timing, charmed by its perfection, and can never duplicate the fine shading of beats. Her son-in-law Henry is her favorite to sing with her, for he too knows many of the old songs, and has a rich sweet bass that ripples like velvet under the silver of her voice. Unfortunately Henry is often in disfavor and we must sing without him. It is of no use ever for me to ask him to sing "St. Louis Blues" or "Coon-shine Baby."

"Mama don't let me sing them low-down songs where she can hear it," he says.

I wonder often what she thinks of the mysterious business that is my writing. Once in the midst of creative difficulties, I said facetiously, "Martha, I'm in trouble. I'll do the washing if you'll write this chapter for me."

"Sugar," she said gravely, "God knows I'd do it if I could."

I recall the time I rang late for my breakfast coffee. It seemed necessary to apologize for the hour, for at the Creek one is not quite decent who is not up with the red-birds.

I said, "I'm sorry to be so late. I worked very late last night at my writing."

She said compassionately, "Oh Sugar, I knows you're tired in the arms."

There is indeed much writing that sounds as though the only possible fatigue to the author were manual, but working as I do with great mental anguish, I could hope that a trace of celebration might register, even for Martha. Pride pricked me, I think, or the need of self-justification that Martha is likely to impose on one, and that day I showed her my published books. She recognized my picture on a jacket and turned the unintelligible pages with a cautious black finger. She put her hands on her hips and threw back her head.

"Sugar," she said, "they ain't nobody at Cross Creek can do that."

3. *The magnolia tree*

I do not know the irreducible minimum of happiness for any other spirit than my own. It is impossible to be certain even of mine. Yet I believe that I know my tangible desideratum. It is a tree-top against a patch of sky. If I should lie crippled or long ill, or should have the quite conceivable misfortune to be clapped in jail, I could survive, I think, given this one token of the physical world. I know that I lived on one such in my first days at the Creek.

The tree was a magnolia, taller than the tallest orange trees around it. There is no such thing in the world as an ugly tree, but the *magnolia grandiflora* has a unique perfection. No matter how crowded it may be, no matter how thickly holly and live oak and sweet gum may grow up around it, it develops with complete symmetry, so that one wonders whether character in all things, human as well as vegetable, may not be implicit. Neither is its development ruthless, achieved at the expense of its neighbors, for it is one of the few trees that may be allowed to stand in an orange grove, seeming to steal nothing from the expensively nourished citrus. The young of the tree is courteous, waiting for the parent to be done with life before presuming to take it over. There are never seedling magnolias under or near an old magnolia. When the tree at last dies, the young glossy sprouts appear from nowhere, exulting in the sun and air for which they may have waited a long hundred years.

The tree is beautiful the year around. It need not wait for a brief burst of blooming to justify itself, like the wild plum and the hawthorn. It is handsomer than most dressed only in its broad leaves, shining like dark polished jade, so that when I am desperate for decoration, I break a few sprays for the house and find them an ornament of which a Japanese artist would approve. The tree sheds some of its leaves just before it blooms, as though it shook off old garments to be cleansed and ready for the new. There is a dry pattering to earth of the hard leaves and for a brief time the tree is parched and drawn, the rosy-lichened trunk gray and anxious. Then pale green spires cover the boughs, unfolding into freshly lacquered leaves, and at their tips the blooms appear. When, in late April or early May, the pale buds unfold into great white waxy blossoms, sometimes eight or ten inches across, and the perfume is a delirious thing on the spring air, I would not trade one tree for a conservatory filled with orchids. The blooms, for all their size and thickness, are as delicate as orchids in that they reject the touch of human hands. They must be cut or broken carefully and placed in a jar of water without brushing the edges, or the creamy petals will turn in an hour to brown velvet. Properly handled, they open in the house as on the tree, the cupped buds bursting open suddenly, the full-blown flowers shedding the red-tipped stamens in a shower, so that in a quiet room you hear them sifting onto the table top. The red seed cones are as fine as candles. They mature slowly from the top of the tree down, as a Christmas tree is lighted.

Because I miss the flowers when the blooming season is over, I begged my artist friend Robert to paint a spray on my old Tole tray. He rebelled, being a true artist who is annoyed by owners' specifications, and wanted to do a stylized landscape on the tray. I sulked and grumbled, and as sulky as I, at last he began the magnolias. He put on a few white daubs and growled some more and let the months pass. Then the magnolia season came around, and he had a jug of the blooms in his studio, and my battle was won. The magnolias were irresistible. Now I have them, imperishable at least for my lifetime, with the inexplicable added loveliness that true art gives to reality. Unfortunately, the tray is now too fine a work of art to put back on its low table, where the convivial and the careless will set down their damp silver julep cups. I have the alternatives of taking it to bed with me, or hanging it inappropriately on the farmhouse wall, or following my guests about like a secret service agent, ready to snatch up the dripping symbols of my hospitality from off the white breasts of the magnolias.

The tree that nourished me in a lean time is still here and will be as long as I can protect it from everything short of lightning. It is not conspicuous when walking through the grove. It comes into its own from the west kitchen window beside the sink. The high window frames it, so that its dark glossy top is singled out for the attention of one standing there, washing dishes, preparing vegetables, rolling pie crust on the table under the window, putting a cake together. The sun sets behind it and is tangled in the branches. In the days when the life and the work at the Creek were new, and the three brothers, for whom the pattern proved within a year to be not the right one, seemed three bottomless capacities for food, and there was no domestic help, the hours by the west window were endless, and the magnolia never failed of its beauty and its comfort. One wanted to cut it down, believing that it sapped the nourishment of the orange trees around it, but another laughed and upheld me, and it was left to raise its leaves, its blossoms, its red cones, to the changing sky. Now oranges scarcely pay for their care and their picking and shipping, and we know that magnolias, like palm trees, are good things in a grove, breeding and harboring many friendly parasites, and I have been alone a long time, and the magnolia tree is still here.

The matter of adjustment to physical environment is as fascinating as the adjustment of man to man, and as many-sided. The place that is right for one is wrong for another, and I think that much human unhappiness comes from ignoring the primordial relation of man to his background. Certainly the creatures are sensitive to this, and while some seem contented almost anywhere as long as food is provided, and perhaps a mate, others cannot accept the change of scene or the cage. Monkeys, I think, do not mind the zoo, but the eagle hunched on his public perch, the panther behind his bars, break the heart with their desperation. My own two animals who came to the Creek with me from urban life reacted as opposites. They were a Scottish terrier, a shy fellow, and a young tiger cat, both city-bred and reared. Both knew town apartment life, the sound of city traffic and the small bed at night behind safe walls. Both had been happy in that life.

Dinghy the Scotty hated the Florida backwoods from the first sandspur under his tail. He hated the sun, he hated the people, black and white, he hated the roominess of the farmhouse and the long quiet of the nights. From the beginning, he sat on his fat Scotch behind and glowered. Perhaps he sensed that his breed and pedigree were not here properly appreciated. Florida is a country of the work-dog, even where that dog is a pointer or setter and so something, always, of a pet. We live a leisurely life, but while our dogs lie, as we, in the sun, they are also expected to serve us, as the Negro serves.

Dinghy was not approved. He was not even understood. There were those who did not believe he was a dog. The iceman professed to be in deadly fear of him. I took Dinghy in the car with me to Hawthorn for groceries, and the clerk came to put the packages in the car. He retreated, shrieking, "There's a varmint in that car!" I am certain that if Dinghy did not know what was meant by a varmint, he knew that humans were not impressed by him. He was accustomed to slavish overtures, the proffered tidbit and the friendly touch. He retired into his mental Highlands and stayed there.

Jib, his tabby companion, was of different stuff. He too had lived the languid life of a city pet, in the house most of the time, fed on ground beef and liver from the butcher, his only excitement an occasional excursion into the back yard after some intrepid city mouse. I was so busy when I took up life at the Creek that Jib was left to shift for himself. He had his warm milk fresh from old Laura, night and morning, but that was all. And where Dinghy turned into a hopeless introvert, Jib thrived.

The jungle that was a terror to the dog was to him enchanting. All the generations of urban life were dissolved in a moment, and he prowled the marsh and hammock as though he had known them always. He returned home with shining eyes, bearing some trophy un-utterably strange, a lizard or small snake. We use the expression here, "poor as a lizard-eating cat," and I think Jib learned they were not the healthiest of foods, for as the years passed I would see him lying in the shade, watching a lizard with no attempt to catch it. He must once have been bitten by a snake, for he disappeared for two days, and came in with his head swollen to twice its size, and very wobbly on his legs. He refused food for two days more and then was himself again, but with a holy fear of anything resembling the serpent. I have seen him jump three feet in the air, like a released spring, at the sudden sight of a curving stick or a ribbon on the floor.

He seemed to sense the unhappiness of Dinghy and made a great effort to teach the Scotty the new delights he had discovered. He brought his lizards to the melancholy Scot and was puzzled by his disgust. He spent hours trying to teach Dinghy to catch a mouse. He would cripple it, cat-fashion, and release it under the dog's nose. Dinghy would move a few morose inches away. Jib would pick up the mouse and push it under Dinghy's belly with one paw, then sit back and wait hopefully for the mouse to slip away and Dinghy to pounce, as any rational animal would do. The mouse would begin its escape and Dinghy would look the other way. At last, with evident lack of relish, Jib would kill and eat his mouse.

Dinghy was returned to the city, lived happily in a bed-in-door apartment filled with the commotion of newspaper people, and fathered many broods of equally haughty and urban Scottish terriers. I am sure that if he had stayed in Florida he would have sired no progeny, out of sheer boredom. Old Jib has lived to be a veritable Egyptian mummy of a cat, lean and desiccated, with an eye cocked to watch the birds and the chameleons he has not disturbed for many years. Life will be for him always a lively matter, even when it is reduced to mere speculation. I drove over the cattle-gap into the grove late one night recently, and my lights shone two bright pairs of eyes, one on either side of the driveway. Old Jib was curled comfortably there, watching with friendly interest an opossum who had come by on his night's business.

There was more of Jib's response to the jungle than of Dinghy's in my own feeling about it. It will always seem strange to me, and though I live to be as thin and dried as he, I shall go into its shadows with a faster heart-beat, as Jib must have gone. Even with my first fear, long since vanished, there was more of excitement, and this is a thing I should not choose to have leave me about anything glamorous and lovely. I was most stirred, I think, by knowing that this was

Indian and Spanish country, and that Vitachuco, chief of the Ocali Indians, was embroiled with the Spaniards somewhere north of the present Ocala—and it may have been here. The word "hammock" comes from the Spanish "hamaca," meaning "a highly arable type of soil." I wanted to name my book "Golden Apples," "Hamaca," and to indicate the triumphs and defeats that different kinds of men have encountered in this hammock country, but it was believed that the name would be so strange no one would buy the book.

I like to think of the Spaniards blazing their trails through the Florida hammocks. The hammocks were the same then as now, and will be the same forever if men can be induced to leave them alone. Hammock soil is dark and rich, made up of centuries of accumulation of humus from the droppings of leaves. The hammock is marked by its type of trees, and these are the live oak, the palm, the sweet gum, the holly, the ironwood and the hickory and magnolia. We have high hammock and low hammock, and oak hammock and palm hammock, and there is likely to be a body of water nearby. The piney woods and the flat-woods are more open and therefore perhaps more hospitable, in spite of their poorer soil and dryness, but the *hamaca* shares with marsh and swamp the great mystery of Florida.

When I had caught the swing of the work so that there was now and then a breathing spell, I moved beyond the orbit of the magnolia tree seen from the kitchen window, and began to learn the hammock and lake edge that with the grove made up my seventy-two acres. I have since bought forty acres from the Widow Lowry, worthless marsh and low hammock that adjoin my east grove, from that peculiar instinct, relic no doubt of pioneer farming ancestors, that makes a landowner want to "round out his block." The grove itself seems safe and open, no matter how high the tea-weed grows, and the red-top. There are times when the evening sun infiltrates so eerily the dense summer cover crop under the orange trees that the green growth seems, not vegetation, but sea, emerald green, with the light seeming to come from high distant earthly places down through the luminous waters. Yet the effect is open.

The old sixteen-acre field is open, too. It is reached through Old Boss' grove, and I remember the sense of discovery when I went through the sagging gate back of his house and came out into the old clearing. It is a fine sweep of field, level for ten acres, dropping to the east to a line of hickories, and to the north melting into a dense six acres of virgin hammock. In the heart of the clearing is a gigantic live oak, with crepe myrtle bushes nearby, and an old well, and though there is not a trace left of any house, one knows this was a home-site, and that children swung from the low-spreading limbs of the oak tree. The field has lost its fertility, and I have struggled with successive optimistic plantings of beans and squash and cucumbers and even, hopeful folly on that neglected soil, young orange trees. But the field is through with the bother of cultivation and will have none of it, and everything withers on its arid and cynical and weary breast. It nourishes only a thick cluster of persimmon trees and wild grapevines, and a spindling grapefruit tree at the edge of the hammock, and a great sweet seedling orange tree among the hickories. The squirrels and raccoons and birds and foxes make a good living there, where a human fails.

The east grove, across the road from the farmhouse, is bounded on the east and south by hammock. This lies around it in a protective crescent. Entering here is a trek into the wilderness. Boots and breeches are required, for the way goes through saw palmettos and is part of the trail where, Tom Morrison says, the snakes cross. Twice each year the moccasins and rattlers move, he says, taking the same path, and back and forth between the east and west groves is a known crossing. It must be so, for I see more snakes on the road there than in any other place I frequent. Once through the dense palmettos the hammock opens out, so that where the old Lowry fence runs the woods make a clear park. There are tall long-leaf pines among the palms and live oaks, so that the earth has a clean carpet of pine needles and brittle oak leaves, and one walks silently over it. The blue-jays nest there, and the hush is broken only by their cries, harsh above the soft slurring of the wind in the tree-tops. I began my hunting there, practicing with a .410 on the gray squirrels that whisked up and down the tree trunks. There was great sport at first in all the hunting. Then it came to sicken me, and now I go to the pines as a guest and not an invader. The squirrels strip half a dozen pecan trees of their crop each fall, but there are a dozen trees more, and when a gray streak of fur flashes by my window of an autumn morning on its way to the rich nuts, I say to it, "Come in and welcome. There is enough for us all."

Down through the west grove, which is the house grove, is the hammock on the shore of Orange Lake that has been from the beginning a true retreat. I went to it often in the early days but have not gone much since life itself has had more to offer. This has been not for disloyalty or for any treachery, but because at all times we turn to what we need only when we need it. It is a matter of indifference to the lake-shore hammock whether I come or go, and so I went to it in my need, as I have gone along the road that nourished me.

To reach it, I might go by one of two ways: through the grove, dipping at the end to a patch of seedling pecan trees and a great bush of trifoliata, the ground thick with blue spiderwort and wild mustard; a ragged fence is here, marking off what had been a garden in a dry time, but now, with the lake high, is damp muck grown rankly in coffee-weed and brambles. I might go persistently through the coffee-weed and the tearing briers and cross another ragged fence, and come out on a cattle trail along the lake edge that crossed into the hammock. Or I might reach it by going to the south pasture and cutting straight through the hammock edge. The border is an almost impenetrable tangle of blackberry bushes and bamboo vines. But by crouching low, a way may be found under the overhanging thicket, and it is found that this too is a cattle trail, and a low narrow way leads through perpetual shadow to the open hammock.

I do not understand how any one can live without some small place of enchantment to turn to. In the lakeside hammock there is a constant stirring in the tree-tops, as though on the stillest days the breathing of the earth is yet audible. The Spanish moss sways a little always. The heavy forest thins into occasional great trees, live oaks and palms and pines. In spring, the yellow jessamine is heavy on the air, in summer the red trumpet vine shouts from the gray trunks, and in autumn and winter the holly berries are small bright lamps in the half-light. The squirrels are unafraid, and here I saw my first fox-squirrel, a huge fellow made of black shining plush. Here a skunk prowled close to me, digging industrious small holes for grubs. I sat as still as a stump, and if he saw me, as I suspect, he was a gentleman and went on steadily with his business, then loped away with a graceful rocking motion. A covey of quail passed me often, so that I came to know their trail into the blackberry thicket where they gathered in a circle for the night, making small soft cries. It is impossible to be among the woods animals on their own ground without a feeling of expanding one's own world, as when any foreign country is visited.

To the west, the hammock becomes damp, the trees stand more sparsely. Beyond is a long stretch of marsh where the cattle feed lazily, belly-deep in water hyacinths and lily pads, then the wide lake itself. There is a clamor of water birds, long-legged herons and cranes, visiting sea-gulls from the coasts, wild ducks, coots, the shrill scream of fish-hawks, with now and then a bald-headed eagle loitering in the sky, ready to swirl down and take the fish-hawk's catch from him in mid-air. Across the lake, visible the four miles only on a clear day, is the tower of the old Samson manse, decaying in the middle of the still prosperous orange grove. From the tower itself, decrepit and dangerous, is a sight of a tropical world of dreams, made up of glossy trees and shining water and palm islands. When I am an old woman, so that too much queerness will seem a natural thing, I mean to build a tower like it on my own side of the lake, and I shall sit there on angry days and growl down at any one who disturbs me.

I dig leaf mould from this hammock to enrich my roses and camellias and gardenias. When I went with my basket one morning a breath of movement, an unwonted pattern of color, caught my eye under a tangle of wild grapevines. A wild sow lay nested at the base of a great magnolia. At a little distance, piled one on the other, lay her litter, clean and fresh as the sunshine, the birth-damp still upon them. Sow and litter were exhausted with the business of birthing. The one lay breathing profoundly, absorbed in the immensity of rest. The others lay like a mass of puppies, the lowest-layered tugging himself free to climb again on top of the pile and warm his tender belly. The mass shifted. The most adventuresome, a pied morsel of pig with a white band like a belt around his middle, wobbled over to the sow's side. He gave a delighted whimper and the whole litter ambled over to discover the miracle of the hairy breasts.

The jungle hammock breathed. Life went through the moss-hung forest, the swamp, the cypresses, through the wild sow and her young, through me, in its continuous chain. We were all one with the silent pulsing. This was the thing that was important, the cycle of life, with birth and death merging one into the other in an imperceptible twilight and an insubstantial dawn. The universe breathed, and the world inside it breathed the same breath. This was the cosmic life, with suns and moons to make it lovely. It was important only to keep close enough to the pulse to feel its rhythm, to be comforted by its steadiness, to know that Life is vital, and one's own minute living a torn fragment of the larger cloth.

4. The pound party

We pay no attention to a newcomer at the Creek. There is no more formal getting-acquainted than among the rabbits in the woods and the birds in the trees. When any one has been here long enough, sooner or later his path crosses that of the other inhabitants and friendship or enmity or mere tolerance sets in. I was never welcomed to the Creek except by Martha, or my presence acknowledged. If I stayed, that was my own business, so long as I minded it. If I did not stay, no one would be surprised and there was no point in making overtures to me. But how was I to have known this and that the Townsends' invitation to a pound party was not a social gesture? I took it at face value.

I knew vaguely that a family lived half a mile away as tenants in Cow Hammock. A lean brown-eyed man who looked like John the Baptist often walked down the sand road in front of my house, scuffling up the dust with long bare feet. A pretty woman with a baby in her arms sometimes walked with him, or followed him an hour later, or sometimes appeared mysteriously with him only on his way back, as though she had gone off to the Creek in the night and he had come after her by daylight. Actually, I found, they fished both from Cow Hammock Landing and from Cross Creek, and one or the other might take the rowboat back and forth. Apparently countless children loitered along the road, like beads set far apart in a string, sometimes in little knots, sometimes singly. They resembled neither St. John nor the woman, but among themselves were as alike as peas in a pod and precisely the color of that vegetable when a little wilted. I began speaking to the children and they answered, not the conventional "Hey!", but "How-do," politely. Apparently none of them went to school, although I believe it was that winter that the school bus began collecting children from the Creek. Once a wagon went by, lurching in the ruts, filled to overflowing with these passers-by, integrated at last into one family. They were the Townsends, and a community to themselves, aloof by choice. There were enough of them to need no other contacts. One day two of the small girls appeared at my back door.

The oldest said rapidly, before she should forget the memorized words, "I'm Ella May, and Mama says we're having a pound party tomorrow evening and she'd be proud did you come."

It came to me that this was the first neighborly gesture I had encountered at the Creek. I was touched.

I said, "I'd be glad to. But what is a pound party?"

"Everybody brings a pound of something. Sugar, or butter, or candy, or a cake. A cake's fine. Such as that."

The evening of the party was clear as glass and I walked the half-mile to the Cow Hammock. Remembering the swarm of little Townsends, and adding a houseful of guests in my mind's eye, I had doubled my largest cake recipe and baked it in a roasting pan. I thought I must be early, for there was no one in the shabby house but the Townsends. The children were watching and at sight of me scattered within.

I heard a sibilant, "Here she comes."

The suspicion had not yet touched me not only that they knew I should be the sole arrival, but that the party had been built around the probability of my innocent acceptance. The Townsends were in their Sunday best, fresh-scrubbed and uncomfortable. The girls were starched, the boys in stiff clean blue overalls and shirts. I was given a seat on a bench along a wall. Behind me a ragged screen over the open window let in a steady stream of mosquitoes, attracted by the oil lamp on the table. Ella May was assigned with a newspaper to sit beside me and fan my legs to keep them from biting me. When Ella May lagged, Beatrice took up the paper. Their work was enthusiastic but inadequate to the ingenuity of the mosquitoes. I slapped furtively. My cake had the place of honor on the bare deal table in the center of the room. A Townsend layer cake dripping sticky icing was pushed modestly to one side. The rest of the refreshments provided by the hostess consisted of a bucket of water, a ten-cent jar of peanut butter and a nickel box of soda crackers.

She said easily, "We'll wait a while to eat, just in case."

I made conversation as best I could. We talked of the heavy crop of blackberries, of the Hamon sow that could not be kept up, no matter how one tried, of the summer rains and of the fishing. Mr. Townsend spoke up brightly when we reached the fishing. Fishing was not only the family livelihood but its delight. The Townsends would have sat all day with poles if they had been millionaires.

"I'll bring you a mess of bream one day," he said.

The talk ebbed. The mosquitoes buzzed and the Townsends slapped automatically. The lamp flickered in a gust of wind.

Mrs. Townsend said, "Be nice, did you blow some, Floyd."

Mr. Townsend echoed, "Blow some, Floyd."

Floyd, the oldest, long, thin and pale, brought out a mouth organ from his pocket and drew up a straight wooden chair. He began to pat his foot before he started his tune. Into the patting came suddenly the whine of the mouth organ. The tune, formless, unrecognizable, was mournful. One sad phrase repeated itself over and over. Other Townsends took up the patting and the rickety floor shook to the thumping. Floyd stopped abruptly.

Mrs. Townsend said to the air, "Be nice, did Preston dance."

Preston was five, the youngest weaned Townsend. The older children seized him and dragged him from the doorway. He hung his head but made no resistance. They seemed to prop him up, then retreated and left him standing alone. Floyd took up his tune. Preston stood staring vacantly. The tune and the party seemed no concern of his. As though one note had set off a mechanical spring, he began to shuffle his feet. His body was still. His arms jerked a little, like a broken jack-in-the-box. His feet shuffled back and forth without rhythm. He might have been trying to keep his footing on a slippery treadmill. This was the dance. I expected him to stop in a moment but he kept it up. The tune, the dance, were endless.

Mrs. Townsend said complacently, "Preston holds out good, don't he?"

The compliment seemed a signal, for he stopped as suddenly as he had begun.

Mrs. Townsend said, "We just as good to eat."

She passed the crackers in one hand and the tiny jar of peanut butter, with a spoon in it, in the other. Eyes followed her hungrily. I refused, to the relief of the eyes. I had a dipper of water and as small a piece of cake as I dared take and yet be courteous. The two cakes disappeared as though a thundershower had melted them. The party was obviously over. Mrs. Townsend accompanied me outside the house and to the head of the path. She looked up into a cloudless and star-lit sky.

"I reckon the threat of bad weather kept the others away," she said placidly.

I inquired about pound parties at the Creek, and my gullibility was verified. Yet the occasion had been truly a party, and the Townsends had done their best to make it festive. I decided that I should go any time I was invited, and should see to it that a larger jar of peanut butter was provided. After the party, the Townsend children and I were great friends. Ella May and Beatrice came almost every day to visit me. Dorsey and Floyd and Glenwood came to do odd chores. They were thin, grave boys and very capable. They moved slowly, like old men, and had the look of age that hunger puts on children. The boys were the right size to climb into the pecan trees and shake down and gather the nuts. The crop was heavy that year, and the filled sacks and baskets amounted to many hundred pounds.

The boys were asked, "What would you do if you had a dollar for every one of those pecans?"

There was silence while the thought of wealth was contemplated.

Dorsey said slowly, "First off, I'd get me a whole plug of Brown Mule tobaccy, all for myself."

Floyd said, "I'd have all I want of rich folks' rations—light bread and jelly."

The questioner went on, "What, no cornbread?"

Glenwood said quickly, "Oh yes. We know you got to have cornbread to grow on."

One week in the next spring the whole family left off its fishing and picked, without enthusiasm, the heavy crop of beans. Their pay on Saturday totalled thirty-six dollars. I thought happily how far this would go. I pictured the big sack of groceries that night, with money laid by for future needs, seed and fertilizer perhaps for a garden of their own. On Monday morning Floyd came to the house.

"Could you let us have two dollars," he asked, "to get us some rations?"

Their money had surely been stolen from them, or the heavy hand of poor folks' luck had made them lose it in some fashion.

"But what happened to the thirty-six dollars you had on Saturday?"

Floyd's pale face was bright with pleasure.

"We bought us an ottymobile," he said.

They were somehow a challenge. I have never known a more exquisite courtesy than the whole family possessed. There were good blood and breeding back of them. I have known no one with more gracious manners. The children were intelligent. Their finances were a problem beyond me and would evidently have to take care of themselves, but it seemed to me that the children's futures held something better than a precarious living fishing on Orange Lake. The two great needs, where I could give tangible help, were their health and their education.

Their green color came from a lifetime of hookworm. I persuaded the mother and father to let the children be treated. The tetrachlorethylene capsules were dispensed free by the state. I obtained the capsules and instructions, and set off for the Townsend house one Saturday night. One by one I handed out the preliminary doses of Epsom salts. I gave orders about no further food. On Sunday morning I trudged back again and saw the capsules safely down the Townsends. I departed with the sense of smugness common to all meddlers, leaving word that in ten days we would repeat the treatment. When the ten days were up, the mother refused point blank to let the children be treated again.

"It made them sick," she said.

"Of course it made them sick. They were eaten up with hookworm."

She shook her head.

"'Twouldn't be safe to give that medicine to them again," she said firmly. "It must of been stale. You can't trust nothin' is free."

I was beaten there, and passed on slyly to the matter of education. Once safely in school, I was sure the visiting county nurse would have a chance for a fresh battle against the hookworms. I would give clothes, I said, to all the children who would go to school. St. John and his wife consulted and it was agreed that Dorsey and Glenwood, Ella May and Beatrice, might condescend to be clothed and to allow the school bus from the village to stop for them.

I am no seamstress, the holding of a threaded needle in my hand producing an acute stomach ache. But a long line of Methodist preachers behind me has left the evil thought in the blood of my brain that the more difficult a job, the more certainly one must apply oneself to its mastering. I bought yards of good gingham and sat hour after hour, developing stomach ulcers, I was certain, at the sewing machine. The girls came for fittings and had light bread and jelly as reward. I turned out creditable dresses, nicely trimmed, and went at the job of underwear. I cut down my own two woolen coats for Ella May and Beatrice. I bought shirts and pants for the boys. I took my bundles with a missionary's pride to the Townsends and modest pleasure was shown in my products. I arranged for the school bus to stop at the entrance to Cow Hammock. I went home and took a large dose of bicarbonate of soda.

The next morning one of the smaller children brought me a dress length of very good silk.

"Mama says will you please make a dress for her."

I took the material to the Townsend house, puzzled, unwilling as yet to be outraged. Mama was on the lake, fishing. I was shown some of Mama's other garments. Mama was a much better seamstress than I—But if the Lord sends forth a strangely agreeable slave to the sewing machine, surely it is pleasanter and more profitable to spend one's time on the lovely lake, dangling a bamboo pole for bream. I left the material and word that my offer to sew for the Townsends applied only to those in need of education, not to those who had advanced in philosophy far beyond me.

The children went to school just long enough to make ownership of the clothes indisputable. Then they were all home again, playing in the sandy yard, or as a special treat, taken along on the fishing parties.

"They didn't like school," St. John informed me gently.

It would be satisfying, if sad, to tell of their tragic maturities. I can only report that they have grown up as healthy as any one else, and within the limits of their congenital leisureliness, are living as active and prosperous lives as their neighbors. I am sometimes haunted by the feeling that it is I who could have learned of the Townsends.

5. *The census*

*f*or learning a new territory and people as quickly as possible, I recommend taking the census on horseback. In 1930 my friend Zelma from the village was commissioned to take the census in the backcountry sections of Alachua County. Zelma is an ageless spinster resembling an angry and efficient canary. She manages her orange grove and as much of the village and county as needs management or will submit to it. I cannot decide whether she should have been a man or a mother. She combines the more violent characteristics of both and those who ask for or accept her manifold ministrations think nothing of being cursed loudly at the very instant of being tenderly fed, clothed, nursed or guided through their troubles. She was the logical census taker for our district. She knew all the inhabitants, black and white, and every road and trail leading to their houses. None of the places could be reached by a main road, and travelling by automobile would leave most of the noses uncounted. She borrowed two horses from the manager of the Maxcey packing house, and on a bright fall morning we set out together.

I had not ridden since childhood. Even then, my mounts had been the weary work horses on the Maryland farm, and my brother and I had been able to ride safely, without saddles, on their broad backs. I was uneasy at first on my lively mare. Then the beauty of the country took me over, and I was aware only that this high vantage point was perfection for the traveller in strange places. Zelma planned a wide circle for the first day. We set out to the northwest and came to the hammock lands across the Creek that bordered Orange Lake. The population was sparse. I could not understand how folk could settle in the bare piney-woods, when here were uninhabited hammock acres, rich of soil, magnificent of vegetation. But the work of clearing hammock is heavy, and land easily cleared and already open is tempting to migrants who are often not aware of the differences in fertility. The sun streamed through the interstices and glinted on the shining magnolia leaves and sparkleberry bushes. Red-birds darted down the narrow trail before us and among the palms twined with trumpet vines, the blossoms the same bright orange-red color as the birds. Coveys of quail whirred away from us.

"It's a —— blessing for us not many Yankees have seen country like this, or they'd move in on us worse than Sherman," Zelma said, and reined in her horse to dismount in front of the first cabin.

We finished the scanty counting along Orange Lake and cut west toward the River Styx. The name chilled me. My mare was obstreperous, and as we moved into a wet narrow road, I thought that all that was needed to make her bolt under me was the sight of a moccasin. As though I had conjured him up, he was there. We were approaching a wooden foot-bridge and the mare, who had balked at all previous bridges, was taking this one of her own accord. The snake lay on a mound of earth to the right of the bridge. He was solidly coiled, an ancestral cottonmouth, taking up as much space as a dishpan. His triangular and venomous head rested flatly on the outer edge of his coils. The mare failed to see him because he lay so still. She was intent on her footing, on the welcome sight of the road ahead. Her careful, dainty hooves passed three inches from the dark sleek head. I loosened my feet from the stirrups, ready to jump free. The patriarch eyed me and did not stir. I decided that such a live-and-let-live philosophy was admirable, and I touched one finger to my hat, saluting a gentleman.

We entered the River Styx gently. Surely, death itself must come as quietly. The open fields, bright in the reality of sunlight, gave way easily to pine lands. The pines grew thicker, the sweet scent of their needles rising. The sunlight was spotty, the shadows of the tall trees wider. Here and there a live oak told of changing soil. Then, imperceptibly, we were in deep hammock. Coolness came in on us. The leaves of magnolia and bay trees shut out the sun, as all dark everlasting foliage must shut it out from the silent places of the dead. The hammock merged into cypress swamp. A trumpet vine dropped flamboyant flowers from a lone palm. The blossoms seemed gaudy and funereal. There were no birds singing from the cypresses. No squirrels swung in and out of the sepulchral arches of the trees. Out of the dimly defined road a great white bird rose, flapping noiseless wings. It was huge, snow-white as an angel of death, with a wide black mourning band around the edge of the wings. I became aware that the soft dampness of the road had turned into a soft rippling. The whole floor of the forest was carpeted with amber-colored water, alive, moving with a slow, insidious current. We had entered the River Styx.

Some English youth, fresh from his Oxford Greek and Latin, some unhappy, outlawed scapegrace, must have named this silent stream. Long ago, before the Big Freeze, Florida was a tropic land of exile. Numbers of younger sons or ne'er-do-wells were sent here from England, subsidized to stay away. Some were given funds with which to establish orange groves, funds they often squandered. One of these, morose, ironic, must have come on this unknown, unsailed waterway. Bitter, perhaps, certainly homesick, he was stuck by the deathly peace and the dark beauty; stirred by the pale water hyacinths, diaphanous and unearthly; and it was truly to him the River of Death, over which, once traversed, there is no crossing back again. Because this country had become as dear as life to me, the river held for me no horror. I wondered if the greater Styx might not be as darkly beautiful. The leaf-brown overflow of water deepened to the horses' knees. The white ibis flapped away slowly and came to rest high in a cypress. Then we were on the rickety bridge over the main body of the stream, and on the other side, and counting children again.

I thought, "It is not given to many to cross the Styx and live to tell it."

We circled back from Orange Lake and across Lochloosa Prairie. We use the word "prairie" in a special sense. We have no open plains, but around most of the larger lakes are wet flat areas thick with water grasses, and these we call our prairies. They are more nearly marshes, yet we save the word "marsh" for the deep mucky edges of lake and river, dense with coontail and lily pads, and for the true salt marshes of the tidal rivers. We found no living soul across this tract. There were trails used by half-wild gaunt cattle and dim, deep-rutted roads travelled only by the lurching turpentine wagons that came with mule and Negro driver to scrape resin from the clay cups on the tapped turpentine trees.

We came out at last on a turpentine still and here the population was black and dense. So many little pickaninnies ran away from the cabins as the strange horses approached, that it was a long job gathering them all in to be counted, and their fancy names and vaguely estimated ages written down on the papers. Zelma knew all the older Negroes and many of the younger ones. She joked with some and sympathized with others, recommended cures for this and that, and promised to send medicine to one, quilt scraps to another, and a pound of little conch pea seed to yet another. She chided one lean brown girl for her immense brood, fathers unknown.

"I know it's too many, Miss Zelma," the girl agreed. "I sho' got to git me a remedy."

By the time we had finished the Quarters, dusk was falling. Zelma knew a short cut back to the Creek. It took us by Burnt Island, and she told me fabulous tales of it in the growing darkness. There was believed to be the grandfather of all rattlesnakes living there. Only glimpses had been had of him, but several reported to have seen his shed skin, and all agreed that it was nine feet long. The "shed" stretches, and the snake could reasonably and conceivably have been seven feet in length. There were wild boars on Burnt Island, savage, long-tusked and dangerous. The place was also a hideout for criminals who preferred the great rattler and the wild boars to the arm of the law. I was not happy when Zelma announced profanely that high water had covered the old road she meant to take, and we were lost.

Darkness and our own uncertainty and the long hours away from the stable made the horses restless. My mare shied at every stick and reared when a hoot owl cried over our heads from a pine tree. Then the full moon rose blessedly and roads and woods and prairie and water were again as plain as by day. We skirted ponds and continued in a general west by south direction. We came out on the Creek road, but three miles away from the Creek. We had been in the saddle from seven in the morning until eleven at night. I ached through the night and in the morning was obliged to move with some caution. Yet my own country had been revealed to me and a twinge of pain was a small price to pay.

The second day we made a wider circle. We found a cabin here and a shack there, where even Zelma did not know folk were living, silent people who gave their statistics reluctantly. We rode down a piney-woods road in the late morning and as the trees broke at the edge of a clearing, we heard a piano. It was a good piano, not quite in tune, and it was being played with the touch of an artist. I thought my senses were playing tricks on me. Surely I heard only the wind in the pines.

Zelma said, "I forgot that woman was buried back here."

The woman left the piano and came to the door. She was in immaculate rags and she had once been lovely. The house was gaping with holes and was stripped bare of all but the most fundamental pieces of furniture. Several thin clean children came to stare at us. The woman was starved for talk with her own kind, and long after the family had been itemized, detained us. Zelma told me her story as we rode away. She had come some twenty years before on a tourist's visit to Florida, a young and beautiful girl of high breeding. Taking in a local square dance as a spectator she had met a young Cracker and fallen absurdly in love with him, for the mating instinct knows no classes. She had married him, and her outraged and prosperous family had left her to her own devices. Her piano was the only salvage from her early life. There are hundreds of handsome and sturdy backwoodsmen who would make good husbands even for such a girl, if her tastes in living were simple. She had chosen a hopeless and worthless fellow who sat idly in the sun as her life fell to pieces about her. The children held her to him. There was something more, too; a pride that would not admit defeat. I came to know her well, and I have never known a woman to make a gayer thing of life with only empty hands to work with. The family was half-starved most of the time. Yet she made a game of hunger, and a meal of fish and cornpone was a festival. I went once to visit with her, when the girls were grown, and found them all strange specters with their faces smeared with something wet and brown.

The woman said, "We have no place to go and no way of going. So we think up our own ways of having fun. We're at the beauty parlor today. We read about beauty masks, so we made a trip to the edge of the lake and dug mud to make our packs."

Martha has served her without pay when her children were born.

She said to me, "She shames most women, don't she? I does all I can for her, 'cause me and the Lord is all she's got to look out for her, and the Lord ain't exactly put Hisself out."

Martha fixed lunch for Zelma and me that day. We reached her house in the afternoon and were famished. She made us biscuits and fried white bacon, and served her best preserves. She had baked sweet potatoes still hot in the wood range and when we left she gave us a paper sack of them to carry with us. Our next stop was at a small Negro cabin and we were thirsty from the salty bacon. Zelma asked for water and a small black boy handed us up cool well water in clean gourds. When he reached up to me, he spilled the cold water on my mare's flank and she bolted like a rabbit. The woods were full of gopher holes and I dared not try to rein her in too sharply, for fear she should stumble. I gave her her head and we tore away madly, and as we went, I scattered hot baked sweet potatoes all over the piney-woods. The mare and I were both trembling when she came to a voluntary stop. I was proud of myself for having stayed on, but all I had from Zelma was her special brand of profanity for having lost the sweet potatoes.

I was sorry when the census was over and done with. The region around me was plainly mapped now in my mind, I knew every one, black and white, and could never again be a stranger. We allowed ourselves to be interrupted for one day toward the end. The day was mild and cloudy. Our friend Fred rounded up Zelma and me to go fishing with him. The bream were on the bed and the weather was exactly right. We protested that we should be finishing the census.

"Now you just as good to come on fishing with me," Fred said. "You'd ought to know, nobody ain't going to give you their census on a good fishing day like this."

6. The evolution of comfort

*W*hen I first came to the Creek, I had for facilities one water faucet in the kitchen, a tin shower adjoining the Kohler shed and an out-house. For the water faucet in the kitchen I was always grateful, for water pumps at the Creek are all placed in relation to the well and with little or no concern with distance from the house. When Martha lived in the Mackay house she had even no well, but must carry water from the Creek itself. My outside shower was acceptable enough in summer, though it meant going damply over the sand to the house afterward. In cold weather—and you may believe the Chamber of Commerce that we have none, or you may believe me that on occasion bird-baths have been frozen solid—in cold weather the outside shower was a fit device for masochistic monks. The icy spray that attacked the shoulders like splinters of fine glass was in the nature of a cross. I shall not forget the early Christmas afternoon, with six men gathered for dinner, the turkey savory in the oven, the pies cooling, the vegetables ready, the necessity if not the desire for the bath borne in on me, and the temperature at thirty-eight and dropping. I emerged shivering and snarled at the indifferent heavens, "The first time I get my hands on cash money, so help me, I shall have a bathroom."

Because of the cold shower, open at the front to a wandering world, an unfriendly shower, I took to watching for rain like a tree-toad. For when the soft sluiceways of the skies opened and the lichened shingle roof shed the waters in a surge down the northwest sheltered corner of the house, I could strip and accept the benediction. When the day was hot the rain was cool. When the day was cool the rain was many degrees warmer, and as bland as perfumed bath powder. The water faucet and the shower, then, could be endured. It seemed to me that I had done nothing in all my life to deserve the outhouse.

It had been years since I had come any closer to one than James Whitcomb Riley's verses on the subject. But I could look back on them almost with nostalgia, for those I had known had a certain coziness and a definite privacy. One of my fondest recollections is of an outhouse in Virginia. It stood under a locust, at the top of a little rise of ground. The terrain before one sloped down past a corner of the flower-bed, bright with balsam and phlox, to a valley where a cornfield was bordered by a line of willows. The blue hills of Virginia lifted in the distance. Three walls of the outhouse were gay with travel posters from Switzerland, the Rhine and Brittany. It was pleasant to follow pensively the depicted trails, highways and views. On the fourth wall hung a sonnet in French, a charming and vulgar and beautifully composed bit of comment on the circumstances in which the reader found himself at the moment. All was conducive to a sense of well-being.

The outhouse on Grandfather's farm was papered with perfectly beautiful colored pictures of reigning queens. Alexandra was magnificent. Wilhelmina was demure and very pretty in pale pink with a pearl and diamond crown. I cannot look today at the news pictures of the stout housewife in tweeds on a bicycle and believe that it is the same woman. The queen of Norway I recall as rather austere, the queen of Italy as blackly horselike. But all were queens, in full color, in décolleté and jewelled diadems. The building had a door with crescent windows and it stood discreetly behind a hickory tree and was reached by a high trim boardwalk bordered with marigolds.

The outhouse that I inherited at the Creek had no boardwalk, it had no queens, no marigolds, it had, amazingly, no door. It stood on a direct line with the dining room windows. One fortunate diner might sit with his back to it. The others could not lift their eyes from their plates without meeting the wooden stare of the unhappy and misplaced edifice. They were fortunate if they did not meet as well the eye of a belated occupant, assuring himself stonily that he could not be seen. For there was indeed a wire screen, and this screen had been, or so the instigator fatuously pretended, modernized with camouflage. Streaks of gray paint zigzagged across the screening. The effect was to make of a human being seated behind it a monster. The monster had gray bolts of lightning for arms and moss-gray tree-trunks for legs. Possibly the head of a human tall enough might have lifted to meet and be shielded by another streak of gray paint, or one short enough might have been veiled entirely, but I never peeked in fascination at any occupant of the infernal box whose face did not gaze recognizably out in a silent and steely torment.

The camouflage, cruelly, worked perfectly when approached from the path. The result was that it was impossible to tell, until too late, whether a living thing was trapped behind it. It seemed for a time that Uncle Fred had solved this problem. Two days after his arrival on a visit he asked in a low, strained voice, "Do you have an old piece of bright flannel I could cut up?" His manner prohibited questioning. I had been here too short a time to have acquired scraps of cloth, but I brought out a ragged quilt, flaming red in color. His face brightened. He went solemnly away and a little later a two-foot-square red flag stood in the middle of the path just outside the outhouse. The technique was obvious and simple. When one went in, one placed the flag in the path. When one came out, one put the flag back inside the outhouse. One went in and put the flag in the path. One returned to the house, forgetting to put the flag back again. The flag stood like a red light against traffic, for hours and hours and hours.

These were only the day hazards. Only a pillar of fire by night would have seemed sufficient comfort and guidance, and this was never provided except by the dubious assistance of lightning. There were provided instead, none the less appalling because harmless, spiders, lizards, toads and thin squeaking noises made by bats. Over all the dark hours hung the fear of snakes. I had arrived in Florida with the usual ignorant terror. If time proved that the sight of a snake was a rarity, there was no help then for the conviction that the next footstep would fall on a coiled rattler. An imaginary snake is so much more fearful than a real one, that I should rather handle a rattlesnake, as I have done since, than dream of one. I dreaded the sunset, thinking of the dark dark box of the outhouse. And once there, even on the blessed nights of moonlight, the small ominous thuds against floor and wall that by day were the attractive little green tree-toads, by night were the advance of nameless reptiles. I would not yield to the temptation of installing in the house the old-fashioned "conveniences," for that was an admission of defeat. I would stick it out and the first cash money should go into a bathroom.

The first cash money from the first orange crop, a good one, disappeared into mortgage and note payments, fertilizer and a Ford, for the seven-passenger Cadillac, a shabby behemoth from more affluent northern days, had literally torn its heavy heart out on the deep sand road to the Creek, and was sold for sixty dollars to a Negro undertaker. He must have towed it with the hearse, for it was past repairing. There was a year of low citrus prices and a year of freeze. Then my first Florida story, *Jacob's Ladder*, brought in the fantastic sum of seven hundred dollars.

The instant that I saw this wealth begin to dissolve as usual, I worked rapidly. I would not do anything so reckless as ordering a complete new bathroom outfit, but would shop around and pick up something second-hand. The boom was over, and in abandoned houses in unsold "scrub divisions" bathroom fittings were gathering rust and discoloration. Inquiry aroused fresh boom hope in various owners of the unwanted houses and a toilet without a seat immediately became worth its weight in gold.

My good friend carpenter Moe was at work on the building of the bathroom. The farmhouse had been built casually in three separate eras, and while the gap between the front and the back was now filled in with a porch, there was nothing but space between the main part of the house and the two large bedrooms with fireplaces that made up a wing. One stepped into the air from what, we decided, was not a French door but an Irish door. That vacuum was providential for a bathroom. It would link the two bedrooms to the house as cozily as though an architect had planned it; a careless architect, perhaps, for a difference in floor levels meant a step down from the first bedroom that has proved no friend to the aged, the absent-minded and the inebriated. Moe was pounding away while I lamented that I should have to go to Sears Roebuck after all. He laid down his hammer and sat back on his heels.

"Why, I know a feller's got a bathroom outfit," he said. "Hain't never been used. Brand new, and he's got no more use fer it than a dog. Feller right over in Citra. You come by for me this evenin' and we'll go make you a trade. Now I'm plumb proud I remembered that feller's new bathroom outfit, jest settin' there."

Moe and I drove to Citra that night. I had the fortunate feeling that time has taught me to mistrust more than nightmares and bad omens. We stopped at a shabby house on a side street and the owner of the bathroom set, presumably so irrelevant to his life, came to the door.

"I told this lady you had a bathroom set you got no use for," Moe said. "Don't say I ain't a friend to you. She'll take it off your hands and pay cash money for it if the price is right."

A small gloomy man scowled at me and did not answer.

Moe persisted, "Ain't you got a set the Baptist preacher give you afore he died?"

"'Tain't a set. It's just the toilet. It's mine, all right, but I ain't exactly got it."

"Ain't it handy, where you can git it?"

The little man came to angry life.

He shouted, "It's in the smokehouse to the Baptist parsonage and I'll git it when I'm o' mind to! They don't want I should take it but they can't stop me. I've had nothin' but meanness from the Baptists all my life and I'll go off with that toilet when I'm ready."

Moe said with deliberate aggravation, "Mebbe you cain't prove it's yourn."

"I got no call to prove it. Everybody knows how it come to be mine. The Baptists was too mean to put in runnin' water for Preacher Wilson, so he give the toilet to me."

"Well, you got no more runnin' water than the Baptists. You want to sell it?"

The legatee pondered in the dusk.

"No," he said. "No, I don't. I tell you—I thought a heap o' Preacher Wilson. He give me that toilet—and it's all I got to remember him by."

Moe comforted me on the way home.

"Like as not it's a no-account thing," he said.

The toilet had to be ordered new after all, but passing over the catalogue lure of a green-pedestalled monument for washing one's hands and face, and a Venetian-style recessed tub—for in spite of the literary windfall, oranges were bringing twenty-five cents a box—I found a second-hand lavatory and a very good tub with crooked legs. The formal opening of the bathroom was a gala social event, with a tray of glasses across the lavatory, ice and soda in the bathtub, and a bouquet of roses with Uncle Fred's card in a prominent and appropriate position.

The royalties from my first book, *South Moon Under*, went mostly for old debts, but the second, *Golden Apples*, brought temporary prosperity again and I decided that nothing is more tangible for one's money than plumbing. New friends had found their way to the Creek and were old friends now, and when there was a week-end houseful, a second bathroom seemed the most hospitable gesture possible. I contracted again for Moe to add one beside my own bedroom. The oldest four of his boys were big enough by this time to give a hand with the carpentering and the small new room was filled with male Sykeses when we reached the point of measuring for the height of the shower. Moe was a realist.

"Git in the tub," he ordered me. "Stand up straight. We'll git this right the sure way."

I stepped in the tub and stood up straight.

"Now whereabouts you want this here stream o' water to hit you? 'Bout there?"

Four pairs of bright Sykes eyes helped us gauge the proper play of water on the bathing form, and I have never felt so undressed in my life. But the Sykeses rejoiced with me in the completed bathroom, and although the linoleum buckled for nearly a year, we all felt that we had achieved unparalleled elegance. If I give an impression of *nouveau riche* when I inform guests pointedly, "The *other* bathroom is beyond my room," I am not bragging, but only grateful. I go happily from one bathroom to the other, and when a flying squirrel thumps on the roof at night, the sound is pleasing, for I am safe inside, and I remember the old Scotch prayer:

> "From ghillies and ghosties,
> And long-legged beasties,
> And all things that go *boomp* in the night,
> Good Lord, deliver us."

7. Antses in Tim's breakfast

I have used a factual background for most of my tales, and of actual people a blend of the true and the imagined. I myself cannot quite tell where the one ends and the other begins. But I do remember first a place and then a woman, that stabbed me to the core, so that I shall never get over the wound of them.

The place was near the village on the Creek road, and I thought when I saw it that it was a place where children had been playing. A space under a great spreading live oak had been lived in. The sand was trodden smooth and there were a decrepit iron stove and a clothes line, on which a bit of tattered cloth still hung. There were boxes and a rough table, as though little girls had been playing house. Only opened tin cans and a rusty pot, I think, made me inquire about it, for children were not likely to carry a game so far. I was told that a man and woman, very young, had lived there for a part of one summer, coming from none knew where, and going away again with sacks over their shoulders when the autumn frosts came in.

What manner of man and woman could this be, making a home under an oak tree like some pair of woods animals? Were they savage outlaws? People who might more profitably be in jail? I had no way of knowing. The Florida back country was new and beautiful but of the people I knew nothing. The wild home at the edge of the woods haunted me. I made pictures to myself of the man and woman, very young, who had come and gone. Somehow I knew that they would be not fierce, but gentle. I took up my own life at the Creek.

The answer to my wonderings was on my own grove and for a long time I did not know that it was there. A tenant house stood a few hundred yards from my farmhouse. It was placed beautifully under a vast magnolia tree and was all gray age and leaning walls. It was a tall two stories and had perhaps been the original home on the grove. It was windowless and seemed on the point of collapsing within itself. The occupants were Tim and his wife and their baby. I saw only Tim, red-haired and on the defensive and uninterested in his work. His job with the previous owner of the grove had been his first of the kind, he said. His weekly wage was low but I did not question it. He had come with the place. His passion was for trapping and the hides of raccoons and skunks and opossums and an occasional otter or wild-cat hung drying on the walls of his house. He trapped along the lake edge back of the grove, and I would see him coming in of an early morning with a dead creature or two in his hands. The well at the barn, in front of the tenant house, was sulphurous and fit only for the stock, and Tim came to my pump by my back door for water for his family uses. I saw his wife only from a distance and made no inquiries about her.

Callousness, I think, is often ignorance, rather than cruelty, and it was so in my brief relation with Tim and his wife. My excuse is that at the time I myself had so much hard physical work to do and was so confused with the new way of living that I did not understand that life might be much more difficult for others. The woman came striding to my back door one day. She had her baby slung over one hip, like a bundle. She walked with the tread of an Indian, graceful and direct. She was lean and small. As she came close I saw that she had tawny skin and soft honey-colored hair, drawn back smoothly over her ears and knotted at her neck. She held a card in her hand and she thrust it at me.

"Please to read hit," she said.

I took the card, addressed to Tim, and turned it over. It was only an advertisement from a wholesale fur house, quoting current prices on such pelts as Tim trapped for. I must have seemed very stupid to her, for I did not know what she wanted. At last I understood that she could not read, that the card had come in the morning's rural mail while Tim was at work at the far side of the grove. Mail, all reading matter, was cryptic and important and it was necessary to know whether she should call Tim from his work because of the card. I read it aloud and she listened gravely. She took it from me and turned to walk away.

"I thank you," she said.

Her voice was like the note of a thrush, very soft and sweet.

I called after her, seeing her suddenly as a woman, "Tell me, how are you getting on?"

She looked at me with direct gray eyes.

"Nothin' extry. They ain't no screens to the house and the skeeters like to eat us alive. And I cain't keep the antses outen Tim's breakfast."

Her statement was almost unintelligible. I myself was troubled by the mosquitoes, for they came up through holes in the kitchen floor and had my legs swollen to twice their size. But my bedrooms were tight and comfortable, and when sleep is possible, one can stand much in the daytime. I had actually not noticed that the tenant house was wide open to the intrusion not only of insects, but of wind and weather. The matter of ants in the breakfast was beyond me. It was only as I came to know the backwoods cooking customs that I knew that enough food was cooked once or at the most twice a day, to last for the three meals. The people were up long before daylight and the remnants of the previous evening's biscuits and greens and fat bacon were set aside for the early breakfast, eaten by lamplight. Where a house was rotting to the ground, ants and roaches inhabited the very wood of floors and walls and swarmed over the family's edibles. The situation of Tim's wife puzzled but still did not concern me. I did not yet understand that in this way of life one is obliged to share, back and forth, and that as long as I had money for screens and a new floor, I was morally obligated to put out a portion of it to give some comfort to those who worked for me. I took others' discomfort for granted and the only palliation of my social sin is that I took my own so, too.

I made another profound mistake in my short time with these two. I asked Tim one day if his wife would do my washing for me. He looked at me, and looked away angrily and spat.

"A white woman don't ask another white woman to do her washin' for her, nor to carry her slops," he said. "'Course, in time o' sickness or trouble or sich as that a woman does ary thing she can for another and they's no talk o' pay."

There was a fierce pride here, then, and above all, services that would be gladly given but could not be bought. I began to understand and then Tim announced that they were leaving.

I asked, "Are you going to another job?"

"No'm. I ain't made for this kind o' work. I don't do it to suit and it don't suit me."

"Where will you go and what will you do?"

"Same as we done before. I only takened this on account o' the baby comin'. A woman's got to have a roof over her then. Us'll git along better thouten no house, pertickler jest a piece of a house like this un here. In the woods, you kin make a smudge to keep off the skeeters. Us'll make out."

They moved on, the proud angry man and the small tawny lovely woman and the baby. But they put a mark on me. The woman came to me in my dreams and tormented me. As I came to know her kind, in the scrub, the hammock and the piney-woods, I knew that it was a woman much like her who had made a home under the live oak. The only way I could shake free of her was to write of her, and she was Florry in *Jacob's Ladder.* She still clung to me and she was Allie in *Golden Apples.* Now I know that she will haunt me as long as I live, and all the writing in the world will not put away the memory of her face and the sound of her voice.

8. The Widow Slater

The Widow Slater and I understood each other from the beginning. She was a violent person and I was warned to beware of her eccentric and unpredictable indignations. I found that nothing about her was unpredictable, for all her being was keyed to the one idea, that whatever is, is good. At the time when I was warned against her, she had just made a local reputation by lifting a shotgun in defiance against the starched white bosom of a county nurse. The occasion was simple and her violence was no contradiction in her character. The order had gone forth from health authorities that all school children were to be inoculated against smallpox or typhoid or something or other. The Widow Slater had refused to have done anything so unnatural and savoring of witchcraft as injecting the blood of a horse in the veins of her offspring.

Her feeling was, simply, that God knows best. What she meant by "God" I do not know, and no two people mean the same thing in their invocation of the mystic Word. My own idea is that those of us who are least positive are closest to the truth. We know only that as human beings we are very stupid and that somewhere beyond us are forces unintelligibly wiser or cleverer or more fixed than we. The forces may concern themselves with us or they may not, but it seems to me, and seemed to the Widow Slater, that people live or die, thrive or pine, quite beyond human reason. In the matter of the inoculation and in several kindred matters I believe that the belligerent mother was wrong. I am only applauding her philosophy.

Her firm conviction that God moves in a mysterious way, His wonders to perform, applied to the delights of life as well as to its burdens and its sorrows. In this, she differed from most "professing" Christians, who see God in everything difficult and unpleasant, but seldom in the natural joys. I have never known a person who had less over which to rejoice, who found more in daily living to rejoice her. She was herself almost constantly ill, local doctors being certain that she had a tumor that required removal. This she rejected, saying, "I come into the world in one piece and I aim to go out the same way. I'll not have a part of me buried here and the rest yon." Yet for all the reverence for the short, stout, untidy body which had been given her, she never spared it. People with a philosophy are usually inconsistent.

She had been a widow for some years and her family was large for one of no means at all. There was a daughter, distant in Alabama. There was Snow, a grave, brown-eyed youth, sullen when I first knew him under the family difficulties. There was Henry, a cripple, with the same indomitable spirit as his mother, who took a course in watch repairing and set up in a hole in the wall in Gainesville and became a personage. There were Alvah and Little Irene. And there was the youngest, Rodney, whose club feet and twisted legs and tortured back made Henry seem an athlete in comparison. Somewhere in the family blood was a strain that should not, eugenically, have been perpetuated. Yet all of the Widow Slater's brood, the "chappies" as she called them, Carolina fashion, had a luminous quality that somehow set them beyond the well and fit and made of them more desirable citizens and friends and neighbors than many a well-cared-for aristocrat.

She was an artist in optimism. Her rented house leaked so badly that beds must be moved and all available pots and pans set under the worst holes whenever the rain fell.

She only said, "You know there's plenty of places in the roof I could get through, and a heap more Irene could," and chuckled at her own description.

In her place I should either have kicked down the walls of the house, or lain down and given up, putting the full responsibility for my care on that Providence that she was so sure watched over the sparrow's fall.

She asked me for work, in an early year at the Creek when I had little to spend for help of any sort. All I could offer was the washing. It was too heavy even for me, though I did it when necessary, and I told her so and did not see how she might manage it. But she insisted and took the unreasonable labor as a favor. She asked to do it of a Saturday morning, when Alvah and Little Irene were home from school to help, and begged to me only that I not hurry her at it. The washing was a long and incredibly sloppy procedure. The Widow Slater dressed always in a Victorian white shirtwaist and a long full-flowing black skirt. She trailed her long black skirts through the puddles of soapsuds splashed around her and carried great dripping armfuls of half-wrung sheets to the clothes line, and was concerned, not with the hardships, but with the weather and the phlox. The weather almost always suited her, for if it was fine the clothes would dry well and if it rained, why, nothing was better for bleaching them. The phlox bothered her for the reason that they grew wild in the yard around the wash-bench and she was afraid of stepping on them.

"They look up at you with little faces," she said, "and it seems treacherous to stomp them."

She reported happily one day that Snow was doing better at his fishing.

"Folkses has woke up a catfish market," she said.

The closest to complaint I ever heard her come was when she would say, as though it were a great joke, "I feel as if I'd been drug between two twisted Fridays."

She made high-spirited play even of our fence-repairing. The fences around Old Boss' orange grove and mine were old and rotten. Her cow Betsy and my Laura, pastured jointly in my sixteen-acre field, were wise in forbidden ways. They went through the old fence as if it were not there, until we learned to fool them. We did this by dragging boughs and brush to the weakest places and propping them up with a plausible look of impenetrability. We had done this through a steaming hot summer afternoon, through the poison ivy, until we had exhausted our supply of camouflage. We stood scratched and perspiring and very dubious.

"Well," she said, "I reckon it may look solid to a cow, but it's a mighty hypocritical kind of a fence."

The word "hypocrite" may have been a favorite in the family. Little Irene came out with it one day. She brought us a katydid to show, cupped carefully in her small grubby hands.

"I caught me a hypocrite," she said.

The widow chuckled.

"That's a jizzywitch, honey," she corrected her.

Irene stamped her bare foot.

"'Tis not. It's a hypocrite. I know, because all hypocrites is long-legged."

The Widow Slater, as I look back on it, did much more for me than I did for her. She trudged from our joint pasture night and morning with my bucket of milk. She gave me settings of eggs.

"Now if your hen," she said, "proves up anyways false to you, I have one setting I'll lend to you."

Most helpful of all, after we were well acquainted, she loaned me Alvah afternoons after school to wash dishes. Alvah saved part of her small pay to buy me a Christmas present. The present was a set of glass wind chimes, and until the day when a strong wind blew them to the floor in splinters, the high thin tinkling sounded to me like the laughter of the child herself. There was something fey about most of the family. Rodney, the cripple, foretold the weather with a strange accuracy. He had always some small pet, a squirrel or chameleon or perhaps a chicken hurt and crippled like himself. I think that "Fodderwing" in *The Yearling* must have been Rodney.

The widow's confidence in me faltered only once. Several eminently respectable souls in the town of Ocala had offered me their friendship, among them the venerable white-haired mayor. It was time to return their hospitality and I invited them for supper. I asked Alvah to come and help me with the serving. She agreed with enthusiasm. The next day she did not meet my eyes. She said in a low voice that Mama would have to think about the question of her helping with the party. I assured her that the work would be light and I would take her home myself. The day of the supper the Widow Slater came unhappily, twisting her apron.

"You been mighty good to Alvah," she faltered. "I'm just obliged to let you have her." She laid a trembling hand on my arm. "Alvah's young," she quavered, "and I look to you to protect her."

I did not know the decorous gathering well enough to tell them that they came to Cross Creek as a menace to a young girl's virtue.

The widow and Alvah and Irene and I all wept when they

moved away to Carolina. Some small stout cord bound us together. Alvah came back to visit Snow a year or so ago and came to see me. She was a tall shy young woman, and it was plain that, thanks no doubt to her mother's standards, much firmer than our fence, her virtue was still not only intact, but, I fear, inviolable.

I think that Snow, the widow's eldest, was her greatest concern. She grieved over him when she left him behind at the Creek. He had already left her leaking roof to shift for himself. She knew that he was fishing for a living but could not find out how or where he might be. From Carolina, she could get no word from him in answer to her letters, and wrote me, beseeching news. I had none to give her, but reported that I saw him pass now and again and he looked well. I could find out no more than she of his mode of life. Her occasional anxious letters kept the youth on my mind. I knew that at one time he had done satisfactory grove work for Old Boss and when I became desperate for male help, I decided to run him down. Tom Glisson told me where I should find him.

"I'm proud his Ma don't know how he's livin'," Tom said. "If she was here, she'd anyways keep him off the dirt."

I did not understand him until I drove down the dim hammock road to the lake edge where Tom told me I should find him. I could not believe that I had come to the right place until a dog I knew for Slater property came from the woods with wagging tail. The camp was a palmetto shack, no larger than six feet by eight. The four corners were sapling cypresses. Palmetto fronds joined these to make walls and were thatched overhead for a roof. Cockroaches ran among the fronds and darted inside the dark box of a home. There was a half-door, the lower half made from a crate and the upper of burlap sacking. I lifted the sacking and saw that he had built a sapling bunk along one side. The pallet on it was filled with moss. A ragged quilt was the only cover. A small rusty stove stood opposite the bunk, its pipe lifting crookedly and precariously above the dry palmetto thatching. I have seen only one other human habitation more primitive and desolate than this. A can of beans had made his last meal. I was glad the widow, grieving for his silent ways, could not see or know.

I left a note pinned on the sacking. The next day he came to work, his face pinched from privation, his overalls shabby. He walked the two miles back and forth each day, and while the wages I could pay shamed me to offer, they were standard in the section. His lean grave young face filled out, and his loose-limbed frame, and decent shirt and cap and breeches replaced the soiled raggedness. He was a fine grove man and we began a relationship somehow beyond that of employer and employee. A bond was forged that will last as long as either of us lives. Yet he was plainly unhappy. He was close-mouthed, and while he expressed anxiety over the grove and my own returns from it under his care, he did not discuss his own difficulties. At long last the truth came out. He was one of those who pined for his own piece of land, and he should never be content until he tilled his own acres, had his own house, and a wife to bring him the cheeriness the widow had brought to her brood. His wages only fed and clothed him. He could not save for his dream in a whole life's span.

When my own fortunes took a turn for the better, my first act was to raise his pay. As time went on, I raised it again, until he was getting twice the rate of other grove workers. This was low enough, by decent standards, yet out of it he could save regularly. We both admired the rich hammock land near his palmetto shack, and one day he came to report that thirty-five acres of the best could be bought for taxes. I sent him to the tax sale and he came back with the tax certificate to the land.

I said, "That land is for you, Snow," and wondered why I had not had the intelligence earlier to go hungry, if necessary, to get it for him. He was one who needed only the slightest edge on life to master it.

We planned his house together, poring, when his work was done, over the mail order catalogue for doors and windows and roofing. He built the house himself in his off hours and on Sundays, and it is a good house. It has old orange trees around it, and a magnolia tree by the gate, and the hammock soil around it as rich as any man needs for making his living. I hope that some day his mother will come and see it. She would say, "Of course he's gettin' along good. A person allus gets out of life what he's entitled to. The Lord sees to that."

One week-end Snow asked to borrow the grove truck.

"I got something I want to fetch from Gainesville," he said.

I said, "Of course. And since you're going, you can bring out the fertilizer I have on order there."

His expression was suddenly strange.

"Sure," he said.

On Monday morning he did not appear. Martha came to the door.

"I got a message for you from Snow," she said. "He couldn't carry the fertilizer Saturday and he's gone to get it this mornin'. He said tell you he was goin' on his own time and payin' for the gas."

"But why couldn't he bring it Saturday?"

"Sugar," she said, "a man bringin' a bed and a bride just ain't got the room nor the notion for a ton o' fertilizer."

9. Catching one young

I bought Georgia of her father for five dollars. The surest way to keep a maid at the Creek, my new friends told me, was to take over a very young Negro girl and train her in my ways. She should be preferably without home ties so that she should become attached to me. My friends traced a newly widowered father of a large family that he was unable to feed as a unit. He was happy to "give" me Georgia, with no strings attached. A five-dollar-bill sealed the bargain. Two months of life with her made me wonder why he had not given her to the first passing gypsy caravan, or drowned her decently.

It is possible that in catching one young, I had picked from too early a litter. No one knew her exact age, but it was somewhere between ten and twelve. At any rate, Georgia was unteachable. I could remember having polished silver, made beds, dried dishes and dusted furniture on educational Saturday mornings at that age, so I knew the thing was possible. It was pure theory as far as Georgia was concerned. She was happy, in fact too happy for a brown child whose lifelong lot it would presumably be to earn her bread by the sweat of her brow. Georgia never moved fast enough to sweat. She had a passion for butterflies and I could never understand how she could put out her hand with enough speed to catch one. I decided that she just sat in the sun watching the butterflies, and sooner or later by the law of averages one lit on her hand and her fingers closed over it so slowly that it was not alarmed. At the moments when she caught the butterflies, the unwashed breakfast dishes were usually sitting as inert as she.

Great effort, after a month, produced the impression on her that not only were dishes meant to be filled with food and the food eaten therefrom, but that after this pleasant process the dishes must be cleansed and so made ready for the next serving. The chain of thought was difficult for her but at last I felt she understood. Progress was being made in teaching her "my ways." Guests came to luncheon and we adjourned afterward to the fire in the living room. I sat comfortably. When the guests left three hours later I went out to the kitchen. The luncheon dishes still sat on the dining table. The kitchen was in the supreme disorder that I achieve when I cook. Georgia sat in the sun on the back steps, playing with a butterfly.

"But you haven't touched the dishes," I said.

"You never told me," she answered.

As I remember, this ended all hope. The ha'nts had something to do with it. It was peculiarly upsetting to be awakened in the night by a figure in the doorway of my bedroom, saying, "The ha'nts has done come." When I insisted that there was no way for ghosts to get in, she informed me, "They comes in thu the cracks." This was unanswerable and so was Georgia. I made up my mind that I would teach her something. Her listless manner lent itself to the lesson. I taught her to announce a meal. I taught her to go to the veranda or the living room and say with her detached air, "Such as it is, it's ready."

And then I gave her father five dollars to take her back again.

Two or three years ago Martha said, "We had somebody you know come see us today. Georgia. She married and got three chillens. She said she used to work for you."

I could only say, "She said she used to do *what?*"

Georgia should have taught me the futility of taking a child and expecting results any sooner than seven or eight years. The theory came from the old plantation South, where already-trained and mature servants carried on while the younger generation was learning its trade. But I tried again. Finances had something to do with it, for at the time I could not afford the wages of a grown woman. I made no down payment on Patsy, but agreed with her grandmother, with whom she lived, to train her, clothe her, care for her, and to pay two dollars a week—to the grandmother. Patsy's mother was "off." This had no connotation of mental aberration. It meant only that she had wandered off with her latest lover and was not in direct communication with her family.

It was probably my fault that I never made much of a success with Patsy. The truth of it was, we had too good a time together. She was as charmed as I with the novelties of flora and fauna and we learned together. When I should have been teaching her to make biscuits and scour skillets, we were wandering in the wildest part of the hammock by the edge of the lake. There we discovered strange flowers and ferns, and a prize of a large planting of the finest yams, left behind unharvested by the previous grove owner. The yams were deep gold and of a size and sweetness and mellowness I have never tasted since. We found turtles laying, and dug their eggs to boil and eat, and Patsy discovered a new world of foods. She began to study everything with an eye to its edibility. A red-bird sang from the pecan tree by the kitchen door.

"Is that ol' reddy-bird good to eat?" she asked me.

"I don't know. But I shouldn't eat him anyway, because he sings so sweetly."

She inquired if I meant to put a certain hen in the pot.

"Why, no. That hen is a good layer. I wouldn't want to eat her."

"Ha!" she said. "If I was that ol' hen, I'd fix to go right on layin'. And if I was that ol' reddy-bird, I'd fix to go right on singin'."

Having Patsy was strangely like having a child of my own; a black one, as though she were a changeling. She must have felt the same way. We walked one day up Old Boss' path on an errand. I was ahead, walking with a hurried gait that I am told is very awkward. My friend Dessie says of it that when I am in a hurry the head is thrust forward, the upper body lying on the wind, reaching for a speed that is quite beyond the legs and feet, carried hopelessly behind. The effect, she says, is that of a wild turkey hen making a getaway. Patsy was a yard or so behind me.

I heard her say, with a curious mixture of pride and affection, "Step it off, Mama! Step it off!"

I am never done with marvelling at the sensitivity to beauty of presumably the dullest and most ignorant souls. The black child Patsy had this response. We went together into the yard one night when the only light was from the stars. She stood motionless by the Oneika mandarin tree. She gave the little chuckle peculiar to her when ideas raced in her small kinky head.

"You can't see the tangerines," she said, "in the dark. But you know they're there, and you think you see 'em. And they look purtier than in the daytime. It's the same with the stars. You see 'em when the sky's plumb black, and that's when they shine the best."

The Negro imagination is dark and rich. As they grow older,

they learn to save it for their own kind, to hide it from unfriendly minds, perhaps, in an alien civilization. But a Negro child will some day make a sad and lovely study for a poet. There was a small grandson of old Martha who came now and then to visit. He found a rare snail in the orange grove and brought it to me to say, "I fotched you this, Missy, for a play-pretty." He brought me once, too, a toad, cupped in careful black paws.

"Look at the little ol' hoppy-toad," he said. "He's got big eyes jus' like our baby."

I do not know whether Patsy would have stayed with me or not, if she had been left to herself. She was snatched away by her mother, who appeared, fat and slovenly and predatory, to claim her. My friends had not foreseen the fact that once a girl was old enough to be of real use, she had more value in a lazy home household than any wages she might turn in. Patsy went away, with a good rudimentary knowledge of housekeeping and cooking, to a turpentine camp where her mother lived with the latest paramour. The Creek always has few Negroes, and Patsy's cousin told me that Patsy, at not quite twelve, was "courting." She seemed to me no more restless than any kitten, but it may be that she saw bright boys' eyes in the darkness where there were none, and that like the mandarin oranges and the stars, they were the more glamorous for being invisible.

*t*he black girl came on foot the four miles from the village. She was barefooted. She strode up the path to the back door, thick-legged, her big toes splayed in the sand. She stopped short and glared at me, as though she meant to strike me. She wore one garment, too short for her erect height. It was of muslin flour sacking, so tattered that the full length of one sweating thigh showed through its multiple rents. She was the dusty black of teakwood. Two short tufts of hair were braided over her temples. They were stiff, a trifle curved, like horns.

She said fiercely, "I hear tell you want a girl. You take me."

She seemed impossible. She looked capable of murder. It would be like having a black leopard loose in the house.

I said, "I wanted a young girl."

"I be's young."

"No. One young enough to teach my ways."

"If I don't do to suit you, you can cut my throat."

It occurred to me that displeasure might work two ways. It seemed necessary to placate her rather than, simply, to reject her.

I said, "A girl your age wouldn't be satisfied four miles from town."

She stepped closer as in menace.

"Town ain't nothin' to me. You don't know. I don't do no courtin'. I don't want no man around me. You jes' don't know."

I said helplessly, "I'm sure you wouldn't suit me."

"Time to say, time you've done tried me. All you got to do is try me."

Futility possessed me.

I said, "I can't pay very high wages."

"Any wages is better than nothin'. I got to get work. I got a use for my pay."

It was her eyes, I decided, that were frightening me. One was blind and white, fixing me with an opaque, unseeing purpose. I made a gesture of despair.

"Right now, this porch floor ain't scrubbed," she said. "You got to have things clean. I be here soon in the mornin'. I got to fotch my things."

She turned on her bare heels to go.

I called after her, "But I don't know anything about you. What's your name? Where do you come from?"

"Name be's Beatrice. I be's 'Geechee. Folks jes' calls me 'Geechee."

She was gone, striding down the path toward some black and Amazonian army that awaited her coming that the battle might begin. I felt dazed and foolish, as though I had been hypnotized by a grotesque idol. She was the ugliest Negress I had ever seen.

The Ogeechee River is tidal and its salt tongue licks far into Georgia. The Negroes of the region, cotton niggers, sugar niggers, rice or tobacco niggers, the sons and daughters of slaves, are of a special African tribe and have kept their identity. They are very black; strong, with a long stride; their bodies straight as palm trunks; violent, often, and as violently loyal. Another black will say, "He's 'Geechee. I'se skeert of him," and a Georgia plantation owner will say, "There's no better Negro in the world if you get a good one."

'Geechee came the next day at daylight and had good strong coffee and crisp small biscuits ready when I awakened. Her "things" were a comb, not the straightening comb of sophistication, but the ordinary kind, toothless from struggles with her knotted wool—and a bundle of letters. That was literally all. I had never seen material possessions at a more irreducible minimum. Even the letters, I thought, were a fancy and could have been dispensed with. I did not know my 'Geechee. She had nothing to wear but the torn shift in which she had appeared, challenging me to accept her. I dressed her. She was bigger-boned than I, but leaner. In my clothes she looked like a battered black rag doll. As the weeks passed I bought her a cautious cheap uniform or two. Even in their white formality she seemed always about to burst into a belligerent dance, tearing her garments from her, prancing naked in a savage triumph. The effect came from her lioness stride, from her unkempt hair which shot in black electric spirals from her skull, and from the white eye with its hypnotic probing. She had been blind in it, she said, since the big fight.

"I dis-remember did I get the lick before they put me in the jailhouse or en-durin' the time they was puttin' me in the jailhouse."

I could have beaten her raw those first months and it would not have mattered. She cleaned my house. She began with the painted wooden ceilings, the hand-hewn rafters where generations of dirt-daubers had built their mud homes. She continued down the painted walls, where roaches had trailed and long-vanished children had drawn pictures. She included the furniture in her sweep, so that polished mahogany emerged pale and unshining. She washed rugs that would go in the washpot. Those that would not, she beat until they hung limp and dustless over the clothesline. She thrashed mattresses in the sunlight. Their tufting covered the yard like full-blown thistles. She ended with the floors. She used six cans of potash, and where there had been soot and grease and streaked varnish and the ochre-colored paint dear to all the South, there were now soft pine boards, luminous with age. There was a hole in the middle of the kitchen where she had followed a stain quite through the flooring.

I shall never have a greater devotion than I had from this woman. She was, as I had thought, not young. Within a week, all fear of her was gone and in its place came the warmth of being watched over and served and cared for. Then she began to drop unintelligible hints. There was something back of the service, something back of the fierce woman. I remembered my first sensing of a fixed purpose.

She said, "I'm doin' to suit you?" and I said, "Yes," and she said, "You trust me, enty?" and I said, "Yes."

One day when she had been with me for some months, making life a good smooth thing, she said, "I got a thing to tell you. I got to have help."

It seemed to me then that I had always known that we were building up to this; that it was not she who was serving me, but I who was destined to serve her.

I said, "What is it?"

She brought a mass of crumpled paper from her breast.

"These is from my man," she said. "Read them."

"My sweet Beatrice," they read, "you got to get me out. I can't stand it. You got to get me out."

One after another, they sang the same refrain. They were written from the state prison.

"You know people," she said. "You can git him out. I got to git him out. You can do it."

I felt like a pawn in the hands of dark forces. Her man was named Leroy. He was serving a twenty-year sentence for manslaughter.

"He didn't do a thing," she said. "This other nigger was layin' for him. He went at Leroy and he bopped him one and Leroy be's strong and he made a pass at him and it done killed this nigger. And you got to git him out."

The 'Geechee had become a part of me. I had little of comfort and that little stemmed from her.

I said, "I'll do what I can," and did not mean to. I needed her more than did Leroy.

I wrote a bland letter to the superintendent of the prison. It was answered as blandly, for I think he understood me. Time passed. Then one day I got the mail from the rural mail-box instead of sending 'Geechee for it, and in the mail was a letter addressed to her from a lawyer. I questioned her.

She said, "You ain't done nothin' for Leroy, when you could. A lawyer that visits at the prison done tol' him he could git him out for two hundred dollars. I wrote him I'd git it, did he give me time."

No shyster lawyer could liberate a killer. I could not endure to have her slave and save and throw away her money on one such. And surely, if this fierce good woman believed in Leroy, he must be entitled to consideration. I felt an unreasonable trust in her judgment and her loyalty.

I said, "Don't pay this lawyer another dollar. I'll see what we can do."

I drove to Raiford and interviewed the superintendent. Leroy had been a model prisoner. The superintendent was an idealist.

"If you can give Leroy a job," he said, "I see no reason why he shouldn't return to normal living. Lack of work when a man first gets out is the usual stumbling-block."

I had made good friends; a state senator, the president of a university. I asked them to wire the Pardon Board, asking for the black man's parole to me. I had a hearing at the state capitol and Leroy was paroled in my care. I drove back to the grove to gather up 'Geechee to go to the prison to collect the man for whom she had starved and toiled and gone ragged.

Leroy was not at the prison when we reached there. He had headed on his release, an hour before, not for the black woman who had done so much for him, but direct to Jacksonville for a round of carousing. He showed up at the grove four days later. He was a slim, sullen, light-brown man with shifty eyes. 'Geechee walked on air. I would pay him, I told him, the customary rural wages, his house and fuel free, and he might have the use of the farm truck once or twice a week. The grove work was not too hard and I would show him all that must be done. I had bought clothes for him, and I gave them a real wedding, with good food afterward.

For a week he languished comfortably under his wife's care. He made no effort to learn the grove work but I did not hurry him. Four years in jail would surely do something to a man's initiative. He could not plunge at once into living. There must be a period of adjustment, as for one who long blind should come with new sight into the sunlight. I made my excuses for him and 'Geechee lost her air of ecstasy. She worked harder than ever, for now she had Leroy's comfort to look after. My own work was never slighted.

At the end of the second week he came to the back door for his Saturday wages. I hold no brief for southern wages, yet many Negroes supported in a rudimentary comfort large families on Leroy's pay, and must pay rent and buy fuel to boot, without the extra wages that 'Geechee brought in. Instead of standing at the door to receive his money, the man pulled it open and brushed past me and seated himself insolently on the bench. He crossed his legs and threw back, his head, narrowing his eyes at me. In a loud voice he began to recite his grievances. He could not live on his pay. He wanted better clothes than those I had bought him. Nobody could be expected to live out here in the woods. It was too far from town. A man had to have his own automobile. He stopped shouting and began to mutter. There was more than a hint of threat in the low growling voice. I who had freed him was an object of hate. My friend Dessie was in the house. She was so certain that the man was about to spring at me that she slipped to her car for her revolver.

He said, "I jus' as soon be in jail as out here in the woods."

I saw 'Geechee slip into the kitchen with tears running down her black cheeks. I was sick at heart. I ordered him back to the tenant house. I locked my house, which stands for weeks in my absence without even the latching of a screen, and drove to town to put in a long distance call to the prison superintendent. There was a silence at the end of the wire.

At last, "The prison is crammed full. We have absolutely no room for him. Send him away at once. You are running a great personal risk. If he can keep out of serious trouble, we'll let him go his way. If he gets into trouble, he'll automatically be picked up again." He sighed. "If I live long enough, I'll learn to recognize the true criminal nature. This man has it."

It was dusk when I reached the grove. 'Geechee, I knew, with her fierce loyalty, would go with him. I could not send her off in the night. I slept uneasily that night, my revolver under my pillow. In the morning she brought my coffee. Her face was drawn and inscrutable.

I said, "Leroy must leave as soon as you've had breakfast. I know you'll want to go with him. I shall be very sorry to be without you. I've become attached to you, 'Geechee."

She said, "I ain't goin' with him. I don't mind him doin' me wrong. He ain't never done anything but wrong to me. But nobody ain't never done for him what you done. He ain't worth killin', the way he talked to you. I wanted to die, listenin' to him."

The world seemed suddenly a brighter place. Then I knew that no new treachery would alter her long loyalty to the man she had known always was worthless.

I said, "It will be better for you to go with him. Then if you still prefer to be with me, you can come back. I'll wait a week or two to get another girl."

She said, "You cain't git along without me. I'se seed. You needs me. I'll go with him. I'll make sure he goes off far enough. I be back Tuesday mornin' on the nine o'clock train."

Sunday and Monday were long. I could not concentrate on my work. I did the household chores absently. I milked the cow and fed the chickens. The grove seemed very silent with no human being about, no man to care for it, no kind black hands serving me in the house. I was so sure that 'Geechee's loyalty to her man would not waver that I very nearly did not go to the village on Tuesday. I made an excuse to myself to go to the village store at train time. The local puffed to a stop at the dingy station and 'Geechee was there. We lonely humans need very little of devotion for contentment. For a moment, this black one-eyed savage woman was all I needed. I touched her calloused dark hand.

She said, "Us'll make out all right. Us'll do better alone."

We drove home to the grove and Mandy the pointer dog leaped up to lick her face in welcome. She celebrated by putting on one of the uniforms in which she was patently uncomfortable and set about putting the house in proper order. The day was fine and sunny, and she drove the cow in at evening and we managed the milking together. After supper she went alone to the tenant house of which she had hoped to make a home. We got along very well on our own. She was sad and quiet. Leroy was living in Jacksonville with another woman and quarrelling with all around him. She had done her best and now a thing was ended and a book was closed. I urged her to let me drop her off in Citra where the Negroes are gay and light-hearted of a Saturday night. I told her to invite them out to her house.

"Surely you can get a new beau," I said.

She said gravely, "You'd ought to know, jus' anybody won't do."

She was as wild-looking as some fresh-caught African slave, but she had given her big heart for life.

It made her happy for me to have parties. She seemed to think that I needed the gayety I urged on her. When the house was full for a buffet supper, she put on her best apron and tied a handkerchief over her tufted head and dashed in and out among the guests, crying the flavor of our foods. When it was time to pass the dessert, she raced through the house with a loaded tray, shouting at the top of her voice, "Sherbet comin' up! Sherbet comin' up!" Her delight was infectious, and friends complain mournfully, now she is gone, that they never had better times at the Creek than when 'Geechee rushed among them, pressing them to drink deep and eat hearty. Once my friend Norton slipped away to my room to steal a nap and 'Geechee discovered him and routed him out. He grumbled that he was sleepy and the room was quiet and her mistress would not mind.

"I minds," she said severely. "You git right out o' here."

She carried her protective instinct to embarrassing lengths. One Saturday night we had the house full after a football game. Half a dozen decided to spend the night. In the morning there were not enough eggs for making the unexpected breakfast and I sent her down the road to Old Boss to see if he could spare a dozen. She reported on their conversation, proud of the way she had protected me.

"Well, 'Geechee," Old Boss said to her, "your Missus had quite a party last night."

"I looked him right in the eye," she said, "and I says to him, 'No, sir, that wasn't no party. That was jus' a few of her kinfolks dropped in to visit her, and she was so proud to see 'em.'"

My life was circumspect, but if I had lived in scarlet sin, 'Geechee would have covered my tracks. A man came from the citrus packing house on business. I was ill in bed and she showed him in to my bedroom without consulting me. I was a trifle embarrassed and when he came again the next day to report on the matter, I said to her, "When I'm in bed and a man comes to see me, I'd a little rather you stood near the doorway."

She showed him in and disappeared. After he had gone and I questioned her, I found that, loyal soul, all the while he was there she had stood sentinel at the front door—watching the highway.

It was after Leroy had gone that I began to realize the source of her occasional high spirits. There were times when she sang so infectiously from the kitchen or over the washtubs that I would stop my work and follow the old spiritual with her. That anomaly, "Prohibition," was still in force, and our liquor was good moonshine from the Florida scrub. We bought it almost openly, bringing it home in five-gallon glass demijohns and siphoning it off into charred oak kegs to ripen. The local sheriff was in cahoots with the moonshiners, arresting only those who did not pay his weekly tribute. A plutocrat was one who could buy 'shine enough ahead of his needs to have always a fully mature supply on hand. The riff-raff drank from hand to mouth of improperly aged liquor, and it was a mark of caste to serve one's "corn" not less than six or eight months old. I managed to put by two five-gallon kegs, for it was enough for friends to drive twenty-five miles to call on me, without offering them raw liquor.

When I breached the first keg, there were only three gallons in it. I was appalled at the rate of evaporation and decided that the modest original price did not prove out so cheaply after all. When I siphoned off the second keg, the contents were two gallons. On that day 'Geechee was unusually blithe. An unhappy suspicion came to me. I questioned her. One may usually spare one's breath in questioning a Negro about a theft, especially that of liquor. The slave status has made the lie a social necessity. 'Geechee freely admitted having helped herself. She had not even bothered to use the siphon. She had simply heaved the keg up on her shoulder when she wanted a drink and poured out a tumblerful.

"It's the onliest way I can make out," she said. "It's the onliest thing that lifts my heart up, times I think I'm jus' obliged to die."

There could be no answer. We compromised by my parcelling out as much as I thought she needed, but it was never enough. Her grief, her burden, was too great. She found her way, like water seeping through a crack, to whatever stores I had locked or hidden. Once when I was away I left her a quart and locked a new keg in my own bedroom cupboard, taking with me the key. When I returned, the lock was undisturbed and the keg was half empty. She had taken the door off the hinges, she told me. Her despair was greater than I knew. I thought that we were getting on very well, when suddenly, just before Christmas, she got hold of a gallon of her own, got rousing drunk, and simply walked away. I woke up to a strangely silent house, with no good sounds from the kitchen of stove lids thumping, no sweet smell of coffee, no murmur of 'Geechee's morning humming.

A freeze came in the night before Christmas. On Christmas morning the pipes were frozen solid, there was no water for coffee, the woodpile was depleted and I had to chop enough for a fire in the living room. I sat huddled over it, longing for the black girl's feet shuffling toward me with comfort and help. There came instead a message from a passer-by that 'Geechee had told that she had not quit me nor been fired. She was only taking a vacation. Time proved what I suspected. She had taken her savings and gone to Jacksonville to make sure that Leroy was being properly cared for.

I waited a long time for her to come back to me. The weeks passed and there was no word. I believe that she was too ashamed of having abandoned me to return without word from me. If I had understood the Negro psychology as well then as now, I should have gone after her. Exasperated with too much cow and too little firewood, I hired a Negro couple, Kate and Raymond. We settled down into a semblance of comfort, and while Kate was pretty and flip and impudent, she was clever and willing, and Raymond's long arms swinging the axe at the woodpile looked to me like the flutter of angels' wings. But life was not the same. That small bright flame of loving devotion was put out, and sitting in front of Raymond's roaring log fires, I was still cold. More than a year went by. It was a good year, with a new gay friend to initiate me into duck-hunting. The hunt on the lake was good, and coming home at night, with supper of quail and red wine and biscuits, and good talk by the fire. But 'Geechee was gone.

In late spring I sailed comfortably from off an intractable horse and broke my neck and fractured my skull. I rode the horse back to the stables and dismissed the incident. No one has ever had an easier experience with a serious accident. I put in a week not too badly, ending with paddling a boat all day while my friend cast for bass. Then the pain became a nightmare and I was a little out of my mind. My good Tampa doctor friend came with Dessie, his wife, for the week end, and said, "You don't seem to know it, but you have a broken neck." X-rays confirmed his easy diagnosis. There were weeks nursed by them in Tampa and the doctor fitted me with a steel brace that I thought gave me the noble look of Joan of Arc in armor, chin lifted, listening to the Voices, but that seemed to strike others dumb with horror. I was ready to go home. I could drive a car, could go on with my work, but I could not bathe nor dress myself nor adjust the brace. Dessie had already given me too generous a share of her time. The doctor knew of a good practical white nurse who would go home with me. I did not want her. I was re-writing a book and I did not want to take time out from it to be polite to her. I wanted 'Geechee.

Dessie drove me to Hawthorn where 'Geechee's mother lived. The girl had been following the strawberry season as a picker. We followed two blind trails. The third took us south to the outskirts of Plant City. We inquired at a Negro soft-drink stand. She was not known by her name of Beatrice. I described her big-boned frame, her one blind white eye. The Negro chuckled.

"You mean 'Geechee. There's a gal us don't fool with. An' you won't find her around no soft-drink stand. 'Geechee got to have somethin' stronger'n that."

He knew where she was living and we drove into the yard. She came out to the car. At sight of me in my apparatus tears streamed down her face.

"Oh, my white lamb," she cried out, "what they been doin' to you?"

She knew why we had come before we told her. She gathered up her pitiful belongings—she was sending her money to Leroy. Dessie drove us home to the Creek. It was like being in the hands of a black Florence Nightingale. All of us, no matter how self-reliant, long, I think, for tenderness. Her big rough hands touched me as gently as though I were made of glass, instead of being almost as sturdy as she. In the bath, she washed and dried me with a feather touch. She lingered over it, giving great attention at last to the toes, and once she chuckled and whispered under her breath, "Such little white footses—." They were little and white only in comparison with her own.

For two weeks she did not touch a drop of liquor. Then the old need came over her, and her breath reeked, and she wavered in helping me from the tub. Sometimes when I called she did not hear me, and Kate came saucily to report that "'Geechee asleep—leas', I reckon she's asleep," and laughed. My heart ached. One Sunday morning two months after she had come, I awoke to pandemonium. Stove lids were being dropped on the floor, or thrown there. Dishes crashed. I heard shrieks from the tenant house. After a long time, 'Geechee reeled into my room.

"Kate an' Raymond's fightin'," she announced. "But don't you worry."

She staggered out and the racket began again in the kitchen.

She came to my door and said, "The bacon done burnt itself up, but don't you fret."

After half an hour she appeared to say, "Kate is chasin' Raymond thu the grove with a butcher knife. But you jes' lay still and don't worry."

I did not see her again. I lay helpless and hopeful, but there was no further sound. It was all hopeless. My breaks were nearly healed, and in her many delinquencies I had found that I could adjust the brace myself. I got myself dressed after a fashion and went to the back door and called her. There was no answer. In late afternoon she appeared, half sober.

She said, "I know I got to go. I ain't no use to nobody. It comes over me and I can't help it. No use foolin' with me, I won't never be no different."

Kate and Raymond appeared sheepishly.

"It was me got 'em drunk," 'Geechee said. "They didn't aim to do it. Kate an' Raymond's all right."

I paid her and told Raymond to drive her home in the truck to her mother.

"I hate to part this way," I said.

"Me, too," and she was gone.

No maid of perfection—and now I have one—can fill the strange emptiness she left in a remote corner of my heart. I think of her often, and I know she does of me, for she comes once a year to see me. I put my arms around her big bony shoulders and she pats my back comfortingly. She is always a little drunk. She goes from one job to another, losing it always for the same reason. The last time she came I was away.

Little Will reported, "The 'Geechee girl was here to see you. She sure was high. She said she tried to go without drinkin', times, but seemed like she'd lose her mind, didn't she have it. She said she knowed she'd still be here with you, could she change. She said tell you they ain't nothin' nobody can do about it."

11. A pig is paid for

i suppose there is nowhere in the world a more elemental exchange of goods than among ourselves at the Creek. The exchange does not even become barter and trade. We merely return favors. Old Boss uses my truck to haul his vegetable crops to the station and I use his mules for my occasional light plowing. We have never sat down to figure which has the higher rental value, for it does not matter. I have the only pecan trees at the Creek, so each fall two or three families pick the crop for me, by their request, and take for pay only enough pecans to last them through the winter. They refuse the actual cash value of the work. As a matter of fact, they could not have been hired. One fisherman borrows a few dollars of me in lean times, and I have a drawing account for fish, never calculated exactly, but well tipped in my favor. Another man borrows between jobs and appears unsummoned when a freeze comes in and I must fire my young orange grove. Sometimes his two or three nights of the cold and arduous work come to much more than he has borrowed and he waves aside the proffered difference.

"You don't owe me a nickel," he says.

I contracted one debt, however, that involved me in so labyrinthine a maze that I thought I should never find my way out of it. It was my punishment, I suppose, for shooting a pig of Mr. Martin's. I never planned to shoot the pig and I certainly didn't know it belonged to Mr. Martin. As a matter of fact, I didn't care. It could have belonged to the devil himself, and many a morning I was sure of it. I am a patient woman as far as other people's stock is concerned. I know stock. If I were a pig, I should search out the green pastures, as did the pigs of Mr. Martin. if I knew where skimmed milk lay white and frothy in open pans, I should push my way under a stout barbed-wire fence and bury my snout in that milk. But even if I were a pig, I can see no reason for rooting up fluffy-ruffle petunias.

There were eight of the pigs. The first thing I heard every morning at daybreak was the whole outfit crashing under the fence and rushing under the floor of my bedroom for a matutinal rubbing of backs against the crosspiece. The rubbing ended, and the grunts, my room stopped shaking, and the commotion passed. I turned over for a nap. While I was napping, the happy congregation moved on to the trays of biddy-mash, the skimmed milk and the fluffy-ruffle petunias. Fluffy-ruffle petunias are delicate plants. The seed is as expensive as gold dust and as fine. It takes weeks to germinate. The seedlings must be nursed by hand. When transplanted, they are the prey of cutworms, of drought, of the slightest adversity. Once brought months later to maturity, the huge multicolored blooms represent beauty flowered into life by the most desperate of measures. So while I could forgive the heavy supplying to alien porkers of chicken feed and milk, I simply could not forgive the fluffy-ruffle petunias. The intruders dug up altogether four consecutive plantings and on the third uprooting I was a trifle demented. I lay in watch.

I discovered that the litter had a leader. He was as pretty a young barrow as I have ever seen, Titian-haired and light of spirit and rounded into delicious curves by his long diet of biddy-mash, skimmed milk and petunias. It was he who broke his way through and under the fence, he who raced joyously under my bedroom to scratch, he who galloped, butt wobbling, tail curling, to the trays of feed and the petunia bed. His brothers and sisters only followed where he led. Where they came from, where they went when the sun had set, I did not know. I knew only that the bright-red barrow was my enemy. One morning I sat on my veranda. The litter was peaceful, ready to lie quietly and decently in the shade. But not the red-bristled fiend. He pranced to the front yard and gave himself with abandon to my fourth planting of fluffy-ruffle petunias. I arose as one in a trance, picked up my gun, stepped to the petunia bed and shot him dead where he fed.

Psychologists might say, trying me before a jury of my peers, that murder lay ready in my heart. The act was not premeditated, yet the will to kill was waiting. I know only that I pulled the trigger with joy and looked down at my fallen foe with delight and triumph. There would be no more battening of outlaw stock on feed and flowers. I wondered to whom the pigs belonged. They were none of my immediate neighbors'. I looked again at the red menace. He was appallingly fat and succulent. I picked him up by his curly tail, put him in my car and drove to Citra. I arranged to have Mr. Hogan dress him, and Ward the storekeeper to store him in his refrigerator. I sent a wire to my friend Norton in Ocala, "Bring ten or twelve Saturday night for whole roast pig barbecue."

The roast pig was perfection. The meat was as white as the skimmed milk and the petunia roots on which it had been fattened.

After, I read aloud Charles Lamb's essay on "Roast Pig." It was a fine evening.

On Sunday, neighbor Tom stopped by and said with a queer look in his eyes, "You been having pig trouble?"

"Yes, but it's all over."

"Could be, it's just begun. You know anything about the man named Martin?"

"Never heard of him."

"Well, he's settled across the Creek. Put out the word he's a man won't be trifled with. Has notches on his gun. I just wondered." He went away.

On Monday morning I heard knuckles pound on the steps at the side porch. A huge man stood there with his broad-brimmed Stetson hat pushed back from his forehead.

"Mornin'. My name's Martin."

"Good morning, Mr. Martin. What can I do for you?"

He shifted his weight.

"Mis' Rawlings, do you remember hit rainin' last Monday?"

"Why, no, Mr. Martin, I don't."

"Well, hit rained. Mis' Rawlings, do you remember loadin' your truck to Dorsey Townsend last Monday?"

"Why, yes. I don't remember that it was Monday, but he borrowed it one day last week."

"Well, hit were Monday. Mis' Rawlings"—he squinted casually at the sky—"do you remember a gun shootin' last Monday? A 12-gauge, maybe. Maybe a 16. Could of been a 20."

"Why, yes indeed," I said. "It was I who shot. I shot a pig. With my 20-gauge. I don't know whose pig it was. It led the pack that came through my stock-proof fences. It tormented me to death. Why, Mr. Martin, maybe it was your pig. The mark was a half-moon in one ear and a bit in the other."

He drew a long breath.

"That were my pig," he said.

He stared at me.

"Of course," I said. "I expect to pay for it. In a way, I had a right to shoot it, because it was an outlaw. In another way, the right is on your side, because in a no-fence county you have the right to turn your stock loose. But I'll pay for it very gladly. Oh, Mr. Martin, I did so enjoy shooting that pig."

He stepped back and studied me.

"Them pigs was practically pets," he said.

"They were very tame," I said. "That was the trouble."

"You could of ketched it with your bare hands," he lamented.

"Yes, Mr. Martin," I said, "but then I wouldn't have had the pleasure of shooting it."

Suddenly I remembered the notches on his gun.

"In a way, Mr. Martin," I said, "I'm sorry. But that's the way I am. I go along quietly for a while, and then out of a clear sky I just don't know what I'm doing. I pick up a gun and I shoot whatever makes me angry. This time it was a pig. I'm so afraid some time it may be a person. After it was over, I'd be terribly sorry. But then it would be too late, wouldn't it?"

He wiped his forehead.

"I don't know what to think," he burst out. "From the beginning, I ain't knowed what to think. I went to all your neighbors, and they all said, 'Oh, no, Mis' Rawlings wouldn't do a thing like that.' But all the time something told me, if you got mad enough, you'd do it."

"It's too bad, isn't it?" I condoled with him. "When I'm so sorry afterward."

He grew confidential.

"I heard the shot and I placed it about here, and my pig come up missing. I stopped Dorsey and I got it out of him he'd heard you shoot. I went to Citra and I found out where you'd had it dressed and where you'd had it stored, and they all said, 'Why, yes, Mis' Rawlings come in with a pig she said she'd shot.' I saw the constable and turned out he was a buddy of yours and he just laughed. I studied and I studied and I decided to have the law on you. I aimed to put you in the jailhouse. And if they wouldn't put you in the jailhouse I aimed to settle it my way. I aimed to make all the trouble for you I knew to do. And now—now you talk so honest—why, I just don't know what to do."

"Don't you worry about it another minute," I soothed him. "Now it's all over, and I'm so sorry, I can't bear to have you worried. You just decide on your price, and whatever that pig was worth to you, why, it's worth the same to me. And if you'd rather have another pig of the same size and pedigree, I'll replace it."

"I don't know how to figure the price," he said. "I'd not of dreamed of selling one of them pigs."

He turned away, then back again.

"I could of stood everything," he said, "but then you went and had a drunken party—and *ate* it."

"Oh, Mr. Martin," I said, "the meat was delicious. I wish I'd sent you some. I never had better pork in my life. And why wouldn't it be good? It had fed on biddy-mash and skimmed milk and fluffy-ruffle petunias."

I suppose that Mr. Martin gave it all up then as a matter in the realm of madness. He went away, murmuring that the pig was beyond price and replacement would be practically impossible. I gave no further thought to pig or payment, waiting for the bill to arrive. The pig was worth several dollars, but I decided that I would pay anything up to fifteen without protest. Or I should go to market and buy its valuable duplicate. And then Mr. Higgenbotham entered the picture.

My relations with Mr. Higgenbotham were already involved. We first became friends over the matter of snakes. Adrenna came mincing to my room one morning as though she were announcing the President.

"Mr. Higgenbotham is calling," she said. "Mr. Higgenbotham wishes to show you a snake."

I put on a house-coat and went to the front door. I knew Mr. Higgenbotham to speak to, for his ramshackle open truck passed the house going and coming on his business of frog-hunting and snake-catching. Mr. Higgenbotham is a small ragged man with hair shaggy in his eyes. He had his campaign planned. As I came to the door, he held up one hand in command, unfurled a crocus sack, and with great drama rolled a large king snake onto the grass.

"There! Look at him! Six foot long! I ain't been getting but forty cents for 'em. I just want you to see. Why, a snake like that is worth forty cents in the woods!"

His grievance, it appeared, was over the low market on snakes.

"You know folks in the up-country," he said, "and I want you to see can you get me a better market for my snakes."

His confidence touched me. I could think of no friend at the moment who might be interested in upping the price on king snakes. But I assured him that I would do my best. A king snake six feet long was certainly worth forty cents in the woods. We became immediately fast friends. The king snake was to Mr. Higgenbotham an individual. It was his pet and its name was Oscar. He put it through its tricks. It coiled like a rattlesnake and struck playfully at him. He tapped it on its glistening head.

"That's enough o' that, Oscar. You wouldn't believe how smart he is. I can't fool him on his rations. I hold a little snake for him, or a mouse, and he takes it as dainty as a lady. Give him a stick or a strip of shoestring and he turns away disgusted. And when I turn him a-loose, he's after the rats in the house like lightning."

Foolishly, idiotically, regretting it in an instant, I said, "That's fine. I have terrible trouble with rats in my attic."

"I'll lend you Oscar," he said. "I want to do something for you, helping me with my business. I'll put Oscar in your attic."

I could have cut out my tongue. Mr. Higgenbotham was gathering up Oscar with enthusiasm, to put him in the attic.

"It's all sealed up," I said. "We couldn't very well get to it."

"We'll cut a hole," he said. "Oscar would have to have a hole, anyway, so he could come down to get water."

I had visions of awakening and staring into the black beady eyes of Oscar, come down for water. The rats seemed pleasant companions.

"It wouldn't be safe," I said, inspired. "My cat is death on snakes."

He put Oscar reluctantly into the crocus sack.

"Well—I'd sure hate to have that happen."

I was so happy to be rid of Oscar that I did my best about the snake market. I wrote to Ditmars and to the Cincinnati Zoo and the Washington Zoo. The replies were courteous and I think amused. The general opinion was that if my friend was getting forty cents for king snakes, he was doing nicely. The big zoos had their own collectors and snakes were a glut on the market. Mr. Higgenbotham was grateful for my efforts, satisfied now with his price. He waved violently whenever his truck passed my house. He usually had a cross-eyed child with him, and I could see him nudge the child, so that it too waved to me. One day Mr. Higgenbotham stopped and came up the path with the unhappy air of a man about to try to borrow money.

"I'm in a tight," he said, "and you're my friend, and I figgered you was the one to help me out. The sheriff's been after me and been after me about a license for my truck. 'I cain't let you keep that thing on the highways no longer without no license,' he said to me. He said, 'I hate to be hard on a poor man, but next time I catch you out without no license, I'm obliged to run you in.'"

"How much do you need?"

"Not but six dollars. I'll give you a mortgage on the truck."

I looked at it. There was not six dollars' worth of usable parts of any description.

"Or," he added, "in a pinch, I could work it out."

The idea seemed feasible enough. I gave Mr. Higgenbotham six dollars and he agreed to work it out in pruning on my orange trees. Days passed, and weeks, and Mr. Higgenbotham passed and re-passed on his frog- and snake-hunting expeditions and did not stop to prune. It is one thing to help a friend in distress and it is another thing to be done. I was on the roadside one day picking up pecans and flagged down Mr. Higgenbotham. It took him a hundred yards to stop. He backed up. The cross-eyed child began waving dutifully.

"Don't speak," Mr. Higgenbotham shouted. "Don't say it. I know what you're thinking. You're thinking I got no intentions o' paying back what I borrowed. Mis' Rawlings, I had the confidence in you not to borrow without I meant to pay it back. I got my plans. You just wait now. The moon won't be out this month without I pay back that six dollars."

He drove off with a flourish and the child waved as far as it could see. The next week the truck stopped at my gate. In the back stood trussed a lean gray razor-back sow. Mr. Higgenbotham walked jauntily up the path.

"Want to buy a pig?" he called.

"It's just about the last thing in the world I want to buy," I said with possible bitterness.

"Couldn't use a pig to trade?" he asked and winked at me. "Can't think of nobody now you owe a pig to?"

Understanding struck me.

"I do owe a pig to Mr. Martin," I said, "but how did you know?"

"Oh, everybody knows you owe Mr. Martin a pig. Now what I got figgered out is this. That sow there is worth six dollars if she's worth a cent. I owe you six dollars. If Mr. Martin takes that sow, you've paid him and I've paid you. Now how about it?"

I looked at the rangy creature in the truck.

"What makes you think Mr. Martin will take her?"

"Well, when you figger on a sow, you figger on more than a sow. You buy you a sow, and directly you've got a litter of pigs to boot. You've got the sow and you've got eight-ten pigs and the pigs'll soon make shoats and you carry the shoats to market and you get good money for 'em and you've yet got the sow. Now I'm carrying that sow there to Mr. Martin's boar hog. You know sows?"

"No," I said, "not very well."

"Well, a sow's peculiar. Times, she'll take, and again she'll not take. It all depends on the moon. Now last moon, she'd not of took. This moon, I figger she'll take. And if she takes—mind, if she takes— Mr. Martin'll take her for the debt. 'Course, if she don't take, I'm the one loses. In that case, I got a dollar to pay for the use o' the boar."

It seemed very complicated, between Mr. Martin and Mr. Higgenbotham and the rental stud of boars and the ways of sows and the moon, but I had little to lose.

"Very well. If the sow takes, and Mr. Martin accepts her for my debt to him, then your debt to me is paid. Right?"

"Righter'n rain," and he drove off with the gray sow lurching in the back of the truck and the child waving.

Time passed and I had no bill from Mr. Martin and no call from Mr. Higgenbotham. The situation was a little delicate, for a lady is not supposed to inquire too closely into matters either of debts or of breeding. Then I ran into Mr. Martin in the grocery store on a Saturday night in Citra. He was cordial. He was effusive.

"You do any duck-hunting?" he asked.

"Indeed, yes."

"A quick shot like you," he said, "I figgered you'd enjoy duck-hunting. Now when winter comes and you're ready, you just get me word and I'll carry you out to the best duck stand on Orange Lake."

Surely something must have been settled. The moon must have been right. In the formality of the store I could not inquire of the intimate relation of the gray sow to Mr. Martin's boar. I longed to say, "Did she take? Are we all square, you and Mr. Higgenbotham and I?"

I said, "The pig I owed you for. The one I was to replace—"

He put out a big hand for me to shake.

"Mis' Rawlings," he said, "the pig is paid for."

12. My friend Moe

Sometimes there are friendships that have no apparent reason for existence, between people set apart by every circumstance of life, yet so firm in their foundations that they survive conditions that would separate friends of more apparent suitability. My friendship with Moe was one of these. Moe said and believed that we were friends because we needed each other.

In the village he said once, "Me and her is buddies, see? If her gate falls down, I go and fix it. If I git in a tight for money she helps me if she's got it, and if she ain't got it, she gits it for me. We stick together. You got to stick to the bridge that carries you across."

If he had never fixed a gate for me, waving aside any offer of pay, leaving a profitable carpenter's job to do it—for I certainly could not be bothered with the neighbors' stock coming in, could I?—if I had never scratched up a dollar for him, Moe and I would have been friends. Beyond our admiration of something in each other that might pass for courage, beyond our mutual helpfulness, there was a warm tenderness that made us like just to sit down together on the back steps and talk about the world as we saw it, while three or four of his boys squatted patiently on their heels waiting for us to be finished.

Sometimes he would wave his arm at them and boom in his deep voice, "You scapers go on, and eat oranges now. Me and her ain't half done talkin'."

He introduced himself on my first Christmas Day at the Creek. He came out with a man named Whitey and it was a formal Christmas call. I was bustling about cooking Christmas dinner, some of the family were there, and Moe and Whitey sat on the back steps and visited with the men. It was long past the country noon dinner hour and I grew uneasy as the turkey browned and the squash and potatoes were done and the hard sauce finished for the plum pudding. I took my outdoor shower and dressed. I delayed, pushing the gravy to the back of the wood range. Moe and Whitey sat on. The turkey was beginning to dry out and the sauce had stood too long on the oyster cocktails in the ice-box.

In desperation, I said, "Dinner is ready. Won't you men join us?"

According to my bringing up, that was the signal for uninvited guests to be on their way. I found that in rural Florida, to refuse an invitation to a meal, if one is there at the time it is ready or nearly so, is to insult hospitality so grievously that the damage can seldom be repaired. Moe and Whitey had of course had their dinner, but to my horror Moe said "Thank you, Ma'am," led Whitey to the pump stand to wash up and came in. The family dinner was ruined for me. The intruders were as unhappy as I, but applied themselves with lowered heads and high-lifted elbows to their plates. Whitey was plainly only a follower and I stole a look at Moe. He was a great burly man with long arms and thick shoulders, slightly hunched from years of labor. His head was massive and beyond a full fine forehead the receding hair was shaggy and leonine. There was the look there of a man who might have been a statesman. He had one of the most beautiful speaking voices that I have ever heard. It had the deep resonance of a bass fiddle.

He plowed his way through the many-coursed dinner without comment. When I served the plum pudding that had taken so long to make and decorate, he looked briefly at the blanched almonds and sugared fruits on the top and scraped them to one side, as I should scrape unexpected insects. The dinner had been one of my best, and it seemed to me from the rough worn clothes and the backwoods speech that it must surely have been a little out of the ordinary for these men. My vanity about my cooking is known and pandered to, and it seemed incredible to me that uninvited guests like these should not only pay me no compliments, but should have put down the choice dishes like so much hay.

I said, "You men have just eaten a typical Yankee Christmas dinner. Now tell me, what is the usual Cracker Christmas dinner?"

Moe lifted his big head and looked at me gravely.

"Whatever we can git, Ma'am," he said. "Whatever we can git."

I should have given the dinner and all my work over it, not to have asked that question.

I heard later that in the village Moe described the meal dish by dish. He spoke even of the edible decorations on the plum pudding that he rejected.

"A meal like that," I was told he said, "a feller don't know what's cold-out rations and what's fancy fixin's. When I seed her face, I knowed I'd ought to of run the risk and et everything."

I do not remember when we became friends. The occasion is bound to have been one when he did me some kindness. It seems to me that it was the hot Sunday morning when he passed by with his boys from a night's frog-hunting and found me in hell. I shall always associate my conception of hell with hot Sunday summer mornings at the Creek. And why Sunday morning? Because that is when the drinking portion of the Negro help fails to arrive.

The Sunday morning that Moe stopped by was one of these. I was without household help at the time and I slept late without hearing a sound on the place to disturb me. The lowing of the cow finally penetrated my sleep and I awoke in a humid heat to an uneasy sense that all was not well. I dressed and went out to the stillness of a desert island. I do not remember which of the procession of Negro men was the culprit, but whoever he was, he was not there.

The cow was old Laura, weather-beaten, gray and gaunt, and the only cow I have known with a more evil nature than hers, is her daughter Dora. Laura was busily and angrily engaged in tearing down the pasture fence. An early daughter, then a calf, little Atrocia, a repulsive creature whom I later traded to a Negro for a week's hoeing, was jumping back and forth through the hole in the fence that Laura had begun. The young bull had broken through the fence by the road, and at sight of me began bellowing and pawing the earth. The chickens, unfed and protesting, got under my feet and tripped me as I made my way through the sandspurs to the pasture gate. It had been fastened with an intricate African arrangement of chains, and by the time I had them loosened and the gate swung wide, Laura had knocked down two more fence posts and was making her way loftily to the barn.

She then decided to be coy, and food being what I supposed she wanted, refused to go into the pen where it waited. She gambolled like a heifer through the grove, her bony hips heaving, little Atrocia at her heels in delight at the sudden friskiness of her aged parent. I was obliged to give up getting her into the pen. I lugged the feed trough out into the open by the barn and brought a bucket of water, for the lake was low beside the pasture and the stock must be watered by hand. I went into the barn for feed. A new sack had to be opened and I bruised my fingers working at the chain-stitch binding. I took a bucket of the feed and emptied it into the trough. Laura was in front of the house eating blue plumbago blossoms and asparagus fern. I climbed up the rickety ladder to the hayloft to pitch down hay, for the bull must have some of this too. A chicken snake and two rats ran across my feet as I lifted a forkful. A leather-winged bat, disturbed from its slumbers in the rafters, swooped out of the loft, brushing my hair. A setting hen under the hay flew into my face and floated to earth, squawking and shrilling. I pitched down the hay and descended the ladder. The next to the last rung broke under me and I slid to the ground and walked limping to the feed trough. Laura had come, eaten all the feed, and was now over by the tenant house. Being full, she had no intention of standing for milking. She had a greedy nature and I lured her back to the trough with another bucket of feed. The calf was only two months old, though weaned, and Laura's bag in mid-morning was full and tight. I had never milked in my life. I had never expected to milk in my life. I should not have tried it now, but I was certain Laura would burst if she were not somehow relieved.

I knelt down beside her, put the milk bucket under her, and tightened my fingers around two of the udders. Nothing happened. With her mouth dripping feed, Laura turned her head over her shoulder and looked at me, as though to say, "What on earth are you doing?" In annoyance, she moved a foot to the side. I moved too. I began again. I constricted desperately, trying to recall the motion I had seen the milkers use. The knack suddenly came to me, and I saw the first thin streams of milk drop into the bucket as though I had brought up pearls from the sea. By this time the second bucket of feed was gone, Laura walked off, and I was obliged to go for the third bucket and lure her back again. She was indifferent, but she had become also a little lethargic, and I got her back to the trough. This time, because she ate so slowly, I got a quart of milk. A sense of proud competence filled me. I was dripping with perspiration and the flies hummed around us. When they stung me, I went frantically on with my milking. When they stung Laura, she switched her long tail across my face. Now she stood immobile, ruminating placidly. With no provocation at all, because the stinging flies were on me, she lifted a hind foot and kicked the bucket of milk into my lap. I looked at her bag. It seemed as full as ever. I went back to the milking. Humanitarian motives had left me, but I did not want a good milch cow to swell up and die. I got another pint, and Laura lifted a hind leg and kicked me square in the middle. There was only one thing left to do. I kicked her in the middle, said to her, "You may burst for all of me," and she stalked off into the coffee-weed. I tottered to the pen to close the gate. It was at this moment that Moe and his boys drew up by the fence and hailed me.

His big voice boomed out, "What you doin' with a milk bucket?"

I leaned weakly on the fence to answer him.

"My man didn't show up and I tried to milk the cow."

"Where is she?"

He was already putting his long legs out of the old car. His boys tumbled out behind him.

"Over there in the coffee-weed. I hope she pops wide open."

I must have begun then to know him as a friend, for he did not laugh. He gave directions to the boys and they scattered to the points of the compass. Two of them drove back the cow. Two made a noose of a rope from the barn. All together they held her tied tight to an orange tree while Moe rested on his heels and milked and stripped her.

"What else you got around here ain't done?"

The chickens had not been fed and water for all the animals had not been pumped. They did that.

Moe said, "Now if that nigger don't show up by evenin', you leave me know. I'll go find him and take a whip to him, leavin' you like this."

He was always indignant when he found me doing work that he considered too difficult or too heavy, and called his boys in a swarm to take over. They were silent, unsmiling youngsters, undersized and pale. They went to school passively, and since they showed no interest in education, Moe was trying to train them in his own profession of carpentering, and was teaching them frog-hunting on the side.

"Them scapers is the best frog hunters in the county," he said. "No fear o' them or their mammy starvin' when I'm done for, long as they can haul in a hundred pounds o' frogs of a night."

The boys smiled then, wanly. The irresponsible night hunting was to their taste. I am sure the carpentering was not, though they did accurate enough work under Moe's critical eye. Moe's true love was an orange grove, and he would have liked to raise oranges for a living. His father, and his grandfather before him, had been superintendent for the Fairbanks grove, one of the oldest Florida groves, of which my choice seven acres in Big Hammock is a part. Moe had lived on the grove as a boy. One day I heard his voice giving orders at the gate. The boys were bringing in a bedstead. It was handmade, spool turned, of pine, put together with wooden pegs. It had the grace of all good handmade things.

"This mought seem like pure trash to you," Moe said, and the boys set the bed down in front of me. "But if you want it, it's yours. It was made for Major Fairbanks, and before he died he give it to my daddy. It's been out in the barn for fifty years. You want it?"

The bed had real value as Floridiana. There are almost no native Florida antiques. Major Fairbanks was not only a famous early grove owner, but the founder and first president of the Florida Historical Society and the author of *Fairbanks' History of Florida* and the *History and Antiquities of St. Augustine*, both now collectors' items.

I said, "It's beautiful, Moe, but it's valuable. You should keep it."

"We got no use fer it," he said contemptuously, not of the bed, but of his household's way of life, which grieved him. "The way I got to figgerin', a thing belongs to be used and used right, and you livin' nice, and havin' a piece o' the Major's old grove, why, you're the one to have it. Been layin' up all these years waitin' for the right person."

The bed is now my own, and it is promised when I am done with it to the Historical Society.

I did not understand it at the time, but as I look back on our friendship, I believe that Moe lived vicariously in my grove and in my "livin' nice." He was intrigued with every detail of my housekeeping. He put in a new kitchen floor for me, saying of the old one through which 'Geechee had scrubbed a hole, "Why, Ma'am, they was places you could of throwed a dog through it." As he worked, he noticed a row of glass jars of huckleberries that I had canned. His grave face brightened.

"Now that's the way to live," he said. "All the good things we got here in Florida, blueberries and blackberries and beans and cowpeas, all them things had ought to be canned and put up on a clean cupboard shelf with white paper on it. That's the way my Ma did. She lived fine, not the way you live, but just as good when it come to cannin' things and keepin' things clean." His face darkened. "I've tried and I've done tried to get my wife to do that-a-way but it just ain't no use. One time I bought two dozen glass jars and I went out by myself and I picked about a bushel o' blackberries and I went to the store and bought a twenty-five pound sack o' sugar and I takened it home, and I said, 'Wife, here's a bait o' blackberries to put up for us for jam and jelly for the winter.'" He hesitated, his loyalty pricking him.

"She probably didn't have time to do it," I suggested.

"She had time. She let the blackberries spoil, and the antses got in the sugar, and I found the jars throwed out in the back yard."

I had light on the matter when I met his mother, who came to visit in the village. Moe brought her out and left her with me for the day. She was of the admirable Florida pioneer type, plump, immaculate, wise and kindly. We talked of her life on the Fairbanks grove and we talked of Moe.

"It like to killed me when he married," she said. "Moe did love bein' to home and havin' things nice. I said to him, 'Son, don't you marry that girl. She ain't your kind and she'll not make you the home you want.' He looked kind o' sorrowful, and he said, real slow, 'I know, Ma. But I love the little old thing.'"

Moe followed the fortunes of my grove as closely as if it had been his own. When I planted ten acres of Valencias across the road where the dingy pecan trees had been cut down and the vacant space had stared at me, he rejoiced with me. We were sure that the new ten acres would make the needed difference between profit and loss. I had put my last hundreds of dollars in the planting and was obliged to watch my simple grocery supplies in consequence. I went to the Everglades in the winter on a hunting trip with Dessie and the Chanceys. The weather in late November was warm when we left Tampa. Cold weather set in the second day at camp. Even so far south, we were obliged to have a roaring camp fire night and morning, and the pond water in which we bathed struck us with icy power. We wore sweaters under our hunting clothes and were hard put to it, as we stood motionless on our deer and turkey stands, not to stamp our feet and clap our hands to keep our circulation moving against the cold. The hunt and the companions were so delightful that I did not think to associate the cold with any menace to my new young grove.

When I returned to the Creek, I found that a disastrous freeze had come in to north and central Florida. Old groves showed much damage, fruit was nipped, and many young groves had been frozen to the ground. I looked across the road to my small frail Valencia trees. A miracle had happened. They had been mounded with earth almost to their tops and below the frozen tips they were safe. No one could have done this but Moe. That evening I drove in to his house to see him.

"Bet you was surprised," he chuckled. "The cold begun comin' in that afternoon and it got wuss and wusser. I drove out to the Creek to tell you somethin' had ought to be done. You wasn't there and Martha said you was off huntin' in the south and likely didn't know it was freezin' up here. Dogged if I aimed to let them trees freeze behind your back. I got my boys together, and Ivey Sykes, and Whitey, and a couple more, and I borried all the spaces and shovels in Island Grove, and we went out and we worked all night 'til sunrise. The wust cold come in about day and by that time we had the job done."

Such things that Moe did for me could never be paid for.

He tried me out a little later. He came out one evening with the boys and sat stiffly on the veranda.

He burst out, "I got to have forty dollars. How about it?" He looked me in the eye with something like belligerence.

I said, "As long as I've got it, it's yours."

The loan caught me very short. I wrote out the check and as I handed it to the man, I sensed in him a feeling of triumph. He returned the money a week later. I happened to know that he had not worked that week. He was only making certain that he could count on me. After that, he borrowed only when he was in dire straits. Sometimes I myself had to borrow the money when half of his immense family was sick, but my credit was better than his. If he could not pay me back in cash, he paid in work worth twice what he owed me.

One summer I decided to make a hurried trip to New York to consult with my editor. I put my car in storage and bought my ticket for New York. My grove man would drive me in the truck to the train at the village stop. The morning that I was to leave, Moe drove out to see me. His face was gray.

He said, "I'm in trouble. Mary's dyin'. Seems like I'm turned to stone. I cain't think. I cain't figger out what to do."

Mary was one of the youngest of his brood of twelve, a shy child with a certain brightness of face the others did not possess.

I said, "I'll come," and drove the farm truck behind him to his house.

The child lay like a crumpled rag doll on her small bed, her blue eyelids closed, her breathing hoarse and labored. The mother sat nearby in a slovenly incompetence. Moe had taken Mary to the doctor two days before, and while there was a chance, he had said, that her illness might pass into pneumonia, there was an equal chance, with proper nursing, of no danger at all. The pneumonia had developed rapidly and literally nothing had been done. Moe had been ill and unable to work and his funds were exhausted. His wife thought the illness was unimportant. The child was plainly in a critical condition.

A heavy downpour of rain had set in, the roof of the farm truck leaked like a sieve, I was dressed for my trip and had only two hours before train time. But my own plans were trivial before Moe's trouble. I drove to Ocala in the rain, arranged for a doctor and a nurse, drew money out of the bank for Moe, and went back to tell him that help was on the way. The doctor and nurse had arrived ahead of me and were working over the sick child. Moe looked at my soaked clothes. He dropped down on the porch of his house and tears ran down the deep furrows of his face.

He said, "I hadn't ought to of let you do this. I reckon you can't figger why I'd take on so over one young un, and me with a whole houseful of 'em."

He wiped away his tears unashamed with the back of his big hand.

"Mary's different," he said. "All them other young uns, and their Ma, they don't pay me a bit o' mind. When I come home, times they don't even pass the time o' day with me, lessen to ask maybe did I bring home meat for supper. They don't none of 'em care do I come or go. But Mary sets by the road and waits for me. She comes runnin' and I carry her in on my shoulder. She calls me 'Bubber.'"

The tears ran like rain.

"I don't know how I'll live if she dies," he said. "I just couldn't make out without Mary."

I took my train for New York, but I had almost forgotten why I was going. I could not get Moe out of my mind. All day, far up into Georgia, the rain fell, and they were Moe's tears, falling for Mary, the only one who cared whether he came or went. All night, the wheels of the train repeated, "Moe and Mary! Moe and Mary!" It seemed to me that I should be obliged to get off the train and go back to them.

I had a brief interview with my editor and hurried home. Mary was safe. She smiled shyly when Moe took me to her bed. The nurse had the sickroom in order and Moe was in his best bib and tucker. His face was luminous.

"I shore went to pieces," he apologized. "When I think o' you comin', all dressed in your best clothes and soppin' wet from helpin' me I'm ashamed. But them things gits made up somehow. I'll git a chance to do somethin' for you sometime. Tell you what I'll do. I'll take you alligator-huntin'. You ain't never been and I'll bet you could write a fine story about it if you saw it yourself."

Moe continued to keep an eye on my grove and on tottering fences, leaking roofs and broken plumbing. He tried to keep his own garden, single-handed, and he brought me always the first of his crop; lettuce, squash, watermelons. He brought up the matter of the 'gator hunt every time he came, but somehow we never got together on it.

"How about that 'gator hunt tonight?" he would say and I would have some engagement that prevented it.

He could not have been much past fifty in age, but he began to break like a man much older. There were increasing periods when he could not do his carpentering and when he could not go frog-hunting with his boys. The last summer of his life he was very ill. He asked if the boys might help with my summer grove pruning. I was glad of the extra labor. At the time Moe owed me twenty-five dollars and since I knew it fretted him, I asked if he wanted the boys' pay applied on the debt. He hesitated.

"No, jest pay 'em right out," he said. "That other's somethin' between you and me."

There was no hope for him. Years of improper food and over-work, of anxiety over the future of his family, above all, I think, despair at not living as he longed to have them live, had eaten at his big burly frame and great gentle mind. He knew that he was going. He sent the boys out for me one day. He sat propped in a chair, his face gaunt, his hair tousled above the broad forehead.

"I ain't goin' to make it," he said and his voice was as deep and rich as ever. "I ain't never taken you on that 'gator hunt like I promised, and I hate that."

A few days later I stopped by his place, drawn by an uneasy instinct. Moe was still propped in his chair. As I stood in the doorway, his breath made a strangling sound in his throat and the big head dropped forward on his chest and did not lift again. The family stood stonily. Only Mary huddled behind his chair with a desperate small face. Only she and I have missed him, finding the world less generous for his going.

13. Residue

I have my own explanation of the cynical Biblical statement that it is as easy for a rich man to enter Heaven as for a camel to pass through the eye of a needle. On the surface, the statement is unjust, for wealth is so accidental a thing, that either its possession or its lack should not be held against any man. Sift each of us through the great sieve of circumstance and you have a residue, great or small as the case may be, that is the man or the woman. The rich, the well-favored, the well-situated, are surrounded with a confusing protective mass of extraneous and irrelevant matter that tends to hide the substance beneath. The poor, the unfortunate, have been put through the sieve and stand nakedly for what they are. A poor and simple man stands with bare outstretched hands at the gates of Heaven, and his essential character is written in broad letters across him, for life has stripped him down to it. Confronted with the fortunate but cluttered man, St. Peter must do a neat problem in psychiatry and estimate, "Now what would this man's honor be if he were starving? He gives much, having a surfeit. What would he give if he had nothing?" Being busy with the checking of admissions to Heaven, it is conceivable that St. Peter is obliged to tell the rich man that he must wait in the anteroom until he can go deeper into his case.

These thoughts come to me when there pass down the road in front of my house those Creek residents whom Life, shall we say, has knocked down and sat on. There are always one or two outright derelicts in the neighborhood, men cast adrift by life, waiting patiently to be cast up on some hospitable and nurturing shore, finding it, often, here. The evil and dishonorable among them do not stay long at the Creek, for we are too busy to be bothered with neighbors we cannot trust. We leave our houses wide open. I sleep alone in my rambling farmhouse with never the latching of a door, and I am away for weeks at a time, with the place as free of access as a public picnic ground. Nothing has ever been taken. Small tools disappear gradually, of course, from my open barn, parts from my tractor and sometimes gasoline from my truck, but this only because some man needs a shovel and a shovel is available; needs a coil or a generator for his broken-down car and a coil or generator sits invitingly in the idle tractor under the shed; gives out of gasoline on his way from the Creek to the village with his night's catch of frogs legs and gasoline waits providentially in the truck. This seems no more predatory than the taking of fallen timber from the open woods, the drinking of water from a stranger's well. Usually the silently borrowed implements are returned as quietly as they went. Sometimes a man says, "I forgot to tell you, I got your Brinley plow. Leave me know when you want it." Sometimes a frog hunter leaves me a fine mess of frog legs or an alligator hide, and I know that this is pay for gasoline.

We know the character of the most destitute drifter. One or two of these are drifters in the spiritual sense, for physically they have come to rest at the Creek. Sometimes that character commands our respect, for its sieved residue is sound, and we do not hold it against a man that he goes in rags and cannot or will not work for a living. One unfortunate is Mr. Tubble, who gets along in life by attaching himself to one stronger than he. All the men at the Creek feel a responsibility for him, and when evil befalls him, usually through the medium of the jug or bottle, they join forces and set out to find him and nurse him back to normal.

He has a trick of "coming up missing." The expression is not as contradictory as it sounds. I, for instance, never come up missing, for it is a known habit of mine to be absent from the Creek without explanation. My car is either under its shelter, the porte-cochère that Moe built and called a "cashay," and I am at home, or it is not under the cashay and I am simply "off." A roving cat does not come up missing, for it is expected of a cat that he ramble. But if a dog of steady habits is not at the door one morning for his breakfast, that dog "comes up missing." A misplaced household object comes up missing. A man, like Mr. Tubble, who needs to have an eye kept on him, is suddenly not in his usual haunts. Mr. Tubble has come up missing. Snow came anxiously to me one day to report that it had happened again.

He said, "We want to borrow your outboard motor. We've all paddled until we're give out. We can't cover all of Orange Lake in this wind, just paddlin'."

"Do you suppose he's drowned?"

"We're gettin' feered of it."

"How long has he been gone?"

"He was seen last on Wednesday evenin', mighty drunk. Not fitten to fish his traps. But he must of set out to fish 'em, for his boat's not there."

"Well, if there's anything I can do, let me know."

"We'll cover the lake with the kicker, then if we have to, we'll portion out the lake and cover it closer. A boat can lodge up against a tussock and you not see it for the marsh grass. The tussocks move around so bad, too."

The next day Snow returned the motor.

"Did you find Mr. Tubble?"

He was plainly disgusted.

"We found him."

"Alive?"

"No more than half."

"Where did you find him?"

"We never did. He come in Saturday night and asked what day of the week 'twas—and what week."

"Where had he been all that time?"

"In a tussock."

"In a tussock? On one of those floating islands? Since Wednesday?"

"Since Wednesday. He'd drawed up his boat beside him and laid down with a gallon jug beside him."

"How did he ever manage to get back?"

"Come a rain Saturday night and fell on him and sobered him up."

"I see."

Snow said, "It's his business, gettin' drunk, but he'd ought to had more consideration for his friends. I paddled past that tussock a dozen times. Now tell me, if you aimed to pitch a long drunk, would you pick out a floatin' tussock to do it in?"

George Fairbanks has both Snow and Old Boss to look out for him, and they do the job with mingled irritation and affection. Yet George somehow needs as little looking out for as any of us and has proved his ability to survive under conditions that would quite finish the rest of us. He has an aloofness, a central integrity, that is his heritage from his good blood. He is the last of a once proud and prosperous line. The great Fairbanks family itself has been sifted by time and circumstance until only George is left to carry the name. He carries it in an amazing body, bony and gangling, with no chin at all, a black mustache, the whole dressed loosely in nondescript garments topped by an immense black Stetson hat. The effect is a parody of the villain in an old-fashioned melodrama. He is gentleness itself, except when corn liquor inflames him and the Fairbanks blood runs hot, and stuttering, he tells any man on earth what he thinks of him.

Fifty years ago, before the Big Freeze, the Fairbanks family owned section on section of the best land in the county. Theirs were the finest stretches of hammock, needing only a few hundred dollars' worth of labor to clear into the choicest citrus land in the state. The fine grove in Big Hammock, where lie my choice money-making seven acres, is still known as the Fairbanks grove. It was Major Fairbanks, of whom I have spoken, owner of my hand-carved pine bed, who was the greatest of George's line. I feel that I should offer George the pine bed, but since every house he lives in eventually burns down, it seems safer with me.

At one time George had a half-blind horse, a parlor organ, a modest income from the Fairbanks estate, administered for him by Old Boss, and the whole of a house. The house was a derelict, too, of gray weathered pine, but it had been a good house in its day, it had two stories, a chimney and a shingled roof that leaked no more than was to be expected after fifty years of Florida sun and rain. George entertained lavishly in those days, the entertainment consisting largely of corn liquor, the guests a queer assortment, mostly crudely painted women who were after George's "wealth." One of them managed to marry him and when she found that his worldly goods were not only extremely modest but were tightly in the wise hands of

Old Boss, the fur flew. He could not accept his betrayal. He came regularly once a week to tell me his grievous story. I have wondered if he hoped I might know a formula for handling a harridan. He is what we call tie-tongued and I strained my attention to understand his morose tale. The phonetics of the cleft palate cannot be intelligibly reproduced.

"I do' see how a woman tin hol' so much meanness," he lamented. "S'e wake up mean, s'e go thu the day mean, s'e go to s'eep mean. S'e thwow things a' me. S'e tuss me. Any man in the tounty but me tin s'eep wi' her."

I think he got an advance from Old Boss with which to buy her off. At any rate, he got rid of her, and soon afterward the horse died, the house burned to the ground, parlor organ and all, leaving only the fine brick chimney standing bleakly, and Old Boss was obliged to withhold cash income from him, providing instead the clothes and groceries he would not buy for himself as long as liquor might be bought instead. He was not discouraged. He moved into a shed left unburned near the chimney and began to look for another and a more agreeable wife. He made tentative overtures to me.

"I been thinkin'," he said. "I dot a Victwola an' twenty-five wecords. Here you are, livin' alone. There I am, livin' alone. I bwing my Victwola an' my twenty-five wecords an' I play for you."

I pled too great a business to listen to twenty-five Victrola records and contrived to discourage him. He was soon safely off on another tack. He courted a widow's daughter somewhere in the woods and stopped by one day to tell me that he was on his way to resolve the issue. It did me good to see the old Fairbanks pride and arrogance blaze brightly in him.

"I goin' to det her told," he said haughtily. "S'e tan't fool aroun' wi' me. I goin' tell her, if s'e want me, s'e gotta take me wight now. If s'e don't want me, there's plenty more rarin' for me!"

❧ ❧ ❧

Mr. Swilley, unlike George, was infinitely humble. Yet in his grotesque way he too had his integrity. We frightened each other almost out of our wits the first time we met. I went out to the barn one morning, and so close to the threshold that I very nearly tripped on him, sat Mr. Swilley. I not only did not know that he was Mr. Swilley, I did not know that such a person existed, or had come to reside in our neighborhood. He looked like a cross between an Indian and one of those travelling quacks known as medicine men. He had dark cavernous eyes, high cheekbones and lank black hair that hung to his shoulders. I found later that he cut his own hair and was dependent for even this rudimentary barbering on the loan of some one's scissors. I jumped back with a startled cry and Mr. Swilley frightened me still further by going apparently into a convulsion. He jerked all over, his head swung from side to side, his arms shot forward spasmodically, his feet flew in my direction, and all the while he let out pained and explosive grunts, "Uh, uh, uh, uh." I had terrified him more than he had me. I learned in time to make some preliminary noise whenever I approached him, preferably some natural woods noise such as the breaking of a stick, for if I called or spoke or came unexpectedly within his vision, he cried out in that grunting pain and jerked like a monkey on a stick. He lived most of the time, I think, in a trance, and I have wondered from what strange and lovely world I brought him unhappily back to life.

He was in my barn that first morning, a cold one, waiting for Snow to come to work, in the hope that the truck would be going to the village and he could get a ride. The truck did happen to be going to town and Mr. Swilley rode in and out on it. Snow came to me with his brown eyes twinkling.

"Don't be surprised at anything," he said. "Mr. Swilley had a dream."

The whole business of Mr. Swilley seemed in the nature of a nightmare, and now Snow was participating.

"Mr. Swilley dreamed," Snow continued, "that his dead mother came to him and told him his troubles were over. 'You got nothin' more to worry about, son,' she told him. 'You'll have a good roof over your head, good clothes to wear, a car to ride in and plenty to eat. The week'll not be out before you meet a rich widow.'"

I had never seen the silent Snow so close to laughter.

"I just thought I'd warn you," he said. "I'm mighty afraid you're the rich widow."

It is unkind to slap a ghost in the face, but I called to Mr. Swilley's dead mother and thanked her to mind her own business. Mr. Swilley came daily to ask for work, though we had none, and for fear that on the strength of supernatural backing he would also ask at once for my hand, I dealt with him through Snow. Snow hinted that the man was starving, so we put him to work as a hoe-hand. He was plainly dejected. Ghosts take a great responsibility when they encourage mortals. Mr. Swilley must have clung to hope, for he made excuses to speak to me. Once he asked me to do an errand for him and brought a handful of silver from his overalls pocket. The nickels and dimes that he handed me were strangely smooth and bright, the design almost obliterated by a tinny covering.

I said, "What on earth is on this money, Mr. Swilley?"

He fidgeted and jerked and stammered.

"Uh-uh-you know-it's quicksilver-for bedbugs."

I wondered how the mercury controlled bedbugs and whether he used it on his dead mother's recommendation but I did not press the point.

At Christmas time I thought of the man's baggy clothes, his still uncut hair, his quicksilver and his dejection, and made up a box for him; a cooked ham, a fruit cake, pecans and candy. I wanted to put in shirts and socks and a sweater, as for Snow, but I feared these personal items might invoke again the shade of his hope-bringing parent. Snow had told me that Mr. Swilley was living on the old Turner place. I knew the Turner house had burned, at a time when George was occupying it, and I had wondered vaguely how Mr. Swilley had been able to build for himself. I made my rounds on Christmas morning and turned with the last box down the magnolia-lined lane that led to the Turner place. The gate had been ingeniously mended with wire, the only sign that the land was used by any one but hunters. For a moment I thought that Snow must be mistaken. There was no possible human habitation in sight. I fastened the gate behind me and went on foot toward the scrawny orange and camphor trees that had once shaded the Turner house. Under the camphor tree was a tin box. True, it was almost as tall as a short man, and about six feet by six, but surely the Townsend boys must have thrown it together for the purpose of playing pirates or G-men. Then I remembered that the Townsend boys did not build things, and certainly would engage in no game as strenuous as pirates or G-men. The box was made of sheets of corrugated tin roofing that had survived the fire. I walked around it. One sheet of tin had been nailed to the adjacent sheet with hinges made of old harness leather. Opposite the hinges was a new lock. This, then, was a door. I walked around the corner and a square of about twelve inches had been cut in the side. This was a window. I poked my head inside the square. I had found Mr. Swilley's home.

It was as dark as a cave. It made Snow's palmetto shack seem as comfortable as a city apartment. One by one I identified the objects that made up the household equipment. A bunk of rough saplings filled one wall. It was covered with pine boughs. The bedding consisted of a ragged patchwork quilt, the work, I gathered, of Mr. Swilley's mother. From the look of the quilt, she had been dead a long time. There was no chair. There was no room for a chair. The near side of the box was filled with a stove that Robinson Crusoe would have considered beyond the pale. It consisted of a rusty piece of sheet iron. Under it ran a length of old stovepipe and fire still smoldered in this. There was one battered pot on the stove. It held a few spoonfuls of lumpy grits. There may have been supplies under the stovepipe but there were none in sight. There were no clothes hanging on the wall, for the only clothes Mr. Swilley owned were on his stooped back, wherever it might be. I could no longer begrudge him the dreams his mother brought him. I pushed my box in the window and went away.

When he came the next day to hoe, he said, "I'm sorry I wasn't to home when you called. I knowed it was you. I got a little somethin' for you, too."

His gift was a ladder of a length he knew I needed. The sides were of peeled cypress saplings. The rungs were hand-carved from straight hickory limbs, set in solidly with wooden pegs. It was a good ladder and it made my box seem very trifling indeed. I suppose he took encouragement from the exchange. Dreams die hard, and perhaps as he huddled on his pine boughs under his ragged quilt his mother came to him again to tell him to keep heart. For he began to prance. When I spoke to him, if I managed to attract his attention without startling him into the jerks, he jumped from whatever he was doing and pranced toward me like an old and decrepit goat. I never saw him negotiate six yards without tripping.

It is still a marvel to me that he did not break his neck the time I took him with me to bring colored Mary's belongings to the Creek. The whole expedition, including Mary, was a mistake. The confidence I showed in Mr. Swilley in entrusting him with the mission was all he needed to assure him that the solution of his life was at hand. I had engaged Mary as a maid, knowing nothing of her but that she was neat, well-spoken, of good honest Negro farming stock near Fairfield, and that she assured me that the lonely job I offered was all she asked of Heaven. Her bed, trunk and boxes that she asked to bring could not be carried in my car. Snow was behind with the tractoring and I asked Mr. Swilley to follow me in the truck to bring home Mary and her worldly goods.

He had assured me that he was a finished driver and mechanic. I believe that this was the first time he had ever driven a car. The truck was in good running order, but I noticed that he called Snow from the field to start it for him. I had the sudden wisdom to tell him that I should drive slowly ahead, and to blow the horn if he had trouble. Four times on curves or at cross-roads the horn sounded desperately and I stopped and went back to find the truck stalled. I started it for him and we reached's Mary's home in the backwoods. She pointed out the things that were to go and said she would call her brother to help. Mr. Swilley protested that for a man of his strength, handling them alone was nothing. He came out first with a heavy old walnut bed which he said it was not necessary to dismantle. He carried it by the headboard, the whole sticking out in front of him as though he meant to use it as a mammoth trap for a bear. I was horrified to see him ignore the wide gate and leap, bed and all, over the fence. The bed crashed down ahead of him, Mary let out a shriek that was to become familiar, and Mr. Swilley picked himself up and flung the bed bodily into the back of the truck. He dusted his hands, flushed with pride, and hurdled the fence back to the house.

I called, "The trunk will go through the gate, Mr. Swilley."

He beamed and waggled his head, poised the heavy trunk jauntily on one shoulder, and again attacked the fence. His intention was not only to jump it, but to soar lightly over it. Mr. Swilley missed soaring by half the height of the fence. One leg cleared it in a blithe arc, the other caught midway, the trunk bounced to earth and flew open, Mary screamed, and Mr. Swilley hung dangling, an almost inextricable part of the fence. He unwove himself, staggered to the trunk, helped Mary to heap things back in it, sat on the lid, fastened it, and heaved it into the truck. He smiled happily and returned for the collection of boxes. Only a little cautious, he took the fence from a standing jump, picked up himself and the boxes from the ground, and we were ready to set out for home. He managed to start the truck this time, and I had gone perhaps half a mile over the winding woods road when I realized that he was not behind me. The road was too narrow and curved for backing or turning around and I went back on foot to where the truck stood motionless with a great roaring of the engine.

"Seems to be stuck," Mr. Swilley panted, and leaped from the seat and threw himself prone to examine nonexistent obstacles.

The truck was not stuck. He had managed to throw it out of gear and had sat racing an impotent engine. The truth came to me now but it was too late. Dusk was falling and we had to get home. I was reminded of the nursery story of the fire that had to burn the stick, so that the stick would beat the pig, so that the pig would jump over the stile, "or we won't get home before morning." I gave Mr. Swilley a belated and elemental lesson in gear-shifting and we were on our way again. He got along nicely for a few miles and hope and success went to his head. In a great burst of speed, he passed me, and the rest of the trip was a nightmare. Mr. Swilley swooped and swerved ahead of me, as though he were trying to take the truck itself over fences. I dared not pass him, for fear he should think it was a coy game. He took curves on two wheels, dogs and pigs and chickens and other cars fled out of his way, and by a miracle he brought the truck in to the home grounds and to rest against the side of the barn.

"We went through some beautiful country," he said.

I was glad he had enjoyed the scenery, for I had seen none. Perhaps his dead mother had told him that the proper approach was the aesthetic one.

I lived through the rest of Mr. Swilley and Mary together. They were sad, strange, violent days, and I would not live them again for the wealth of India. Mary began promisingly, keeping my house as clean as a laboratory. Martha brought me the first word that all was not well.

"Sugar," she said, "I think you'd ought to know. Mary comes down to my house almost every day and tells me she's starvin' to death. Says you don't give her a thing to eat. Says she has to walk to town and buy herself a little somethin' with her own money."

I was horrified.

I said, "Why, I give her exactly what I have myself. I buy enough of everything for both of us, and I thought I made it clear that she was to help herself."

"You don't need to tell me, Sugar. I knows your kitchen and I knows your ways. I just figgered you'd ought to know."

It occurred to me that perhaps my steaks and chops and asparagus and lettuce were not to the taste of a country woman. Perhaps Mary longed for cornpone and cowpeas and white bacon.

I said to her, "Mary, if you don't like what I happen to have to eat, help yourself at any time to cornmeal and bacon and things like that, and fix whatever you want for yourself."

She looked at me with cold glittering eyes and made no answer. A few days later she began shouting. She was at the washtubs and a wave of angry shrieks came to me, as though she were driving off an assailant. I ran to the back and she stopped instantly, bending low over the tub.

"Mary, what's the matter? Why were you screaming?"

She looked up innocently.

"I never opened my mouth," she said, and dipped a sheet up and down in the water.

The shouting began to have a rhythmic pattern. It came regularly every six days. Once I awakened in the early morning grayness and heard her in the kitchen. She seemed to be throwing pots and pans about the kitchen, shouting as she threw. The shouts lifted to the familiar shriek. I looked at my watch. It was five o'clock. Suddenly the sound ended and she was gone. At the usual hour of seven o'clock she was back in the kitchen. She brought me my coffee quietly. I could not believe that the quiet woman serving me capably was the one I had heard before daylight.

One night I told her that I must have coffee early the next morning, at six-thirty instead of seven-thirty. I must leave promptly at seven to drive to Jacksonville where I was meeting a party at nine, I said, to go on a trek to Fort George Island. I set the alarm clock and gave it to her. I awakened in the morning with the uneasy sense of lateness. It was a quarter of eight. The kitchen was silent. A light rain beat on the shingled roof. I dashed to the kitchen and put on the coffee pot and returned to my room to dress. I could not now possibly reach Jacksonville in time, and since the party was large, it could not wait for me, and I must drive to the village and telephone that I could not join them. As I poured a cup of coffee, at a quarter past eight, Mary sauntered in.

I said, "Didn't your alarm go off? Did you oversleep?"

She said jauntily, "Oh, the alarm went off all right. I was up at daylight. But it was raining, and I didn't care to get wet."

I said, "You could have thrown a quilt around you. You had all day to change your clothes."

I turned and looked into her eyes and knew instantly what I should have known before, that she was as mad as a March hare.

Bits of her history had seeped out in her outbursts. She had mentioned a northern hospital where, she said, she had worked. I asked my doctor to investigate. Word came back that she had indeed been at the hospital, not as an employee, but as a patient in the insane ward. She had a long record as a manic-depressive. She had had a quiet spell, and while attention was relaxed, she had escaped, back to Florida.

My doctor said, "You can't get rid of her fast enough. With that type of insanity, you're likely to wake up one morning and find her standing over you, with a maniac's strength, with an axe."

She had driven me almost as insane as herself, but in her quiet periods she was sweet and gentle and infinitely pathetic. She needed a minor operation, and it seemed to me that her mental illness might possibly be traced to the physical one. I took her to the hospital, paid for the operation, nursed her at home afterward, and she was patient and grateful. She was entirely recovered and there had been no shouting. She asked to spend a week end at her father's farm. I took her there and told her I should call for her at Fairfield, at the store, about ten-thirty Sunday night.

"I may be a little earlier than ten-thirty," I said, "or a little later. If I'm early, I'll wait for you, and if I'm late, you wait for me."

At ten-thirty-five Sunday night I was at the store. There was no Mary. The village was dark. I waited until eleven-thirty and drove home. On Wednesday there came a note in Mary's very good handwriting.

"I came to the store at ten-thirty," she wrote, "and you were not there. The weather was inclement so I returned to my father's house. You may come for me."

I wrote, "Dear Mary: I shall not come at all."

With Martha tiding me over until I should find some one else, I realized that I had been living in the heart of an electrical storm. My ragged nerves eased their tension and peace filled the Creek beneficently. A year ago Martha went to Fairfield for the bean-picking.

"Mary was pickin' beans with us," she reported. "She sent her love to you."

My last days with Mary ran concurrently with my last days with Mr. Swilley. Together they were part of a dark tortured unreality. After the expedition to bring her belongings, he took to sitting in the yard after his work was done. Two or three times I asked if he were expecting a ride, or needed something.

"I'm just waitin'," he said.

Between Mary's shrieks and Mr. Swilley's waiting, I was in a fair way to become a psychopathic case myself. I longed to send him packing, but there was no other work at the Creek, and I could not endure to think of the tin box without even a pot of grits boiling over the stovepipe. All I could do was to provide hoeing and to ignore the long-haired derelict who squatted under the orange trees. One day he was blessedly gone and did not appear again. Snow brought me good news of him.

"Mr. Swilley found his widow," he said. "I reckon she was rich, like his mother promised, for they live in a right good cabin by the edge of a little stream and I see an old car setting out in front."

I can only hope that the widow keeps control of the car. I dare not conjecture, if Mr. Swilley is the answer to her dream, her own mentality and appearance.

The Bernie Bass family is prospering. They can now afford to buy milk for the children. It makes me feel as good as when I have a stroke of luck of my own. As long as Bernie has a job, the somehow terrible matter of the dime cannot arise again. When my cow Dora and Lady, the heifer, came fresh at the same time, I sent out word to the Creek that any family with children could have skimmed milk without charge. Any one who wished to pay might have it at the rate of three quarts for ten cents. The milk was skimmed after only eight hours in the ice box and was even then as rich as city milk. I had the Raney family and the Basses in mind. The Raneys were too lazy or too shy ever to send and the Basses did not, I am sure, for pride. They could not pay and they would not accept the milk without it.

Mrs. Bernie Bass came lately to arrange for milk, two of the boys stubbing bare toes behind her. She untied a fifty-cent piece from a handkerchief and paid, with an immense satisfaction, in advance.

"A dime of that," she said, "is what I owed you a'ready. I reckon you don't even remember. Near about a year ago, I come to you to carry a dime for the little one's lunch. But I hadn't forgotten."

I had not forgotten, either.

Mrs. Bernie Bass is a small thin woman. She flutters like a nervous mother bird. The first time I met her, after the Basses had moved into the tenant house in Cow Hammock, she came running, calling out in the panic that I associate with her. The woods fire that had been smoldering around us for days had fanned into fresh flame and was closing in on her house. She was alone and needed help.

"I been fightin' and frammin' 'til I'm wore out. I hate to see the house go for lack of help."

I called the men from the grove and we all pitched in and fought fire. It is hard and evil work. A shift of wind helped us save the clearing.

Long later, when the woman called from my gate about the dime, her voice held the same distress as when the fire menaced.

"I do hate to worry you," she said, and brushed her hair back from her forehead. "I know you'll do it, but I shore hate to ask. It's the little one. Bernie ain't had no work for the longest. He didn't have no dime to give him today for his school lunch. I just found out he went off on the school bus without no dime. He gets two of them nickel packages of raisin buns for his lunch. Seems like they fill him up better than anything else he can get. It's a heap to ask, but could you drive in to the school and give him a dime? I'll pay you back just as soon as I can."

"Of course. I'll go right away."

"It's a heap to ask, but I just had to."

A day without food is a trifle to the adult Basses.

"He ain't but seven," she apologized. "He's so little to go all day without his rations."

The repayment of the dime a year later was a triumph. The putting down of money in advance for milk, when it could have been received free, was the winning of a major battle. When one has a basic integrity, one's standards are high. A dime becomes a banner.

Grampa Hicks lived in a palmetto-log shack at the edge of Cross Creek. His brown old face was beardless. He wore one blue mail-order shirt, "Chieftain" brand—loyalty forbade his buying the cheaper "Big Yank"—and one pair of blue pincheck pants until they dropped from his unlaundered body. He lived, slept and fished in them. He was also loyal to "Three Thistles" snuff. He considered "Railroad" fitten only for niggers and "Buttercup" for women.

He existed by the illegal trapping of fish in Orange Lake and by renting other men's rowboats, without permission, to fishermen from Jacksonville. If a customer's outboard motor lacked gas, he shuffled mysteriously to the other side of the bridge across the Creek, where lay beached other boats and motors, and returned with fuel. If a stranger to these parts needed liquor, so that when the fish didn't bite he could spit on his hook, cuss and take a drink to get them started, Grampa went into the underbrush beyond his shack, returning with a catsup bottle of 'shine. If catfish were scarce on his own lines, he ran the other fellow's.

Man's law is one thing, God's another.

One Sunday morning we asked Grampa to go fishing with us. He knew where the bream were biting and we had had no luck for weeks. He spat.

"I don't fish on Sundays," he said haughtily. "I wa'n't raised up that-a-way."

Mister Marsh Turner might have been called a vagabond, but never a derelict. I shall always be sorry that the high sheriff did not know what I knew about him. The law called him troublesome, and certainly his ways and his live stock did not make for peace in the environs. But I think of him still as a man peaceable at heart, and definitely a gentleman. The Negroes, who are infallible snobs, recognized the mark of high caste that illuminated his drunkenness and his violence and spoke of him always as Mister Marsh Turner.

He lived across the Creek on the old Turner place with his elderly mother. Why the decaying house did not fall down around their ears, especially when he was in a mood to hurl furniture through the windows, I do not know. He owned considerable numbers of hogs and cattle. They roamed at will over the woods, our county being open range, and crossed the bridge and intruded on our side of the Creek. We are accustomed to ordinary pigs and cows that root and browse harmlessly. But Mister Marsh Turner's stock seemed to share his lawlessness. The hogs were of the large razorback variety and fought the Creek dogs at sight. No fence could resist their attacks. They went through them, over them or under them. Once in my house yard, they broke into the feed room of the barn and turned over feed barrels with a din like thunder. They devoured young and unwary chickens in their stride. The Turner cattle were almost as bad. They were led by a big bony range bull who once went so far as to gather my two milch cows into his harem and to refuse to allow them to enter my lot for the evening milking.

I had heard tall tales of the Turner doings but I had never seen him. Almost every Monday morning Martha had a racy account of his Saturday night drunk. He was as addicted to music as to liquor and thought nothing of walking uninvited into a frolic and taking the fiddle away from the fiddler and playing his own tune, independent of the rest of the music. One Saturday night he played the guitar all night on the courthouse steps in Gainesville, where a sleepy sheriff took him over at dawn, still picking the strings. Jail was almost his week-end home. He paid his fine amiably on Monday morning, went home, got drunk again, and becoming enraged, took out his fury by throwing whatever he could lift inside the house or out. It was all harmless enough and Mother Turner did not seem to mind. When his activities had spent themselves and he had slept it off, he arose quickly, ate heartily and set about making new table and chair legs to replace the broken ones. I got these reports from Martha.

"Whatever Mister Marsh Turner do wrong," she said proudly, "he set in and make right."

One morning I reached the limit of my patience with his stock. The bull crashed a new gate, the Turner cows and heifers and year-lings followed, and I awoke to a veritable stampede around and around my bedroom. I sent word to Martha to tell him, when next he brought the Turner washing to her, that something must be done and if necessary I would do it. The law gave a property owner certain rights against true outlaw stock and if the law proved indifferent, I should not continue so.

The next day a bay horse trotted smartly to my gate and a long graceful figure wavered in the saddle, then dismounted and swayed up my path. It was indubitably Mister Marsh Turner and he was unbelievably drunk. I had a moment of panic in which I could picture him lassoing me and mounting me on the back of the offending bull, for I knew his imagination was as vivid as mine. I went to the door and called "Good morning," politely. He continued his zig-zag course up the path. When he reached my steps, he took off his broad-brimmed black Stetson with a flourish, swept it across his breast, and bowed almost to the ground.

"I am Marsh Turner, callin'," he said.

"Your stock," I began.

He held up one hand to stop me.

"I been told," he said, "I been told my stock has been a-botherin' of you. The next time them cattle and them hogs comes over here a-botherin' of you—" he bowed deeply and unsteadily again—"them's your cattle." He put one hand on his heart. "Them's your hogs."

He turned with dignity and swayed down the path, out of the gate, closing it carefully behind him as a countryman should do, and managed to mount the bay. I never saw him again.

I was distressed when his gentility, however violent, was removed from our terrain. He gave an air to the Creek that is gone with him. None of us is so dramatic, so picturesque, or drinks with such originality. I do not know the truth about Mister Marsh Turner's death. I have heard several versions. The one I choose to believe may be apocryphal. It is certainly, though spectacular, the most plausible. Mister Marsh Turner had tried the sheriff's patience for a long time. As the story goes, on the previous Saturday Marsh had taken his hurling proclivities when inebriated into the house of a total stranger. When he finished throwing things, he shot holes through the north wall of the house. No householder relishes the idea of a tall, dark, handsome, drunken intruder's stalking into his home and pitching the furniture out of the window. A shot-up wall is of course insult added to injury. He could not be expected to know that the stranger's habit was to make full restitution. A warrant for Mister Marsh Turner's arrest was, to say the least, in order.

The sheriff went to the Turner homestead to serve it. He found Marsh leaning against the doorway, oiling his shotgun. Marsh turned with no surprise. The gun was at an ominous angle in his hands.

The sheriff called, "Put down that gun."

Marsh took a step toward him and said quietly, "Sheriff, this here gun is for you."

The sheriff shot and Marsh fell and it was the end of glamor at Cross Creek. If the tale be true, I am the only person who knows that when Marsh spoke, it was without menace. He was offering the sheriff the offending gun exactly as he had once offered me his trespassing hogs and cattle.

14. Toady-frogs, lizards, antses, and varmints

I do not profess to know all there is to know about frogs, lizards, ants, and varmints. I have learned enough, however, in years of enforced intimacy, to turn them from aliens into friends, or at least into bowing acquaintances. I should have been prepared to like frogs. One who has heard a northern spring come in on that silver chorus should make decent obeisance to the singers and all their related family. The frog Philharmonic of the Florida lakes and marshes is unendurable in its sweetness. I have lain through a long moonlit night, with the scent of orange blossoms palpable as spilled perfume on the air, and listened to the murmur of minor chords until, just as I have wept over the Brahms waltz in A flat on a master's violin, I thought my heart would break with the beauty of it. If there is not a finished tune, there are phrases, and there is assuredly a motif, articulated, reiterated. I searched long in my mental attic before I remembered where I had heard the sound before. It is the high thin jangle of Chinese music, overlaid with the pattern of glass wind-chimes, such as Alvah had given me for Christmas.

If frogs an inch long have never been carved in apple-green jade, they should be. Nothing else could repeat the jewel-like perfection of this diminutive species. Their eyes are tiny moonstones. I am sure of this, for I just stepped off the veranda and turned back a spider-lily leaf to look at one and make certain. They are also as soft and smooth as satin. I know this, too, for the variety is the one that clings to the wetness of the shower-bath pipe and drops on my skin.

They appear in June, full-fledged, and do not seem to change their size all summer. Martha calls them the rain-frogs. They are inch-long, animated pieces of pale green enamel. Self-conscious jewels, they seem to choose their setting. I find them until the first frost on the pleasanter side of a lily leaf. Spider lily leaves are preferred, being roomier, but a large Amaryllis will do. At night, or when the sun is not too fierce, they lie in the inner trough of the thick spiked leaves. When the sun is high, or when the rain comes down tempestuously, they cling with tiny cream-jade vacuumed feet to the under side of a leaf. They roll their moonstone eyes. They quiver slightly if their perch is shaken. They move only when actually dispossessed, taking off in a long leap that is almost a flight.

They are a celestial breed of frogs and in season are found in apartments suitable to reincarnated Chinese emperors—large yellow allamanda blossoms. The flowers are trumpet-shaped, two inches deep. The chosen few among the frogs lie all day in these deep golden caves, contemptuous of a less luxurious world. I have no doubt that prevailing winds blow in their breakfasts and their teas of insects. There is an uncanny resemblance between the frogs and the buds of the allamanda. Until they open, the buds are precisely the size and shape of the frogs. Until well along into yellow prematurity, they are even the same shade of green. They have the same snub nose, the same little bulges of two eyes. It is easy to imagine that the more royal frogs are born in the allamanda blossoms, giving the buds their shape. It seems as though there must be a mystic affinity between the flower and its inhabitant. If I were a theosophist, I should certainly revere the tiny frogs as the living shape of Chinese aristocrats, who, even in an enforced humility of form, maintain an archaic arrogance. It would surely, I decided, be lêse majesté to scream at one in the shower bath.

The Widow Slater, however, always screamed at them.

"I'm as skeert of a toady-frog as of a snake," she said. "I don't want a thing to do with anything can swaller fire and shot."

Some connotation from Elizabethan witch days still clings in these Anglo-saxon parts to a frog or toad. "Eye of newt and toe of frog" in the litany of Macbeth's witches has its counterpart here. It is not the only trace of Old English in the Florida interior, for the backwoods people come of a line that stems back to Chaucer. The fire-swallowing of the Widow Slater's complaint I cannot vouch for, but I have it on reliable authority that a toad will swallow buckshot until he can hold no more. The legend is old in American folklore, for Mark Twain used it in his famous story, "The Jumping Frog of Calaveras County." Fred Tompkins and my friend Moe testified to holding a toad hypnotized with a light and slowly rolling the small lead pellets toward him on the ground. He scooped them in solemnly, they said, until his paunch protruded like an alderman's. When released from the spell of the light, he hopped an inch at a time with the heavy thud of a coin-filled purse. Whether a toad believes the balls of lead to be some new delicacy, or whether his appetite is an indication of his ancient witchery, I cannot say. I can only hope that the experimenters were humane enough to do as in Twain's

story, and turn the surfeited creature upside down until he was relieved of his indigestible burden.

Although the Negro and the backwoodsman call the toad a
hoppy-toad and the frog a toady-frog, they make the common dis-
tinction between a frog and a toad.

The large edible frogs of lake and marsh have been a boon to
the otherwise unemployed of Creek and village.

My profane friend Zelma, the census taker, said, "The b——s
killed the egrets for their plumage until the egrets gave out. They
killed alligators for their hides until the alligators gave out. If the
frogs ever give out, the sons of b ——s will starve to death."

The frogs show no signs of giving out, for even the improvi-
dent and needy do not take the small ones, so that there is always a
new crop coming on. When you order frog-legs in a Northern
restaurant or hotel, there is a good chance that you are served frog-
legs from Orange Lake and the Creek marshes. The hunters are
paid a high price for them, for the Boyt brothers of Citra get seventy cents a pound wholesale, as middlemen, and I must pay fifty
cents for the dressed legs. On a dark night, Orange Lake seems to
be dotted with will-o'-the-wisps, and these are the lights of the frog
hunters.

Fred Tompkins took me frog hunting one shadowy night up
the winding channels of the Creek. Later in our friendship, I should
have known that he was up to mischief. Fred is Puck incarnate, in
spite of being a Spanish war veteran, a deputy sheriff, and the constable at Citra. He paddled our boat Indian-soft along the reed-
filled shore, in and out of coves choked with coontail and water
lilies. I lay in the bow, according to his instructions, playing a flashlight on the lily pads. Sometimes the bright eyes of water spiders
caught the light and deceived me. When the light picked out the

hypnotized eyes of a frog, they gleamed like two drops of dew. Fred paddled close.

"Now just reach out and get him," he said.

I reached out a cautious hand. At the moment of what seemed certain capture, the frog straightened out his legs like a jackknife unfolding and was gone. We repeated this aggravating procedure for two hours.

At last, I said, "You just can't catch them this way."

Fred said, "Me and the Boyts gets 'em."

I turned and flashed the light in his face. His eyes were two brown pools of laughter.

"There's something you aren't telling me," I said.

He slapped his knee and could hold his delight no longer.

"Didn't I tell you 'twas the light holds 'em? What happens to the light when you reach for 'em?"

"Let me try again."

What happened to the light was that when I reached for the frog, my hand threw a shadow and the spell was broken. By reaching slowly to the side and then behind the frog, capture was as simple as though the frog were asleep.

I said, a little irritated, "Now we'd have had lots of frogs, if you'd told me. This was foolish."

"Well," he said, and chuckled, "no fool, no fun."

Now that my lesson was learned, the moon had rolled daybright from behind the clouds, silvering the water and the shaggy-headed palms on the horizon, and the flashlight was useless in the brilliance. We came home with two frogs. Skinning them was embarrassing. Peeling back the green glovelike skin from the white flesh of the legs is like pulling off a small boy's breeches. When they came to table, they affected me as alligator steak does Fred, but for another reason.

"The longer you chaw," he says, "the bigger it gets."

For when I thought of the frog chorus, and wondered if I had ever listened to these two particular voices, I felt as though I had just had a hearty meal on Kirsten Flagstad and Nino Martini.

I find lizards altogether ingratiating. The red-runner lizards are the least attractive, in spite of their shining red and brown and orange, for they are the most snakelike of the lizards. They run to body and tail, with very little visible leg. They are shy, and slither out of sight in a flash. The Negroes and many of the whites believe them to be poisonous, but this is rural fiction.

The small gray lizards have a catholic taste in dwelling places. Every abandoned house is full of them; they live in the woods; they live comfortably in your home with you, wondering what you are doing there, but tolerant on the whole of your intrusion. They are the color of old cypress shingles, with bellies of rich cobalt blue, and there is nothing more impudent unless it is a mocking bird. They are one of the few creatures who really look at a human being, returning stare for stare. They roll their many-faceted eyes and cock their heads, and I do not think it is my imagination that they feel complete contempt for the human race. One sat so long beside me on the veranda steps, looking me up and down with an icy loathing, that I took a small stick and began to tap him lightly on his tail. He was at first more curious than annoyed, as though this were a new puzzle in human behavior. Suddenly he whirled and bit stormily on the stick. Then he flicked his tail and sauntered a few feet away with his back to me. He made it plain that he could easily have attacked my fingers, if he had cared to bother.

The little chameleons are definitely friendly. Yet they are detached, like friends with their minds on other matters. They are partial to a warm bed that a human has slept in and expects to sleep in again that night. They have to be lifted from it by the tail, which surprises you by breaking off in your fingers. They clamber slowly, gracefully, up and down screens. They watch you for hours with bright small eyes. They enjoy being brought into the house on a bunch of roses, to serve on the dining table for ornament, shading obligingly from their favorite sage-green through taupe to a pinkish mauve, according to their passage over leaf or stem or blossom.

They have amazing acrobatic tricks in their repertoire. I watched one do a neat piece of tight-rope balancing on top of the wire fence. Their tiny pointed feet have a suction grip, but even so the wire seemed something of a problem. The chameleon reached a fence post and lay there resting. I wondered why he did not slide down the post to the more navigable ground. He knew what he wanted and where he was going. He may have noticed a cluster of dragonflies or a swarm of midges in the adjacent orange tree, for he gathered his three-inch length together like a horse before a hedge and flung himself at least two feet out and up to the tip of an orange bough. The most ambitious chameleon I have ever seen was swallowing a butterfly twice as wide as he himself was long, the body almost as large as the swallower's. When I first noticed him, he had the butterfly's head in his mouth and the wings stuck out on either side like vast and ferocious mustaches. I stood and laughed at him and he eyed me furiously, switching his tail. I said, "You'll never do it," and went on about my business. An hour later I passed by again and all the butterfly was down except for the wing tips. As I watched, he gulped and the job was done.

They live solitary and free-lance lives, meeting only to make love or to fight. I presume the fighting is among males in season. Among some ferns at the foot of an orange tree I saw such a commotion, such a shaking of fronds, that a miniature earthquake might have been in progress. Separating the ferns, I found two chameleons locked in a death embrace. By some wizardry, each had the other by the throat and there they meant to stay. When I pulled them apart, they did not resume their battle, but turned their joint fury on me. No *Deus ex machina* of the human tribe they had so often contemplated with curiosity and contempt was to be allowed to interfere in a championship fight between chameleons. When I took my last glimpse of them, they were glaring after me, heaving up and down on their small stomachs, their throats inflated into enormous rose-pink bubbles. I think this inflation of the throat must be emotional, for I see it when I know that one is angry or amorous. I could not guarantee that it is not also, ignominiously, a digestive symptom, for I see it too when the chameleon is lying quietly in a spider lily, and when I happen to know that he has been there long enough, in the midst of abundant insect food, already to have had his dinner. Yet I feel such confidence in the brittle intelligence of these tiny replicas of dragons, that I have convinced myself that even then he is, stormily, thinking.

Ants have played havoc with my belief that anything is interesting when known. Having come prepared to loathe crawling things and stayed to admire them, I came full of copybook reverence for the ant and remain filled with the desire to exterminate the last one. In a still predatory world, good and evil are not fixed values, but are relative. "Good" is what helps us or at least does not hinder. "Evil" is whatever harms us or interferes with us, according to our own selfish standards. The ant as a symbol of industry, of social organization, of superb community instinct, has been extolled by science as well as the Bible. But for whom does the ant function so industriously and so socially? No one has troubled to point out that it is for the ant.

In the tropics and the semi-tropics, the ant is a major pest. When in the spring the orange trees put out their new growth of tender frail leaves, overnight those leaves may curl in on themselves into a hard twisted mass incapable forever of taking in the nourishment of sun and earth for the growth of tree and fruit. Examination shows the under side of the leaves a mass of small green aphis, or plant lice, sucking the sustenance of the leaves and so of the tree. A few of these come in on the wind from other infected areas, but most of them are moved there, fed, cultivated and milked, by the ants. The aphis is known as the ant's cow, and school children are taught to be intrigued by the conception. The analogy is no more charming than if one's neighbor moved his herd of cattle into one's garden. In the same fashion, the ant brings in and nourishes the cottony-cushion scale, which can turn a thriving young grove in a few weeks into a Dali-esque nightmare of brown sticks. Agronomists have discovered of late years that the cottony-cushion scale has its enemy, an imported Japanese variety of ladybug, whose sole food is the scale. Without this one food, the Japanese ladybug perishes, and all through one summer I traded to the University's citrus department boughs covered with cottony-cushion scale, in return for Japanese ladybugs. The balance of nature is a mysterious thing, and man must fight on one side or the other with caution, or he will find that in his battle he has exterminated some friendly element. Old-timers in citrus growing do not believe in much of the spraying for unfriendly parasites, and some of the moderns are agreeing, for in destroying them, the friendly parasites are also destroyed.

Ants in the garden are psychic. They set up housekeeping in their intricate nests with no apparent adjacent food supply. Somehow they know that the next day the owner of the garden will plant lettuce seed. Their larders are swept and waiting, and the night after the lettuce seed bed has been watered down in the fatuous hope of its sprouting, the ants move in en masse and carry it home. Local custom scatters hominy grits around any freshly planted bed of small seeds, but from its inefficacy, I think it must be intended only as a propitiatory rite, for the ants first take away the seeds, then return to make off with the grits.

Ants in the house seem to be, not intruders, but the owners. Of all things they seem the least aware of human beings. Even a cockroach will scuttle at sight of the mistress of the kitchen, but a colony of ants goes ahead with its thievery under her eye and fury. Every other creature that comes to mind sees us with bright eyes as man-things and enemies. I have often wondered what appearance we make to the ants that they so ignore us. We must loom up to them with the detachment of a storm cloud, and when human hands take away the feast of the cake, or shake the busy thieves from the cold biscuit, it must seem as though only a strong wind had disrupted their activities. This is not flattering and it may be that my dislike is born of a deflated ego. It is disconcerting, too, to be outsmarted. I lost a birthday cake placed on a pan inside a basin of water sitting on a table whose legs were bound with ant-proof "Hoodoo Tape," because I forgot, and the ants did not, that a wire leading from the wall to an electric fan on the table made the easiest of runways.

Oddly, for all their sweet tooth and their innocent love of aphis milk and lettuce seed, ants are fiercely carnivorous. It is meat for which they would tear you limb from limb. Eat your lamp chop in the tropics while you may, for if you are gone from the room long enough to identify a new butterfly, you will return to find your plate already under fire. The small red sugar ants are omnipresent, but they distress me only mildly, perhaps because they are so small. I do not particularly mind a few floating in my coffee. When little black Ben protested the ants on his cold cornpone, Martha overrode him.

"Chile, antses is fine fo' the stummick-ache," she said suavely.

He wanted plainly to insist that he had no stomach ache, but did not, for experience had taught him that Martha would have an answer for that, too.

One Saturday night I heard a Negro boy ask for a cinnamon bun in Cap'n Howard's store.

"There you are, boy. The last one."

The Negro was suspicious before the storekeeper's heartiness.

"Lemme look, boss. Uh-huh. Hit's got antses."

"What's the matter with you, nigger? A few ants don't matter."

"No suh, boss, a few don't, but this bun am all antses."

Before I left another black boy made the mistake of handing over his nickel without looking at the package. Cap'n had the nickel and he had the antses. He walked slowly out of the store, picking them out by the dozens with a sorrowful philosophy.

Philosophy of a sort is possible toward all the ants except the black stinging ant. He at least is enough aware of humans to fling himself on their flesh if they step within a foot of his path. He jumps with an insane frenzy, doubling up his body in an effort to sink his jaws to the bone. His bite is liquid fire and the infinitesimal speck of acid poison is so potent that it has been estimated that if he were the size of a rattlesnake, he would kill in a fraction of its time. I do not know of what use even to himself his venom may be, for as far as I know, he does not use it to numb or kill and does not eat living tissue. His function with small dead things may correspond to that of the scavenging buzzard, for a dead mouse or snake or bird is covered within a few minutes by a black voracious swarm.

I include termites deliberately among the ants I have accepted philosophically. I have read lately that termites are not ants, but a scientist might as well try to convince me that woodpeckers are not birds. I include termites in spite of the fact that I have known for some time they were eating my house down, or up. The front living room seemed to sway one day when I leaned against it. I sent for Moe, who began ripping out the old hand-hewn pine boards. When he had finished, one sound board was found to have been holding the wall together.

"It's a hell of a wonder," he said, "the roof ain't fell in on you."

It was termites, of course, and the marvel was not that they were there, but that they had not demolished the old farmhouse years ago. Its resistance, Moe said, came from having been built of solid fat pine, whose resinous juices are distasteful to the insects. I am no great seeker of silver cloud linings, but I have had few blessings in disguise greater than the devourers of my front living room wall. For when the room was laid bare to the light, I realized that it had been a dark, almost unhappy room, cozy only on cold winter evenings, when the open fire is all one wants of comfort, and what goes on in the outside world is of no importance. Moe replaced the walls and two small windows with French doors, all the way across the front of the room. Now the sunlight streams in across the veranda and gives the long shabby room an elegance that comes from being one with the sky and clouds, the orange trees and the palms, with the red birds like moving flowers across the panes. And when the winter's-night coziness is wanted, the long linen curtains may be drawn, and the hearth fire lighted, and the old snug closeness is still there.

A plausible youth with a tank on a truck once tried to persuade me to let him "exterminate" my termites. I needed no proof that they were with me, but he burrowed under the house to make his point and after frightening a setting hen from her nest near one chimney, emerged with termites clustered in dozens on his shirt sleeves. For a hundred and twenty dollars, he would guarantee that they would make no further depredations for a period of three years. I was afraid that it might turn out like the boy with the cinnamon bun, that he would have the hundred and twenty dollars and I would still have the termites. And forty dollars a year seemed a good deal of money for any purely destructive activity. I consulted Moe.

"Now the only way you can cold-out exterminate them knockers," he said, "is to tear down the house and burn it. And enough of 'em'll be laying up waitin' to set right in on the new house. Don't think I ain't had an eye on them sills and joists. I figger it'll take them termite jessies about five years more to finish their meal. Then I aim just to set in and put you in a new set o' floors and underpinnin's. And it ain't goin' to average you no forty dollars a year."

"Starting with new good pine, how long should the job be good for?"

"Hit'll take a batch o' termites a good twenty years to eat out the bottom of a house. If it's fat pine, now."

"Well, I have an idea about twenty years may see me through. We'll gamble on the house and me holding out together."

My race with the termites against time has a sporting element. Having lived long enough already to know that a world may turn upside down in twenty years, I am leaving my termites to their gnawing. Who knows but that some insect enemy may appear to wipe out their solid existence, while my own topsy-turvy world in that period may stabilize? At the moment, the odds are of course with the termites.

"Martha," I asked, "just exactly what is a varmint?"

"Why, a wild-cat be's a varmint, Sugar," she said. "Skunks be varmints, an' 'coons an' foxes an' 'possums. Minkses, too. A panther be's a varmint, an' a bear. All them wild things, Sugar, out in the woods. Tigers be varmints, an' lions. A lion," she said earnestly, "he'll kill you right now. We ain't got tigers an' lions, praise God, but did we have, they'd be varmints."

She pondered.

"But a cow, now, Sugar, hit ain't a varmint. Nor a hog. Them's beas'es."

She chuckled.

"Heap o' folkses be varmints," she said.

A varmint then, is any one of the wild things in the woods either definitely predatory or of no domestic service. A human varmint is one who possesses skulking qualities and may be expected to be "low down." We use the epithets "bastard" and "son of a bitch" freely in these parts, and the former in particular is not a fighting term, but may even be used with a certain amount of affection. It is objectionable only when it is literally true, and then, of course, one would never use it. When I stayed in the Big Scrub with Leonard and his mother, he complained about unfriendly activities of his cousin. He referred to him as to many others as "that bastard." To my surprise, his mother, accustomed if never reconciled to his language, took violent issue.

"Now you're throwin' off on my sister," she said. "She's a good woman. Don't you go callin' her boy a bastard."

Leonard grinned amiably.

"All right then," he said, "call him the pimp."

She was satisfied.

"That's a whole heap better," she said. "The pimp."

In deference to her feelings, her nephew was thenceforward "the pimp."

But when we call any one a varmint, we mean it.

Of "all them wild things out in the wood," the panther remains the only one in Florida still gilded with the bright legend of fear. To hear a panther scream is to add a new horror to the catalogue of evil. I have heard the sound twice, once above the Ocklawaha River and once in the wilds of Gulf Hammock near the Suwannee River. It is the shriek of a vampire woman, an insane shrill tremolo, half laughter and half moan. Any two or three generation backwoodsman can tell of a child pounced on at the edge of a clearing; of wagons followed; of the sight of a lithe body like a tawny ghost, with its head in the gallberry bushes on one side of the road and its tail in the myrtle on the other. Soon after the last panther in the Big Scrub disappeared, the one I had heard, Fred Tompkins thought he had run afoul of its ghost.

"I'd put Raymond Boyt out of the boat at Eureka," he said, "and was paddling up to Orange Springs to the camp. Night overtakened me and I begun to feel a mite creepified. You know how black it gets on the Ocklawaha, the way them banks lifts up, and the trees thick and the water dark. Direckly I catches sight of a pair of eyes halfways up the left bank. They was wide apart and I knowed whatever was behind 'em had considerable size to it. Thinks I, could be that's a deer, come down to water. Now you know the law says you can't fire-hunt deer at night, and I says to myself, 'Was I to bop one to them eyes, will the law call it fire-hunting?' Then I decides 'tain't a deer, for the eyes is too redlike. A deer's eyes shines green, like a dog's. The current was carrying me close, and thinks I, now whatever 'tis, 'tain't a-going to set there quiet and me passing it. I ain't aiming to have nothing dropping down on my shoulders in a plumb dark night on the Ocklawaha River. So I lifts my gun and I bams at the eyes. You know I usually hit what I aims at. Well, them eyes don't blink no more nor quit looking at me. I fires again, Bam! and the eyes is still there. I shoves in a fresh shell and I shoots one more time. Them eyes goes right on looking at me.

"Fred, I says to myself, that ain't natural. You get out of here right now. You know I ain't superstitious, but when a pair of eyes I'd done shot at three times was yet there, I figured something was wrong. It come to me about that panther had disappeared from along the river. Fred, I says to myself, do you reckon you've done been shooting at that panther's damn ghost? You got to make allowance for the black night, and the creepified feeling a river'll give you in the dark. I sold out. I didn't say nothing to the men at camp when I got there. Next morning my spirits had done rose, and I says to myself, Fred, you ain't going to take a licking from no damn pair of eyes you shoot at and they don't shut. So I paddles back up the river to the place I figured was about right. I goes up a ways and drifts back down. And you know what? I'd done shot a wild-cat in a scrub oak tree, and it was laying in a crotch of the tree, and when I hit him, he had no place to go but to lay right there in the crotch, and them eyes was as dead as my great granddaddy, but they'd gone right on looking at me. Now you know I'm plumb proud I went back and found that thing, or I'd of figured all the rest of my life there was a damn panther's ghost on the Ocklawaha River."

The panthers now in Florida are a few in Gulf Hammock and a number still in the Everglades. Somehow the fiction had built up that there were none in the state. A few years ago, hunters from Arizona brought their pack of dogs to the Everglades to hunt panther. Outsiders laughed at the idea. Panthers were taken in plenty and still prowl the 'Glades, killing deer and cattle. No one knows what became of the last one in the Big Scrub. I was startled to find "tygers" listed among Florida's wild animals in the *Travels of William Bartram*, but a footnote explained that while these were called panthers in Pennsylvania, the Carolina and Florida natives called them tygers. The name has disappeared in the hundred and fifty years since Bartram's chronicle, and even the old-timers call them only "painters" or "panter-cats."

The panther's half-cousin, the wild-cat, seems only a cross, naughty boy. Although wild-cats were hunted with hounds at Cross Creek thirty years ago, and although the snarling cry kept me awake the first night I slept here at the grove, and a large one has been haunting my duck-pen of late, I am not personally acquainted with the animal. I should like to be, and should not be afraid, for it is I who would be the object of terror. A wild-cat is more bashful than a squirrel. He spits like any self-conscious cat, not sure of the world's intentions. He is probably never more than three feet from nose to tail. I missed close acquaintance with a whole wild-cat family one gray dawn in the heart of the scrub. In the dew-moist sand road were the tracks of a mother wild-cat and her kittens. They had seen or scented us and had turned off into the dense undergrowth of gall-berry and scrub oak. The treads were so fresh that the sand was crumbling into the depressions made by the paws. Leonard and I paid our respects to maternal feeling and did not follow. The mother's track was perhaps four inches in diameter. Those of the kittens were the size of ordinary house cats'.

The smaller varmints may all be identified by their tracks. The long pointed hand of the 'coon, the dainty, birdlike mark of the skunk, are unmistakable. All these smaller creatures are delightful on close acquaintance, and the young of any of them may be made a fine pet. An old colored man at Micanopy guarantees to make a household joy of any skunk. His price is a dollar and a half.

"I only gits me a dollar profit," he explains, "count o' havin' to spend fifty cents for Hoyt's Cologne 'fore my old woman'll leave me come in the house again. To say nothin' o' havin' to wash all over. To say nothin' o' my feelin's."

In the light of one's feelings, a dollar profit for removing a skunk's musk-sack seems little enough.

My own closest association with a skunk embarrassed me because of the picture it gave me of my Negroes' conception of my psychology and habits. My friend Dessie was spending the night at the grove. Early in the morning I heard a commotion in the chicken coop where two fryers were penned for fattening. I called Dessie and she came from her room with her revolver. We went together to the coop.

She said, "That's a skunk in there."

I said, "But I don't smell anything."

"You don't always smell a skunk."

I said, "I'll bet you a dinner that it's not a skunk."

I held a flashlight while she peered into the coop. Her revolver barked and barked again. An unmistakable odor sailed suffocatingly from the coop.

I said, "You win," and we laughed noisily.

The next morning I said to black Raymond, "You weren't much help last night. You must have heard the commotion. Why didn't you show up?"

"I heered the ruckus all right," he said. "But I heered you shootin' and I heered you laughin' and I figgered you was just playin'."

Some years ago I met a tame raccoon for the first time. It belonged across the Creek to Mrs. Guthrie's small boy. I was enchanted by her account of its friendship with the family watch dog, a dog who is the only one of my experience to bite me. It had never occurred to me to be afraid of a dog. I thought I knew the secret of handling vicious dogs, which is to walk calmly and steadily toward them, calling, "Come here, boy." This might have worked with the Guthrie dog if I had known that he was dangerous. I walked into their yard one day when no one was at home, in search of permission to hunt across their fields. The dog walked quietly behind me and as I crossed what to him was the boundary line permitted to intruders, he as quietly sunk his teeth in the calf of my leg. I had on heavy boots, but I carried the bruise and soreness for weeks. News that this dog was friendly with the boy's raccoon seemed to me spectacular.

I have unearthed the notes that I made at the time. They are lyrical and useless. I could not foresee that I should have a pet 'coon of my own at a later day and that he would make a farce of them. They may possibly apply to the average pet 'coon, but they most assuredly do not apply to Racket. I have a strong suspicion that he was an individualist.

Note: A young pet raccoon needs far less discipline in the matter of housebreaking than the most aristocratic puppy.

Correction: Racket refused outright to be housebroken. He knew what he was doing and he did it on purpose. He waited for women in their best dresses. He did not like women, anyway. He tricked them. He climbed amiably on the shoulder of the wife of a university president, in gray lace. She said, "He likes me! Isn't he cunning!" Then—. He *knew* what he was doing.

Note: A 'coon is as clean as most human beings. It washes its dear little hands and face with a frequency that Mrs. Guthrie urges her small boy to emulate. Any food except a plate directly from the table, the admirable creature washes carefully before eating.

Correction: Racket didn't wash anything. He liked dirt.

Note: When punished, it cries pitifully, like a child.

Correction: When punished, Racket bit pieces out of you.

Note: It snuggles confidently and touchingly in human laps and on human shoulders.

Correction: Yes, but see correction above for ulterior motive.

Note: The entente cordiale between a pet 'coon and the family dog speaks movingly for the strength of environment as against the pull of heredity. There are unplumbed depths of possible relations between man and beast, and beast and beast.

Correction: Racket did everything possible to make a tramp of my young pointer, Pat. He played with him, indeed, but so strenuously that the dog came whimpering to me to be gotten out of the clutches of an indefatigable small ball of gray fur who gnawed all day on his legs and tail. Racket seduced Pat into going into the marsh with him beyond the grove. They would disappear in the morning, and toward dusk the dog would come limping home, utterly exhausted and covered with marsh mud. Racket would come home the next day, as fresh as a daisy, and having been in the open for thirty-six hours, would make for the top of the bookshelves for his own purposes. He would then head for the kitchen if not caught at it, swing himself up to the table where an extra pan of milk usually sat, and would climb into the pan for a bath. Trailing milk all through the house, he would find the cringing dog and begin to chew.

Note: A 'coon has a most ingratiating curiosity.

Correction: Racket was curious but not ingratiating. He learned to open screen doors from either side. There are eight screen doors in the farmhouse and it was impossible to keep all eight locked all the time. Life wasn't worth living if you had to go around locking screen doors. Racket preferred to pull one open and come in when you were not looking. It was no fun to come in under your eye and be stopped from whatever he had thought up to do. I was having dinner on the veranda. My new silk-lined coat was on the chair, for the spring evening was cool. Some one called me from the rear and I left the veranda. When I returned, my dinner was gone. It was liver and bacon and French fried potatoes. Racked had slipped in through the front screen door. I didn't so much mind the dinner, but he had taken it from the serving platter and moved it to the silk lining of my new coat to eat it—liver and bacon and French fried potatoes.

He could open all the ice-box doors. One day the colored iceman let out unholy shrieks. He had not noticed that the door of the ice compartment was ajar. He swung it open, and there sat Racket on top of the cake of ice, eating raw breakfast bacon.

Note: A pet 'coon has a deep capacity for personal devotion.

The Guthrie 'coon sleeps with the boy, his little iron-gray body under the covers, his strange black-masked face on the pillow beside the child's, like a changeling brother.

Correction: Racket was only devoted to Racket. He had no desire to sleep with me, but if I left one of my bedroom screen doors unlatched, he liked to slip in about midnight, nip my ear with teeth like hypodermic needles, and slip out again.

Note: A 'coon learns early to eat everything the family eats. He soon takes to canned salmon, cooked fish and scrambled eggs.

Correction: Racket was half grown before he would touch anything but rich warm milk. How so ferocious an infant clung so long to the bottle, I do not know, unless he knew that it made the most trouble. He was brought to me as a baby. A colored boy brought me two in a cracker box, and remembering that Uncle Barney Dillard had told me that of twin young of many animals, one would have a mean eye and one a kind eye, I picked. My mistake—I picked Racket. I fed him from a baby's nursing bottle and in a few days he had learned to lie on his back and balance it on his stomach with his hind paws, gripping the top with his forepaws. In a week, he had learned, when done with the milk, to chew the rubber nipple to bits. It took more nipples to raise him than to raise the Dionnes. When offered canned salmon, cooked fish and scrambled eggs, he growled menacingly and I hurried to replace his so-called natural foods with milk. If insufficiently warm or with too low a percentage of cream, he took a chunk out of my hand.

He weaned himself in a way possible only to Racket. I have a friend who is addicted to my Alexander cocktails, for my thick Jersey cream blends smoothly with the gin and crême de cacao to make a perfect Alexander. I made a shaker of them one afternoon and we sat on the veranda with new-filled glasses in our hands. Racket came swinging in, jumped into my lap and reached up his small human hands to see what was in my glass. He growled when I tried to lift it out of his reach. Most animals are Puritans about liquor and turn away their heads in disgust at the smell of it. I not only wanted to avoid being bitten, but I was certain that Racket too would be content to jump down like a good boy when he scented the gin. I put the cocktail to his pointed nose. He clutched the stem and drank the whole cocktail and licked the glass. It was over in a moment. W. C. Fields never tossed down a drink with greater speed or gusto.

In a few minutes, Racket was paying the piper. Not that he minded, for he held his liquor, but his eyes crossed and his legs would not support him. He wabbled about, as cross-eyed as an owl, and disappeared. I saw no more of him and was busy the rest of the afternoon seeing to preparations for dinner, for guests were coming. When they arrived, I led the women into my bedroom to take off their hats. Racket was on my pillow, sleeping it off. I was grateful, for it would keep him out of the way while we dined on the veranda. Half-way through dinner I heard a pattering of little feet and Racket came swaggering out. He hunched his shoulders like a prizefighter. All his bearing was that of a bully who has come into his own. He was cold sober and pleased with himself. He swung under the table. I suppose he nipped a female ankle, for one of the women let out a shriek and tossed a pair of frog-legs to the floor.

I said nervously, in the manner of one trying to pretend that all is well, "Oh, he won't touch it. He won't take anything but milk."

Racket pounced on the frog-legs with a snarl and ate them bones and all. He ate six pairs. He never touched milk again. He was a man. A fellow who could down two ounces of gin could do anything.

I gave him up gladly. There was no use in turning him loose in the woods, for I think he would have come home to nip me at midnight from ten miles away. A farmer once reported seeing him, swaggering in his small leather collar, five miles from home. I took him to Ross Allen's zoo, thirty miles away, to be penned. A year later he led a jail break. He worked at the latch of the cage until he opened it. He took five other 'coons with him to freedom.

A year ago Little Will heard a commotion late at night on the steps of the tenant house. He opened the door and flashed a light. An enormous 'coon was digging in a box of rubbish. He growled and jumped at the man, then turned coolly on his heel and sauntered away into the darkness. Something tells me it was Racket.

15. *The ancient enmity*

"**A**nd the Lord god said unto the serpent, Because thou hast done this, thou art cursed above all cattle, and above every beast of the field; upon thy belly shalt thou go, and dust shalt thou eat all the days of thy life:

"And I will put enmity between thee and the woman, and between thy seed and her seed; it shall bruise thy head, and thou shalt bruise his heel."

GENESIS 3:14–15

Fear of the serpent is inherent in most animals. A placid mare has bolted under me like any wild filly at sight of a coiled moccasin by the road. I have seen my cat jump with arched back like a witch's cat, at the unexpected movement of a garter snake. All hunters have seen their bird dogs tumble backward to avoid a snake. If avoidance is impossible, the dog comes to an unforgettable point, obviously not on birds, a point that is one long tense quiver of distress.

I believe that, contrary to Biblical implications, fear of snakes is not inherent in human beings, but is planted at an age so early that memory draws no line for its beginnings. Fear is the most easily taught of all lessons, and the fight against terror, real or imagined, is perhaps the history of man's mind. The average man or woman says, and believes it, "I have an instinctive horror of snakes." Yet babies and small children, who might be instinctively terrified at sight of a large animal such as a cow or dog, show no fear of snakes, but reach out their hands to them, and have even been known to handle venomous snakes without harm.

I came to Cross Creek with such a phobia against snakes that a picture of one in the dictionary gave me what Martha calls "the all-overs." I had the common misconception that in Florida they were omnipresent. I thought, "If anything defeats me, sends me back to urban civilization, it will be the snakes." They were not ubiquitous as I expected, but I saw one often enough to keep my anxiety alive. A black snake actually ran at me, and a chicken snake thrust his face into mine from a pantry shelf. These were harmless, I knew, but none the less revolting. I took my first faltering steps of progress through sheer shame. In a section where the country women possess great physical fearlessness, I felt feeble-minded to find myself screaming at sight of a king snake that asked nothing more than a chance to destroy the rats that infested the old barn. I forced myself to stand still when I saw a snake in the weeds of the neglected house yard, at least long enough to determine its non-venomous nature. The only poisonous reptiles in Florida, I knew, were the rattlesnake and the cottonmouth moccasin, which I had already seen with horror, and the coral snake, which I did not know.

My determination to use common sense might have been my undoing. One late winter day in my first year I discovered under the palm tree by the gate a small pile of Amaryllis bulbs. The yard was desperate for flowers and greenery and I began separating the bulbs to set out for spring blooming. I dug with my fingers under the pile and brought out in my hand not a snake, surely, but a ten-inch long piece of Chinese lacquer. The slim inert reptile was an exquisite series of shining bands of yellow and black and vermilion, with a tiny black nose. I thought, "Here is a snake, in my hands, and it is as beautiful as a necklace. This is the moment in which to forget all nonsense." I let it slide back and forth through my fingers. Its texture was like satin. I played with it a long time, then killed it reluctantly with a stick, not for fear or hate, but because I decided to cure the skin for an ornament on the handle of a riding crop. I salted the hide and tacked it to a sunny wall. I showed it proudly to my friend Ed Hopkins, who was teaching me the Florida flora and fauna.

He said, "God takes care of fools and children."

The snake was the deadly coral snake. Its venom is of the cobra type, killing within a few minutes by a paralyzing of the nerves. The old terror was back again, and it seemed to me that I should never now be able to pass beyond it. I had no fear of death as death, but the medium was another matter, and one is certainly entitled to one's prejudices in so personal a matter. I found that I had still the blind, unthinking, "instinctive" horror of coming on a poisonous serpent. Nothing could warm the frozen column that replaced my spine at the thought of finding myself face to face with a Florida diamond-back rattler. In a varied life I had discarded one physical fear after another, finding them harmless when confronted. I said, "I am only afraid of the intangibles." Yet even such intangibles as poverty and loneliness might be, simply, accepted, and so disarmed. I discovered that for me rattlesnakes represented the last outpost of physical fear.

I discovered this when Ross Allen, a young Florida herpetologist, invited me to join him on a hunt in the upper Everglades—for rattlesnakes. At the moment I was passing through one of those periods of emotional distress that all of us experience, when some personal catastrophe has tumbled our house of cards about our ears. My small world had crumbled. I should have said offhand that there was nothing left to frighten me. Instantly I realized that I was numb all over at the thought of going out of my way to encounter rattlesnakes.

I am something of a fatalist, in that I believe in a fatalism that stems from one's own adjustment, or lack of it, to circumstance. The Chinese call this "luck character," and it is the same thing. This rather out of the way invitation had been laid on my doorstep like an unwanted foundling. There was no better time to see the thing through; to go down in defeat and hysteria before my fear; or, by facing it, to rip away the veil of panic that stood, perhaps, between me and the facts. I got out of bed, where my mental agony was causing physical symptoms, and packed my bag.

Ross and I drove to Arcadia in his coupé on a warm January day. I said, "How will you bring back the rattlesnakes?"

"In the back of my car."

My courage was not adequate to inquire whether they were thrown in loose and might be expected to appear between our feet. Actually, a large portable box of heavy close-meshed wire made a safe cage. Ross wanted me to write an article about his work and on our way to the unhappy hunting grounds I took notes on a mass of data that he had accumulated in years of herpetological research. The scientific and dispassionate detachment of the material and the man made a desirable approach to rattlesnake territory. As I had discovered with the insects and varmints, it is difficult to be afraid of anything about which enough is known, and Ross' facts were fresh from the laboratory.

The hunting ground was Big Prairie, south of Arcadia and west of the northern tip of Lake Okeechobee. Big Prairie is a desolate cattle country, half marsh, half pasture, with islands of palm trees and cypress and oaks. At that time of year the cattlemen and Indians were burning the country, on the theory that young fresh wire grass that springs up from the roots after a fire is the best cattle forage. Ross planned to hunt his rattlers in the forefront of the fires. They lived in winter, he said, in gopher holes, coming out in the midday warmth to forage, and would move ahead of the flames and be easily taken. We joined forces with a big Cracker named Will, his snake-hunting companion of the territory, and set out in early morning, after a long rough drive over deep-rutted roads into the open wilds.

I hope never in my life to be so frightened as I was in those first few hours. I kept on Ross' footsteps, I moved when he moved, sometimes jolting into him when I thought he might leave me behind. He does not use the forked stick of conventional snake hunting, but a steel prong, shaped like an L, at the end of a long stout stick. He hunted casually, calling my attention to the varying vegetation, to hawks overhead, to a pair of the rare whooping cranes that flapped over us. In mid-morning he stopped short, dropped his stick, and brought up a five-foot rattlesnake draped limply over the steel L. It seemed to me that I should drop in my tracks.

"They're not active at this season," he said quietly. "A snake takes on the temperature of its surroundings. They can't stand too much heat for that reason, and when the weather is cool, as now, they're sluggish."

The sun was bright overhead, the sky a translucent blue, and it seemed to me that it was warm enough for any snake to do as it willed. The sweat poured down my back. Ross dropped the rattler in a crocus sack and Will carried it. By noon, he had caught four. I felt faint and ill. We stopped by a pond and went swimming. The region was flat, the horizon limitless, and as I came out of the cool blue water I expected to find myself surrounded by a ring of rattlers. There were only Ross and Will, opening the lunch basket. I could not eat.

Ross never touches liquor and it seemed to me that I would give my hope of salvation for a dram of whiskey. Will went back and drove his truck closer, for Ross expected the hunting to be better in the afternoon. The hunting was much better. When we went back to the truck to deposit two more rattlers in the wire cage, there was a rattlesnake lying under the truck.

Ross said, "Whenever I leave my car or truck with snakes already in it, other rattlers always appear. I don't know whether this is because they scent or sense the presence of other snakes, or whether in this arid area they come to the car for shade in the heat of the day."

The problem was scientific, but I had no interest.

That night Ross and Will and I camped out in the vast spaces of the Everglades prairies. We got water from an abandoned well and cooked supper under buttonwood bushes by a flowing stream. The camp fire blazed cheerfully under the stars and a new moon lifted in the sky. Will told tall tales of the cattlemen and the Indians and we were at peace.

Ross said, "We couldn't have a better night for catching water snakes."

After the rattlers, water snakes seemed innocuous enough. We worked along the edge of the stream and here Ross did not use his L-shaped steel. He reached under rocks and along the edge of the water and brought out harmless reptiles with his hands. I had said nothing to him of my fears, but he understood them. He brought a small dark snake from under a willow root.

"Wouldn't you like to hold it?" he asked. "People think snakes are cold and clammy, but they aren't. Take it in your hands. You'll see that it is warm."

Again, because I was ashamed, I took the snake in my hands. It was not cold, it was not clammy, and it lay trustingly in my hands, a thing that lived and breathed and had mortality like the rest of us. I felt an upsurgence of spirit.

The next day was magnificent. The air was crystal, the sky was aquamarine, and the far horizon of palms and oaks lay against the sky. I felt a new boldness and followed Ross bravely. He was making the rounds of the gopher holes. The rattlers came out in the mid-morning warmth and were never far away. He could tell by their trails whether one had come out or was still in the hole. Sometimes the two men dug the snake out. At times it was down so long and winding a tunnel that the digging was hopeless. Then they blocked the entrance and went on to other holes. In an hour or so they made the original rounds, unblocking the holes. The rattler in every case came out hurriedly, as though anything were preferable to being shut in. All the time Ross talked to me, telling me the scientific facts he had discovered about the habits of the rattlers.

"They pay no attention to a man standing perfectly still," he said, and proved it by letting Will unblock a hole while he stood at the entrance as the snake came out. It was exciting to watch the snake crawl slowly beside and past the man's legs. When it was at a safe distance he walked within its range of vision, which he had proved to be no higher than a man's knee, and the snake whirled and drew back in an attitude of fighting defense. The rattler strikes only for paralyzing and killing its food, and for defense.

"It is a slow and heavy snake," Ross said. "It lies in wait on a small game trail and strikes the rat or rabbit passing by. It waits a few minutes, then follows along the trail, coming to the small animal, now dead or dying. It noses it from all sides, making sure that it is its own kill, and that it is dead and ready for swallowing."

A rattler will lie quietly without revealing himself if a man passes by and it thinks it is not seen. It slips away without fighting if given the chance. Only Ross' sharp eyes sometimes picked out the gray and yellow diamond pattern, camouflaged among the grasses. In the cool of the morning, chilled by the January air, the snakes showed no fight. They could be looped up limply over the steel L and dropped in a sack or up into the wire cage on the back of Will's truck. As the sun mounted in the sky and warmed the moist Everglades earth, the snakes were warmed too, and Ross warned that it was time to go more cautiously. Yet having learned that it was we who were the aggressors; that immobility meant complete safety; that the snakes, for all their lightning flash in striking, were inaccurate in their aim, with limited vision; having watched again and again the liquid grace of movement, the beauty of pattern, suddenly I understood that I was drinking in freely the magnificent sweep of the horizon, with no fear of what might be at the moment under my feet. I went off hunting by myself, and though I found no snakes, I should have known what to do.

The sun was dropping low in the west. Masses of white cloud hung above the flat marshy plain and seemed to be tangled in the tops of distant palms and cypresses. The sky turned orange, then saffron. I walked leisurely back toward the truck. In the distance I could see Ross and Will making their way in too. The season was more advanced than at the Creek, two hundred miles to the north, and I noticed that spring flowers were blooming among the lumpy hummocks. I leaned over to pick a white violet. There was a rattlesnake under the violet.

If this had happened the week before, if it had happened the day before, I think I should have lain down and died on top of the rattlesnake, with no need of being struck and poisoned. The snake did not coil, but lifted its head and whirred its rattles lightly. I stepped back slowly and put the violet in a buttonhole. I reached forward and laid the steel L across the snake's neck, just back of the blunt head. I called to Ross:

"I've got one."

He strolled toward me.

"Well, pick it up," he said.

I released it and slipped the L under the middle of the thick body.

"Go put it in the box."

He went ahead of me and lifted the top of the wire cage. I made the truck with the rattler, but when I reached up the six feet to drop it in the cage, it slipped off the stick and dropped on Ross' feet. It made no effort to strike.

"Pick it up again," he said. "If you'll pin it down lightly and reach just back of its head with your hand, as you've seen me do, you can drop it in more easily."

I pinned it and leaned over.

"I'm awfully sorry," I said, "but you're pushing me a little too fast."

He grinned. I lifted it on the stick and again as I had it at head height, it slipped off, down Ross' boots and on top of his feet. He stood as still as a stump. I dropped the snake on his feet for the third time. It seemed to me that the most patient of rattlers might in time resent being hauled up and down, and for all the man's quiet certainty that in standing motionless there was no danger, would strike at whatever was nearest, and that would be Ross.

I said, "I'm just not man enough to keep this up any longer," and he laughed and reached down with his smooth quickness and lifted the snake back of the head and dropped it in the cage. It slid in among its mates and settled in a corner. The hunt was over and we drove back over the uneven trail to Will's village and left him and went on to Arcadia and home. Our catch for the two days was thirty-two rattlers.

I said to Ross, "I believe that tomorrow I could have picked up that snake."

Back at the Creek, I felt a new lightness. I had done battle with a great fear, and the victory was mine.

It would be impossible for me ever to feel affection for a snake. One may be ever so interested and tolerant, but prefer work dogs to lap dogs, dogs to cats, cats to horses, and almost any living thing at all, to snakes. But with the conquering of the horror, it has been possible to watch the comings and goings of various reptiles with conjectures as to their habits and to consider them as personalities.

A king snake lived for several years in a hole beside the front gate. When the first strong sun of spring, in February or early March, struck into the ground, he appeared, a majestic fellow, fresh shed, in yellow and black. His favorite place was coiled on top of the first post to the right of the gate. This was probably a good vantage point over the passing of rats and mice, frogs and smaller snakes. He seemed to enjoy being within sight of human activity and lifted his slim bright-eyed head with interest when any one went in or out of the gate. He was very ornamental and when he did not appear on his post I felt a certain anxiety about him. I had sweet-peas planted on the fence one year and often worked and weeded among them as he watched me a few feet away. Sometimes he slid gracefully into his hole, leaving a careless half-foot of tail hanging out, as though hostage to his friendly confidence. He was itchy one season at shedding time and nothing pleased him more than to have fingers stroke his back. He lay quietly, rippling his muscles as one does under the touch of a masseur. He had some sort of rapprochment with my cat, for I often saw Jib pat the exposed tail playfully but gently. The king snake withdrew it without hurry and Jib followed with an unmolesting claw-sheathed paw. Perhaps they divided their extra rats.

Jib's relations with black snakes did not seem so friendly. The one who lived under the kitchen came out one morning with a broken tail, tell-tale slashes at its tip. The innocuous black snake is both brave and impudent. I walked close to a slim ebony beauty with its smooth narrow head high above the grass. My purpose was only to admire at close range but he resented my attention. He made a running attack at me. Quite naturally, I jumped out of his way. It reminded me of the utterly ignominious evening when a skunk chased me down the road for several hundred yards. Discretion in both cases seemed the better part of valor. The black snake turned and ran at me again. He switched himself arrogantly as long as I stood near. When I went away, he retired in the opposite direction, probably well pleased with himself as a ferocious and awe-inspiring fellow. The fastest living thing I have ever seen was a black snake crossing a bed of hot ashes with a mouse in his mouth. We use the expression here, "Fast as a black snake," and I can amend it to, "Fast as a black snake with his belly burning."

I have been obliged to wage unceasing war on the chicken or oak snakes. If I left them to themselves, we should never raise a biddy or a young Mallard duck. The snakes ignore nests of new-laid eggs through the winter. When nesting time comes and the peanut hay in the loft of the barn is full of the game hens setting, and the Mallards begin to set under the Turk's-cap bushes and along the fence row, the chicken snakes appear from nowhere. Usually they wait for their feast until the night the hatching begins and swallow the wet chicks and ducklings as they pip their shells and emerge, for an instant, into the unfriendly world. It is heart-breaking to leave one of the Mallard mothers hovering her new brood contentedly one night, and in the morning to find her childless, fluttering and crying in her distress, the trail of a chicken snake leading away from the nest. Little Will and I watch with constant vigilance at these times and the first squawk of a hen, the first almost human cry of a female Mallard, one or the other of us dashes to the nest. I once shot a very large chicken snake who came to a nest in one corner of the duck pen while the mother was out getting a bit of green for herself. He had a duck egg in his mouth and rolled his yellow eyes at me as he distended his jaws to swallow it. I did not want to shoot and destroy the other eggs and poked him with the gun barrel to force him to a place more convenient for my purposes. He merely wrapped his tail around the mesh of the wire pen, for purchase, gulped down his egg and opened his jaws over another. This was too insulting and I gave him one shot in the tail. He withdrew then, the egg still in his mouth. It was halfway down before I managed to destroy him.

I have never actually seen a rattlesnake on my land, though the east hammock is a crossing place for them. I see them sometimes on the road at the edge of my place, always moving too rapidly for me to get hold of a hoe or a shotgun. One was killed at the corner where my house grove joins that of Old Boss, and the hoe-hands in summer, or Snow and Little Will on the tractor, come across half a dozen or so in the grove in season. I admire the great beauty of the diamond-back rattler and feel that as snakes go, he is very much of a gentleman.

The cottonmouth moccasins make free of the house yard and I have killed several large ones a few feet from the house. My friend Ross feels that I fail him in not taking them alive for him. I have a guilty moment, thinking of the wasted venom that he would milk from them for scientific and medical purposes, but I am forced to prefer the death of a poisonous snake in my yard to not knowing at what moment it will strike the dog, the cat, one of the Creek children coming for milk, or appear under my own feet in the darkness. I have no particular fear of the cottonmouth, for he is sluggish and easily killed, but he is revolting in appearance. He is darkly nondescript in color, he is fat and greasy. He slithers. When I look at him I think of Martha's shuddering summing up of the reasons for her dislike of snakes, "Ain't got no footses an' kin slide so!"

I think the motion of all snakes, if watched and studied long enough, would move any lover of rhythm. I can understand why a cobra sways to music. The way of the serpent is the way of music. I have sat on the veranda watching the movement of a green tree snake rippling in and out among the orange boughs; watching a black snake flow like water in a dream among the leaves of a poinsettia, or lie like a Japanese brush stroke along a spider-lily leaf, and felt that I watched the poetry of motion. Ruth St. Denis caught this serpentine grace in some of her Oriental dances. I should like to have seen her use, as the Hopi Indians use the rattlesnake, the coral snake, in all its jewelled enamel—properly de-fanged of course, as a scientist has recently discovered the Hopi rattlers to be.

I shall always feel an interest in snakes, after my exposure to Ross' wisdom and knowledge, but it will never extend to making one welcome in the house. I was obliged to deal unconventionally a few nights ago with a small cottonmouth in the guest bathroom. The screen door leading on one side to the porch had been left ajar and he had wandered in, attracted perhaps by the light burning there. If the light had not been on, I should have stepped on him in the dark on my way to my own quarters, for he was directly in my path. He was small and young but he was belligerent and quite as venomous as though he had been six feet long. My first thought was of my .22 rifle or my shotgun on the back porch, but I knew that if I left the visitor he would slip away, and I could think of many places where he might reappear that would be less convenient than his present one. Too, it seemed absurd to fill the bathroom floor full of holes. The

Negroes would be sound asleep in the tenant house and could not hear me call. It seemed to me also that I should feel very foolish having Little Will come from his bed, hoe in hand, to face so small a creature. I looked around the room behind me. On the chest of drawers were two books. One was the Sears Roebuck catalogue, a hefty volume. I heaved it at the moccasin. It hurt him enough so that he went into convulsive coils instead of slipping under the bathtub and I knew I could approach closer. The other book was a copy of one of my own writings, *The Yearling*. I took it and finished off the moccasin. I told Little Will next morning of the encounter, and the method by which I had dispatched the intruder. He chuckled.

"It sho' do come in handy to write books," he said.

16. Black shadows

I am not of the race of southerners who claim to understand the Negro. There are a few platitudes dear to the hearts of these that seem reasonably accurate. The Negro is just a child. The Negro is carefree and gay. The Negro is religious in an amusing way. The Negro is a congenital liar. There is no dependence to be put in the best of them.

Back of these superficial truths lies the mystery of the primitive African nature, subjected precipitously first to slavery and then to so-called civilization, the one as difficult and unjust as the other. The Negro today is paid instead of being rationed. He is left to shift for himself for the most part instead of being cared for. In the South his wages are a scandal and there is no hope of racial development until racial economics are adjusted. Meantime, he continues to be, ostensibly, childish, carefree, religious, untruthful and unreliable. Back of it all is a defense mechanism as ingrained as the color of his skin. He could adapt himself to the injustice of his position and to the master white race only by being childish, carefree, religious, untruthful and unreliable.

The prettier side of the picture does indeed lie in the possibility of real affection between individuals of the two races, conditioned by the fact that one is master, and the other, for all of Lincoln, still a slave. The servant has two weapons. He can make life not worth living for his employer. And he can walk out. When a southern Negro uses neither of the two, it is likely to mean, not necessarily that he is well treated, but that he is truly attached to master or mistress. And he can feel an actual love, and yet make life miserable or walk out. Therein lies his unpredictability, and beyond the half-truth of its fact is a mental and emotional turmoil past the comprehension of the most old-school southern aristocrat who ever slurred his witticisms over a mint julep.

I have made one grave mistake in dealing with Negroes at the grove. I have expected that, given justice and kindness, a reasonable attitude toward their problems, and wages higher than the customary ones, they could carry considerable responsibility and learn to discipline themselves. I should have known better. I should have understood that only in rare instances can a Negro work for long on his own initiative. For long years since actual slavery he has been told what to do and what not to do. He has used his little time of freedom to cut loose, to escape for the moment the lowliness and the poverty and the puzzle of living. Left to himself to work toward an unseen goal without jurisdiction or direction, no matter how reliable ordinarily, he realizes suddenly, not that he has responsibilities, but that he is free, he is on his own, and he pounces without warrant on that freedom as though it were already the Saturday night he had earned. I do not blame Kate and Raymond for going wild. I blame myself for asking of them what most of us manage so painfully and so inadequately for ourselves.

Kate and Raymond came after 'Geechee and ahead of Martha's daughter Adrenna. The long line of Negroes has come and gone like a string of exploding firecrackers, each one arriving on the smoking heels of another and departing as violently. Most have gone in insanity, mad love affairs, delirious drunkenness and shootings. Their shadows lie long and black against the pattern of the Creek. Kate and Raymond began promisingly. Raymond was long and lean and very black, as strong as an ox, and in deathly fear of small Kate. She could make him run in terror, not only with the butcher knife, but by lifting her little brown hand or her strong shrill voice. He was a good grove man and I have often lamented his passing from the Creek. Kate began impudently and on the defensive. She had never done housework or my kind of cooking and I had to begin at the bottom. She learned quickly and praise warmed her.

I left off feeling as though the sword of Damocles hung dark and pointed over my head. I began to trust the fragile hair by which it was suspended. I went to the Carolina mountains for the summer to cool the malaria in my blood and to begin a book. Kate and Raymond assured me that all would go as well as though I were at the grove in person. I mailed their weekly pay and had in return an occasional penciled note, "The groav is fine. we is fine."

Of course they were fine. They were having the time of their lives. It would have been a simple insurance to have delegated Fred to pay them for me, to let them know there was still authority over them. In my stupidity I pounded my typewriter happily and drank in the good mountain air. Autumn came and the mountain ash and maples and sourwood were gold and crimson. I think I might still have lingered, but my brother was coming from Alaska for the hunting season. We were renewing a joyous relationship after a separation of ten years. I wrote ahead to Kate and Raymond, specifying house cleaning, dressed chickens in the icebox, and enclosing money and a grocery list to be filled.

I drove in to the grove at dusk on a Saturday evening. The farmhouse was dark. The atmosphere was silent and ominous. No one came to meet me as my car crossed the cattle-gap and swung into the yard. I went into the house. It had not been swept or dusted all summer. Spiders were comfortably in every corner. I went to the icebox. There was ice, only, I imagine, because Kate and Raymond had used it for cooling drinks. There should have been several pans of milk, for the cow had been fresh when I left. There was one small pan. It had the thin bluish look that showed the cow was nearly dry. She could only have dried up by being improperly and erratically milked. There was nothing else in the box. I shut the door. I heard a step. Kate came to the porch, walking rigidly and with glazed eyes.

I asked, "Where's Raymond?"

She waved a vague arm.

"He to the house. He don't feel so good."

"Where are the chickens I wrote you to have dressed?"

"Oh, they ain't no mo' chickens. Varmints got 'em."

"But there were fifty-four young chickens when I left."

"Yessum. Varmints got 'em."

I knew the nature of the varmints. We lose a few fryers from skunks and 'possums, but a watchful man can always catch them at their depredations after the first kill.

"Why isn't the house clean? Where are the groceries?"

"They wasn't time to do nothin' when your letter come. They wasn't no money in it nohow."

The letter had been sent ten days before and there was money in it. I gave Kate a dollar and told her with a calm that I had never expected to own, to send Raymond in the truck to the village for bread and coffee for my breakfast. I dismissed her, for I could not trust my temper. I told myself to go and make a highball and hold steady. I went to the locked cupboard where I had left Bourbon. There was nothing there. I looked up to the ceiling of the cupboard. The square cut for ventilation, covered with a tightly nailed screen, was ajar. The cupboard had been entered by going into the attic from a similar vent in another room and entering to this one. There were no food supplies in the pantry and in my exhaustion I went to bed hungry. Morning brought the same silence as when I had driven in the evening before. I dressed and went to the kitchen. Kate sat dreamily.

"Raymond ain't never come back," she said.

I drove six miles away to Citra. The recalcitrant and completely happy Raymond had been seen at a Negro boarding house. My truck sat in front of it. I called. Raymond staggered out with blank and stupid eyes. He was cramming fried fish into his mouth. Nothing has ever enraged me like that fried fish, I suppose because I was so hungry. I told him he was fired. I arranged to have the Boyts drive the truck home for me. Then I thought, appalled, of my brother's coming within the next day or two.

Well-trained city Negroes simply will not work in the country, miles from their kind. There were plenty of field-hands, like Kate, delighted at the thought of being elevated to housework, who could be trained into good servants. But the job takes from six months to a year. I had sweat and toiled with Kate, doing most of the work myself as I taught her. Given a little time, I could discipline Kate and even Raymond back into shape. There was no time for anything. Meantime, my brother's comfort depended on my being free to hunt and prowl with him, and on coming home at night to an orderly house and a waiting and edible dinner. He was driving more than three thousand miles to be with me, and I did not intend to ruin his visit with my domestic difficulties. It was no moment in which to fire Kate or to set up a rigid discipline. I told her that I had fired Raymond but would keep her on trial. She applauded heartily. Raymond had been the root of all evil. Left to herself she would have been a model of deportment. I remembered Raymond shrinking from her voice and hand. It is of course part of the slave psychology to blame any one else, mother, father, husband, child, to save one's own hide. Kate settled down demurely and when my brother arrived he was unaware of the volcano sizzling under the charm and peace of the Creek.

"I can't get over the ease and smoothness of this life," he said, and I smiled blandly.

"It's wonderful, isn't it," I said.

We were home only for breakfast and dinner and to sleep. We "did" Florida exuberantly. I was amiable with Kate and she was suave and amiable with me. She had acquired a sweetheart, she told me, and Raymond was a thing of the past. She would never forgive him for the great wrong he had done both of us. I saw the sweetheart slip in at night, and it seemed to me that sometimes I saw Raymond's long legs swing over the fence, but as long as the beds were made, the floors swept and dinner prepared, Kate might be a black Cleopatra for all of me. A healthy hell would pop when my brother had gone and I would get us all straightened out and off to a fresh start— probably, I thought, with the penitent Raymond back again, working better than ever for having sinned. Hell popped, but it was not healthy and it was not of my making. Toward the end of his visit, a week-end deer hunt was arranged for my brother. We left before dawn on a Saturday morning and reached home again at midnight Sunday.

As we drove in, I heard the cow bawling. She was standing beside the barn. The car lights showed her bag at bursting point. She had plainly not been milked or fed or watered since we had left. My dog yelped from the back porch. He was locked in. His feed and water pans were bone dry and the porch showed that he had been there since Saturday morning. In the house the beds had not been made. Our Saturday breakfast things had been carried out on a tray and the whole business dumped higgledy-piggledy on the floor of the pantry. My brother blew up like a geyser.

"I've seen what you have to put up with. We're going over to the tenant house and run that black ape off."

I tried then to explain, but the time had passed for sound psychological explanations. I had given them too much leeway, without supervision, and was only paying the penalty for something that could be straightened out. I had wanted his visit free and comfortable. A period of strict discipline after he had gone would take care of everything. It was too late. We had had colored help in our Washington days, but he had been only a child when we left the city and Negroes were as strange to him as though he had never known them. He had been in the Northwest where foreign labor was sometimes an ominous thing. Nothing could convince him now that I was not in peril of my very life.

"This is dangerous," he said, "and I am not going to leave you here alone without cleaning house before I go."

I tried to murmur my tale of the long training, of what cleaning house would mean.

"Get your gun," he said.

I gasped.

"We don't need guns. All I have to do is stamp my foot and they're in deathly terror. Kate would almost die in her tracks if we shoved a gun at her."

He looked at me pityingly.

We went to the tenant house like an invading army. Arthur strapped a focussing flashlight to his forehead. He carried his big-game rifle, a Winchester .30–40 with a telescopic sight. I had my revolver meekly in my hand. It began to strike me as extremely funny. My giggles impressed him of course as hysteria. He patted me protectingly.

"Everything's going to be all right. Just don't lose your nerve. Don't let them see you're afraid."

I whooped and he held me and poured brandy down my throat.

We crept to the door of the tenant house. Arthur threw it open with a magnificent gesture and turned the flashlight on the bed.

"Don't anybody move!" he shouted. "We've got you covered."

We had an amazing assemblage covered. Three occupants of the bed raised up and blinked in the light. In the middle was Kate, modestly dressed in a long-sleeved, high-necked flannel nightgown. On one side of her was the sweetheart, and cozily on the other side was Raymond. Raymond and the sweetheart were buck naked. All three were so drunk that their wooly heads wobbled on their necks. Kate was the first to come to her senses. The light glinted on the telescopic sight of the Winchester rifle. She let out a blood-curdling shriek and leaped from the bed.

There began a strange community dance. Dance is the only word for it. Kate gyrated, flailing her arms. The long flannel nightgown swirled around her bare shifting feet. The sweetheart rolled from the bed and jumped up and down, reaching spasmodically into midair in hope of finding his breeches. Raymond raised to a sitting position, collapsed on the bed, raised again and collapsed, rhythmically. As Kate spun around and around she shrieked, the sound keeping time to her spinning and the sweetheart's jumps. Around it and through it Arthur pranced. He is six feet four, thin and gangling, and looks like a cross between Daniel Boone and Abraham Lincoln.

"Don't let them rush you!" he bellowed. "Keep your man covered!"

I wanted to say, "The only rush they'll make is for the great open spaces," but it was no moment for trivial conversation. "My man" whom I was covering found his pants. I kept my head turned away from him and my revolver leveled in his general direction. Out of the corner of my eye I saw the pants ascending with the jerky motion of a broken escalator. Raymond had given up. He lay prone with closed eyes, waiting for Nemesis to descend as it willed.

Arthur waved the Winchester rifle under his nose and shouted, "Get up!"

Raymond was past getting up. I do not think he even heard him.

Kate left off her whirling and begged, "Raymond, honey, the man gwine kill you where you lay. Get up, honey!"

Raymond opened one eye, groaned, and closed it again. Arthur pranced to the bed and reached in with one of his long arms and heaved Raymond to his feet.

"Keep your man covered! I'm taking care of this one."

"My man" was trembling against the wall. Love nor money could not have made him stir. Kate rushed to cover Raymond's nakedness.

"Put somethin' over you, honey," she crooned.

Raymond fumbled for the sheet and held it hopefully behind his back.

"In the front," Kate moaned. "Honey—in the front!"

I made the mental note that, passing sweetheart or no, Raymond was her truelove. For an instant, I planned our future together.

Raymond would be back, chastened and capable, the sweetheart would slink on his way, I should never again ask of them more than they could do, and life at the Creek would go on smoothly and better than before. Then I knew that something was finished. One's relations with Negroes are like love affairs. When they end, they end. Kate packed their suitcase and flanked by lover and husband, set out down the road toward town in her flannel nightgown.

My brother was happy at having saved me. When he reads this account, it will be his first inkling that I should have chosen differently. I adored being "protected," for I had never had it in my mature life before. But I was sad. The only compensation was in finding, now that it was over, that Kate had turned into a thief. She had taken a considerable amount of money from my brother's wallet, there were missing some of my best clothes and several pieces of my mother's silver. Yet even there, I understood. We had so much and she had so little. We tossed our wealth about carelessly. Surely we would never miss such trifles out of our abundance.

There was an interim, as always, when old Martha came in to take care of me and to tide me over. Between all the explosions she is here, steady as a lodestar. She is utterly incompetent and serves a spoon for the eating of scrambled eggs, and her inabilities grieve her more than they do me.

"Sugar," she mourns, "I wisht you'd ketched me young. You could of learned me anything."

She had a daughter, Adrenna, in want of a job. Adrenna would please me. Adrenna came, and I was in deeper than I had ever been before. A new black-and-white love affair was in the making, and doomed from its beginning. Adrenna drove me perfectly mad at first. She claimed to be able to do everything and could do nothing. When I corrected her in any detail she went to pieces. It took me several months to realize that she was in great fear not only of me, but of her own ignorance. When I proceeded on the tacit theory that in spite of her own protests she knew nothing of the amenities of living, and taught her as kindly and as patiently as I had taught Kate, all went well. I never made a really good servant of her, never a really good cook, for her mentality was not up to it. But as time went on she learned certain dishes and certain menus by heart, like a parrot, and I could order a fixed meal with the certainty that it would be edible. And the usual love built itself up between us.

I could not believe at first that not only was Adrenna man-crazy, in her early forties, but that she could rope in almost any Negro man on whom she concentrated. Trying to see even through male Negro eyes, I could not detect the faintest trace of charm. She was slovenly, she received her suitors in untidy rags, even when good dresses of my giving hung in her cupboard. She wore her kinky hair in tight pig-tails, like Topsy, or combed them out into an alarming piece of shrubbery that stood up around her thin face. She was knock-kneed. She was not young. But when she swung that shingle-butted rear down the road, the Negro men followed and were entranced.

She said, as a fact, "You needs a good man on the place."

I said, "Indeed I do."

"You jes' leave it to me. I'll get us a man. One that'll suit you and one that'll suit me."

Her efforts to trap a man, who should please me by day and her by night, fell between two stools. One by one she lured them in, and one by one they were incompetent in one capacity or the other. She was not discouraged.

"I'll get us one directly can do everything," she said.

I began to be embarrassed about it. Our search was flagrant. We had a succession of Negro men who occupied one half of the tenant house while she occupied the other, and while I tried one aspect and Adrenna tried another. There was Enmon, who pleased me immensely, and was the best grove and yard man I had ever had. Enmon was obliged to leave, reluctantly, he assured me, because a rival suitor of Adrenna, and a much larger and more imposing suitor, threatened to cut his throat with a razor and Enmon was sure he meant it. Jeff Davis was promising. He already had a wife, who came with him to the Creek, but what were wives to Adrenna? The wife was city-bred, owned a good house, stayed here briefly and in fury, and drew Jeff Davis back to her solely by the power of her worldly goods. I had a message from him lately that his wife had left him and he would like to come back, and was Adrenna still with me? But meantime Adrenna had gone, and I have Adrenna's brother Little Will, most satisfactory for the moment, and I have the perfect maid, and again it was too late.

Adrenna really worked on Sherman. She had known him in the hey-day of her youth and she told me that he was everything either of us could ask. We drove to the farm where he was working to interview him. I was frank and Adrenna was coy. I took lessons that day from her technique. Sherman rose to the bait. He longed to come to us, but he was share-cropping and could not leave until the crops were marketed.

Adrenna said to me, "You jes' leave it to me. I'll get him for us."

By the time Sherman's crops were in and he sent word that he was ready for come what might, Adrenna was off on another tack. She had roped in Samson. Jeff Davis—Sherman—Samson. She was nothing if not ambitious. Samson looked too good to be true when she brought him to the door for my approval. I never knew where or how she found him. He was tall, light brown and handsome. He could do and had done, he said, anything and everything—grove work, garden work and house service and was an expert driver and mechanic. I sighed with relief.

Adrenna said demurely, "He wants us to move to Miami when us is married, but I tol' him you'd more'n likely make it worth his while jes' to stay here."

I jumped into the breech to make it worth his while. I would stake them to their wedding, with a grand wedding breakfast afterward, and I would pay him more than I had ever dreamed of paying before. Adrenna had taken not only Samson, but me, into camp. I took them to the judge in Gainesville to be married, and when Adrenna admitted that she was "divo'ced," the judge did not question it, though I knew that three more or less legal husbands were still in the offing. But I was desperate and so was Adrenna. I gave them ten dollars for the wedding party, they went fourteen miles away to Hawthorn for a week-end honeymoon, and returned to the tenant house to settle down into what Adrenna and I had both looked forward to as unmitigated bliss of one sort and another.

I think that Samson failed Adrenna before he failed me. At least it took me longer to find out that his boasts were based on thin air. Out of doors he knew nothing of grove work, inside the house he did not know a knife from a fork, and when he tried the first time to drive the farm truck I heard such a clashing of gears that I thought the car was on its last legs. But he had the growing hand. He was an expensive gardener, and I luxuriated with a sense of guilt over the miracles he worked with flowers. I had delphinium and Canterbury bells for the first time. I had always wanted a rose-bed, but since I had had to stand threateningly over previous workers to get the commonest flowers weeded and watered, it had seemed useless to attempt the care of roses. Samson begged me to put them in the garden.

"I kin really make roses," he said earnestly.

I ordered the bushes from Texas, red and pink Radiance, Etoile de Hollande, Talisman, Lady Hillingdon, Ophelia and Luxembourg. Samson had roses for me in little over a month. It was immensely elegant, and for what I was paying Samson, who spent most of the day in the garden, while the grove languished and Adrenna did the milking for him, I might as well have bought American Beauties from a florist. I decided that it would be a warm winter and I really did not need a new winter coat. Adrenna had become completely necessary to me, we were very much *en rapport*, and if the only way to keep her was to pay her ornamental husband to raise roses, paid he should be, and if I went over the hill to the poorhouse, I should go magnificently, with armfuls of roses.

I sensed dimly as the winter went on that Adrenna and Samson were feuding with Henry. Henry is Sissie's husband and Sissie is Adrenna's sister and Martha's daughter. Martha had come from across the Creek to live in the old Mackay house. She dropped hints that I ignored. Sissie and Henry lived in the little white-washed shack at the edge of the Creek by the bridge. When Martha suggested to me that I "kind o' notice the way Henry's actin'," I decided that Samson and his lordliness irked him. I began to realize that Samson irked me, too. He was courteous, he was a beautiful specimen to look at, he was raising roses, but I just didn't like him. Adrenna was cryptic. I closed my eyes to the tension. We had worked too hard to get us a man to ask questions now.

New Year's came, and I went to Daytona for the holidays. I was sitting in a café when a long distance call came in. The Gainesville sheriff was trying to reach me.

"A man that works for you, Samson, was shot and isn't expected to live," he said over the wire. "The hospital wants to know if you'll guarantee his bill."

"Who shot him?"

"Another one of your Creek niggers. Name of Henry. We've got him locked up."

"I'll guarantee the bill. I suppose the man will be thrown out in the street if I don't."

I thought bitterly that if socialized medicine came, it would be because of things like this.

I reached the hospital by night. Samson was still alive. The doctors had taken one look and ordered him not to be touched, not even for X-rays. Henry had put three loads of No. 5 shot in his belly from a distance of a few yards. Adrenna was my greatest concern. I found her, and usually so careful not to touch me with her clean brown hands, she threw herself on me. She must stay in town, I told her, to be near the hospital, and I would come again the next day. The Mickens family has ramifications all over the state and there was an aunt, Big Ham, with whom she could stay.

Tom Glisson told me all that was known of the shooting. He had heard the reports of the gun, then Adrenna's screams, and had run down the road. He had loaded Samson into his truck and taken him to town. Adrenna stood in the back of the truck like a Flying Victory, shrieking all the way to Gainesville. Henry had given Tom the gun and gone along with him peacefully to surrender. It was a Sunday and Tom had combed the town for a sheriff, deputy or policeman.

"You know," he said, "there wasn't a piece of law in the place."

He had bullied the hospital into taking the wounded man, had beaten on the door of the jail until he roused some one to take in the meek and drooping Henry, and had given clues as to where I might be located by telephone.

"I was sure tempted," he said, "to turn around and bring everybody right back here to the Creek and nurse Samson and try Henry our own selves."

Samson lived. Not even the doctors knew how he did it. He lay for days, green-white and bleeding. Then suddenly he opened his eyes when I went into his room, smiled weakly and announced that we needn't worry about him. His time, he said, had not come to die. The best explanation of his recovery was that his size had saved him. The shot that would have gone entirely through a small thin man, had largely embedded itself in his thick flesh. The pellets began to roll out of him. Every time the nurse changed his bed, she gathered up a handful. Some would stay in him as long as he lived. My mind jumped ahead to the inevitable repercussions. Henry would now face no murder or manslaughter charge. At most, it would be assault with intent to kill; a few years in the penitentiary. What would Samson do? Would he bide his time, until Henry should emerge from jail? I sounded him out cautiously one day. He held no malice toward Henry.

"Henry done wrong," he said simply. "But I forgive him."

He was most concerned about his hands and about my garden. His big hands had caught a part of the load and it was doubtful whether he would regain their use. He held up the thick bandages.

"I jes' got to git these back," he said. "I been layin' here thinkin' about the garden. Ain't nobody but me goin' to take keer of it right. Them roses had ought to been fertilized yestiddy. I figgered it up. I got to git back my hands."

I came away in tears. Something in the man's nature was truly big. Then I realized with horror that for all my admiration I still just didn't like Samson. The thought came to me that his forgiveness was both bland and unnatural. What had he done to provoke Henry? Adrenna was more enigmatic than ever. She stayed with Big

Ham and went three times a day to sit by her husband's bed. But when I came on her sitting there, she was staring blankly ahead of her, as though she sat as a duty by the unmourned dead. I tried to draw her out about the shooting. She was evasive. It had just happened, that was all. Henry was afraid of Samson. Had Samson done anything to make him afraid? Henry was just afraid. An unholy suspicion came to me that Adrenna the flirt, Adrenna the butt-switcher, was back of it all. Was it possible that she had egged Henry on? I shall never know.

Samson was ready to leave the hospital. His belly wounds had healed and only his big hands were bandaged. With a few operations on the remaining shot, he would recover their use. I arranged to take him back for these. I was to get Adrenna at Big Ham's and then we would pick up Samson.

"Big Ham want to meet you," Adrenna said. "She say she got somethin' to say to you."

Big Ham's place was a neat little cottage on the outskirts of Gainesville. I drove to the door. Adrenna waved. An enormous black woman waddled toward my car. She walked with a fixed purpose, a little ominously.

She shouted, "This the woman?"

I wondered if she blamed me for something, if she thought I had not done enough, or had done it improperly. She reached the car and leaned into the window and peered at me belligerently.

"Look at me," she said.

I looked at her meekly.

"I want to look in your face," she said. "I want to look in the face of the white woman has got such sympathy for the black one."

Her voice softened.

"Say me your name."

I said it. I did not use the "Mrs.," as one does usually with this race. I gave my full name as one does for a document. She repeated it after me, accurately.

"I want to carry your name to the Lord," she shouted. "I gwine pray for you. And when I carry your name, I want to carry it straight, so the Lord know exactly who I mean."

She turned and strode back to her house. Adrenna got into the car and we gathered up Samson at the hospital and we drove home.

A story so full of black nobility should end idyllically. It ended in complete confusion. The aftermath brought me into my one conflict with Old Boss, who presumably had nothing to do with it. Samson was back at the Creek. He wandered around for two weeks while his hands healed, then went at the garden. He could use them well enough to work around the rosebushes. I longed to like him and could not. Then the question of Henry arose, like a ghost materialized. All the Creek, it seemed, wanted Henry back. Sissie and the babies were desolate. I sent them money secretly. I found that I, too, wanted Henry back. But justice was justice, and whether or no we loved Henry and could not love Samson, I decided that justice should prevail. Meantime, the rest of the Creek lined up solidly to stand with Henry.

I think it made me angry that they all went behind my back. If they had come to me and told me that they wanted Henry, we might have worked it out. There was Samson's lack of ill feeling to take into consideration, and the fact that none knew what he and Adrenna had done to provoke the attack. I was pushed into the position of persecuting Henry, my favorite, in the name of Samson, the stranger, and I loathed my situation. The next thing I knew, Henry was free. He was reported camping across the Creek where Sissie joined him of nights. He was afraid to come home and face my vengeance, they told me. Adrenna rolled her eyes and was non-committal. I wanted to wring her scrawny neck. We were in this mess because I had trusted her to get us our man, and now I was left holding the bag, the whole Creek lined up against me. Samson was terrified, or pretended to be.

"That man aims to finish me," he said, but there was a false note in the way he said it.

I went to the sheriff's office to make inquiries. The sheriff was bland. Henry had been let out of jail for lack of evidence. I did not see what more evidence a court of law could require than three loads of No. 5 shot in an unarmed man's belly. I pressed the sheriff and threatened to take the matter to the state's attorney and the governor. The truth came out. Old Boss had gone to the judge, a lifelong friend, and had told him, simply, that Henry was his man and he wanted him released. The judge released him. That was all there was to it. All, except that now I was aroused, and felt that I could not allow so flagrant a miscarriage of justice to transpire.

I swore out a new warrant for Henry's arrest. The sheriff hedged, for Old Boss and the judge antedated me. He could not find Henry, he said. I told him where Henry might be found, and on threat of exposing the sheriff himself, Henry was promptly found and clapped back into jail to await trial on charges of assault with intent to kill. It was an unhappy time at the Creek, and I was the most miserable of all. Nobody wanted Samson, for all his virtues, and everybody, myself included, wanted Henry, for all his faults. But justice was justice and my dander was up. I grieved for Sissie and sent her more money. Martha shared the opprobrium heaped on me, for it was believed she had put me up to my cruelties. Actually, she was on Henry's side, too. She received anonymous letters, threatening her life if she stayed at the Creek. We do not know to this day who sent them, but they came from Henry's cohorts. Martha would have stayed it out, but Old Will got in a panic and they moved to Gainesville.

Henry languished in jail, from which he wrote Sissie. Adrenna presumably stood with me on the side of right, and she stole the letter and brought it to me, for her honor was now involved as well as mine.

"My dear sweet wife. When the trial comes up, you are to testify that Samson threatened me. Just forget what happened, and say that Samson come at me and I had to shoot in self-defense."

Back of Henry, as I found, was a lawyer hired by Old Boss and Tom Glisson. I was angrier than ever. Then Martha slipped back to the Creek to see me.

"Sugar," she said, "everybody want Henry back. Nobody don't want Samson, especially Adrenna. You ask her."

I asked her. I was appalled.

"Samson jes' don't fit in at the Creek," she said. She burst out, "The man 'bout to drive me crazy. I ain't never really liked him. I figured he'd do for you and me, but he ain't. What do he do? How do he spend the nights? He spend 'em drinkin' coffee and quarrelin'. Please get rid of him for me—jes' this once."

I gave in to mass opinion at the Creek.

"Samson," I said, "you're not happy here, are you?"

"Might be," he said, "did Adrenna seem satisfied."

"But you and Adrenna aren't getting on together, are you?" I persisted.

"No'm. Nobody couldn't say me and Adrenna is gettin' along."

"Wouldn't you rather be some place else?"

"Reckons I would. Cross Creek is the most queerest place and the queerest people I've ever knowed."

I gave him a month's pay, with guilt and shame in my soul, and Samson was gone. Adrenna thanked me profusely.

"I won't never make us a mistake like that again," she said.

Meantime, Henry was in jail. Sissie came to me, babe in arms. Martha came to me. Old Will came. Tom Glisson came to me.

"You know, all this trouble is really your fault," he said.

I had felt that, too, but I did not know why.

"I figgered you'd learned your lesson from Kate and Raymond, and them eatin' all your chickens and raisin' Cain on the highway, but you ain't quite learned it. Don't you know that truck of yours causes more trouble at the Creek than a dose of smallpox?"

I said, "What has that to do with Henry?"

"You let Adrenna and Samson and Henry go off on that truck. They got drunk and hard feelin's come up. Who's to blame for the hard feelin's, I don't know, but I do know if there's trouble, Adrenna's back of it. We want Henry here. Old Boss needs him to work on his grove. The rest is up to you."

Henry's trial came off, as great a farce as could come before a court of justice. I had decided what I must do, for peace at the Creek is a vital matter. In a private courtroom, the judge called us to order. Henry was represented by the lawyer. There was no prosecuting attorney at all, the judge announcing that he would act in that capacity. I was the first witness called, and the entire population of Cross Creek leaned forward in its seats, and may God forgive me, I said blandly that my testimony was of no value, as I had not been present when the shooting occurred and had my evidence only from hearsay. A long breath of relief filled the courtroom. The lawyer stared at me. He called his witnesses. The testimony was completely irrelevant. Bernie Bass, a satellite at the moment of Tom Glisson, stood up blithely to say that he had come down the road in time to hear Henry beg piteously of Samson, "Don't you come any closer." Tom Glisson took the occasion to express, with no bearing on the case, his low and suspicious opinion of Adrenna.

"Judge, you can just bet she was back of it."

Adrenna rolled a baleful eye at him, and now that Samson was safely away from the Creek, and Henry destined to be back again, testified so noncommittally that one would have supposed her merely to have passed by, a stranger, on the unfortunate occasion. Samson, gazing mournfully at the steely Adrenna, told a story less larded with imaginative fabrications. Yet back of him were unsaid things. It came to me that I had never been in a court of justice less touched by truth and honesty. Henry is a born actor. He stood, a drooping picture of outraged innocence, and told a story of the danger from Samson in which he had lived; of his shooting at the last moment, when Samson strode toward him with threats and in menace. The judge did not trouble to point out that Henry had stolen Old Boss' shotgun some hours before Samson had passed by; or that Samson had stood outside the gate when Henry shot him. I longed to tear the farce to tatters, to demand an authentic trial. Yet Sissie sat rocking the baby, and Martha had told me that she was carrying another, and who would look out for her? And paradoxically, for all of Henry's guilt, I knew in my heart that he was not dangerous. A thing like this would never happen again, and the social value of jail in any case lies only in prevention. I sat still and heard the judge announce that the case was dismissed, again, "for lack of evidence."

I went up to him and said, "I've let this mockery go through for reasons of my own. I just want you to know nothing has been put over."

He sputtered, "I'll have you up for contempt of court."

"Oh no, you won't. You don't dare."

And he did not.

He said, "You understand, having signed the warrant, you are responsible for the court costs."

I said, "I am not," and I never heard another word from the matter.

The assembled witnesses listened, big-eyed. I gathered them together outside in the corridor, Martha and Old Will, Henry and Sissie, Adrenna, Tom Glisson and Bernie Bass and the lawyer.

I said, "Now we all know this has been as crooked a business as the Creek ever got mixed up in. Samson is all right, but the rest of you wanted Henry back. And if there's ever any trouble at the Creek again, it won't ever reach a court. I'll take care of it. And if there's any shooting, I'm going to do it."

We shook hands all around, and the lawyer asked me to support him when he ran for the state legislature. The dove of peace flew with us to the Creek and nested in the orange trees. Henry went humbly about Old Boss' work, Sissie had her new baby, the hard feeling against Martha's presumed intervention died down and Tom Glisson intimated that it would be good to have old Aunt Martha back with us again, and I built an addition to the tenant house that is hers for life. Adrenna settled down again to the business of finding a man who should suit both of us. I met Old Boss on the road a few weeks later. At first I thought that our long friendship had ended. Then he put out his hand to me and his blue old eyes twinkled.

"Next time," he said, "we'll talk things over."

Martha took great pride in the matter. Old Boss' son-in-law, Mr. Williams, kept a vicious dog at the Creek.

Martha said, "Us got a new boss at the Creek. Boss o' Cross Creek now is her—and Mr. Williams' Pat."

I wish sadly that I might report that Adrenna found us our man. She worked hard at it. At last she decided that between us we were undertaking too much. She would look out for herself and I should have to do the same. Without warning, she eloped with a brown youth half her age. She found too late that it had been a mistake to let him know that she had a fortune of a hundred and thirty dollars in postal savings. Robert had married her for her money. When her wealth was gone, Robert was gone, too.

Martha had meantime been pulling her usual strings. She announced that her favorite son, Little Will, was visiting opportunely at Sissie's and would be charmed to have my job. We moved Little Will smoothly into the job and the tenant house. A left-over lettuce hand, Alberta, was staying there, too, for lack of a place to go. In the Jeff Davis days, Jeff had brought her in from a nearby town to set out our lettuce plants and when Jeff's wife lured him back from Adrenna's clutches, Alberta was left behind. It was natural that, with very little preliminary courting, Little Will married the left-over lettuce hand. I had an optimistic moment in which I thought I might train Alberta to my work. But as soon as the homeless orphan for whom we had all felt so sorry was safely married to a wage-earner, she announced that her working days were over.

Martha, of course, filled in. She tried with all her wiles to keep the job open until the inevitable day when Adrenna should drift back home again. Much as I loved Adrenna, I could not look forward happily to future man-hunts. There came to me, in answer to prayer, a reward for my sufferings, the perfect maid. She is well trained, as good a cook as I, well educated, with almost my own tastes in literature and movies. She loves the country, she loves my dog, she loves company dinners, she dislikes liquor and has no interest in men. The Lord taketh away but the Lord also definitely giveth. Blessed be the name of the Lord.

I expressed as much to Martha. She was at first obstructive. When she hinted that I could not possibly be pleased by a girl from Reddick, and advised me darkly not to spend money on refurnishing her room, for she was certain not to be here long, I knew that she was up to her old tricks of manipulation. I had not won perfection to have it snatched from me, even by Martha. I talked to her frankly and for the first and only time, brutally. Idella was satisfied, I said, and I was more than satisfied with her. I would keep her if it meant throwing every one else out. Adrenna could not come back even if she wanted to. I played my last card, and for once Martha did not see through me. If I could not live comfortably at the Creek, I told her, I should sell my grove to Yankees and move away. Martha gave up gracefully and joined me in pæans of praise for Idella.

I said, "You know what I've been through with maids. I feel perfectly sure that the Lord sent me Idella."

She sighed.

"Reckon so, Sugar. The Lord stands high, but He sees low."

She meant, I think, that the Lord had seen through her.

If, even with the Lord on my side, providing Idella, I imagined that Martha would allow Adrenna to pass from our lives, the dream was fatuous. Martha has just brought Adrenna here for a "visit." She showed up with a four months' old baby, of exactly the right age to be a memento of the vanished Robert. This she denies, quite simply. The baby was born to a neighbor, she said, who was going to throw it away.

"I told 'em I'd raise it," Adrenna said, "rather than them jes' throw it in the garbage."

Adrenna has been jobless since she left and she needs a major operation.

"I decide I rather have the operation here," she said, "so's I can be home, at the Creek."

I had a sinking sensation. The baby, Betty Jean, is bright and ingratiating. I can see Martha behind the scenes, managing, manipulating. I am doomed to pay for the operation and doomed to help

Adrenna raise the baby. Perhaps Martha is looking ahead to the day when the Lord reached down His hand to the Creek and turns her over to Abraham's bosom. Perhaps she sees Adrenna replacing her in the addition to the tenant house in her old age, and Betty Jean serving me in mine. Martha will have a finger in my pie from beyond the grave.

17. Our daily bread

I hold the theory that the serving of good food is the one certain way of pleasing everybody. A Readers' Club, in advertising its wares, advises one and all to turn to books when love and liquor fail them. Love and liquor are admittedly fallible comforters, but who is to agree on books? One man's meat is another man's poison more certainly in literature than in gastronomy. Conversation is fallible, for not all want to talk about the same things, and some do not want to talk at all, and some do not want to listen. But short of dyspepsia or stomach ulcers, any man or woman may be pleased with well-cooked and imaginative dishes.

Cookery is my one vanity and I am a slave to any guest who praises my culinary art. This is my Achilles heel. Dorothy Parker has a delightful verse dealing with the abuse she is willing to take from her beloved, and ending, "But say my verses do not scan, and I get me another man. For my part, my literary ability may safely be questioned as harshly as one wills, but indifference to my table puts me in a rage.

My recognition of cookery as one of the great arts was not an original discovery, but it is as important a one for the individual woman as the discovery of love. My mother and her mother had been famous cooks. When I read Della Lutes' *A Country Kitchen*, I wept in nostalgia for my Michigan grandmother's dinner table. My mother was as great a cook, but there was a taint on her art, for she did not consider it a notable accomplishment and she refused to teach me. Also, she worked so hard at it, with so little joy, no matter how capable a maid stood at her side, that she was exhausted, with a migraine headache, when a special feast was ready, and could not touch any of the magnificent dishes. I watched her in the kitchen with utter fascination, and since she apparently used no recipes, but combined her inherited knowledge with her own natural gift, I came to the secret conclusion that cooking was a matter of instinct, and that surely it must be in my blood. This belief was as fatuous as the belief of most people that they could write if they cared to take the time for it.

My instinctive cooking proved, in my maturity, a thing of horror. It bore no relation to that of my mother and my grandmother. The climax was dual, two shocks following closely on each other. One night at dinner a plate of tomato mayonnaise salad was heaved at my head. There was nothing wrong with the salad, but every other dish on the table was inedible. I began to wonder if heredity might not be a snare and a delusion. A week later my mother-in-law came to visit, and while she ate my meals gracefully, courageously and without comment, she had no sooner returned to her home than there came to me in the mail a copy of the *Boston Cook Book*, even ahead of the conventional bread and butter letter.

I was not offended, but grateful, and I studied Fanny Farmer as a novitiate the prayer book. Lo and behold, my memories of my mother's dishes suddenly fitted in with the new exactness and I could duplicate her secret recipes, her heart-melting egg croquettes, her chicken in aspic, her potato puffs, her white almond cake. Science, art and instinct joined hands in a happy ring-around-the-rosy. I had solid rock under me. I have often thought that if I should be quite destitute, provided I had a modicum of health, I should enjoy making my living as a cook, but it would have to be in an establishment where the cream and butter and cooking sherry were not stinted, for life at the Creek with Jersey cows has unfitted me for skimmed milk and margarine. And I should buy cooking sherry with my last dollar.

The new foods that I found in Florida were a challenge and I have learned more about cookery in my years at the Creek than in those that preceded them. Some of my best dishes are entirely native and local and I shiver with delight when a stranger pokes at something and asks dubiously, "What is it?" then, urged to taste, is wreathed with smiles and says, "It's good, even if it's rattlesnake." Rattlesnake is of couse eaten as a delicate hors d'oeuvre, but of all the queer things I have served or eaten, this alone is not among them. It is sheer prejudice, no doubt, but I know too well the heavy, rolling black and yellow bodies to relish a morsel from their midriffs.

William Bartram gives a pertinent account of a similar divergence of taste. The occasion was a trip to Florida, near St. Augustine, with his father, the botanist John Bartram, at a much earlier date than William's famous travels of 1773.

"Some time after we had been rambling in a swamp about a quarter of a mile from the camp, I being ahead a few paces, my father bid me observe the rattlesnake before and just at my feet. I stopped and saw the monster formed in a high spiral coil, not half his length from my feet: another step forward would have put my life in his power, as I must have touched if not stumbled over him. The fright and perturbation of my spirits at once excited resentment; at that time I was entirely insensible to gratitude or mercy. I instantly cut off a little sapling, and soon dispatched him: this serpent was about six feet in length, and as thick as an ordinary man's leg. The encounter deterred us from proceeding on our researches for the day. So I cut off a long tough withe or vine, which fastening round the neck of the slain serpent, I dragged him after me, his scaly body sounding over the ground, and entering the camp with him in triumph, was soon surrounded by the amazed multitude, both Indians and my country-men. The adventure soon reached the ears of the commander, who sent an officer to request that, if the snake had not bit himself, he might have him served up for his dinner. I readily delivered up the body of the snake to the cooks, and being that day invited to dine at the governor's table, saw the snake served up in several dishes; gover-nor Grant being fond of the flesh of the rattlesnake. I tasted of it, but could not swallow it."

At the Creek I was obliged to learn all over again the simple matter of "bread." Bread to me had always been the baked wheat loaf, white or of the whole grain. One drew a line only between homemade and baker's bread. This is not "bread" to the Creek at all. If I asked a neighbor for some bread in an emergency, I should re-ceive a pan of cornbread. It is the staple bread and the young Townsends were correct in believing that one must have it to grow on. Bread as I once knew it is called "light bread," and healthy ap-petites despise it for "wasp's-nest bread," with contempt for its tex-ture and its filling qualities. There are gradations of cornbread. True cornbread is made elegantly with milk and eggs and shorten-ing and is considered, rightly, good enough for any one. Then comes cornpone. It is not so rich, leaving out the eggs and usually the milk, and is made in a skillet on top of the stove. Below cornpone is hoecake and this is made simply of cornmeal, salt and water, very thin in texture, and fried in a skillet if one has fat for frying, or often in a Dutch oven or over a hearth or camp fire. The field hands of slavery times and the soldiers in the War Between the States baked it on a shovel or hoe held to the open flame. When made of good sweet water-ground meal, it is crisp and palatable, much like Mexican corn-chips.

I do not know where, among the cornbreads, to place hush-puppies. There are elevated Floridians who turn up their noses at hush-puppies, but any huntsman would not exchange a plate of them for crêpes suzettes. They are made and served only in camp, or when one is frying fresh-caught fish informally at home, with the returned fishermen clustered comfortably in the kitchen while the cook works. Hush-puppies have a background, which is more than many fancy breads can claim. Back of them is the hunt, the fishing trip, the camaraderie, the grease in the Dutch oven aromatic to hungry sportsmen. First, you fry your pristine fish, boned and filleted, rolled in fine cornmeal and salt and dropped into sizzling fat. You lift out the fish, golden-brown, and lay them on pie plates close to the camp fire. While they have been frying, you have stirred up your mixture: fine white cornmeal, salt, a little soda or baking powder, an egg or two or three if the camp be affluent, and, if you want hush-puppies de resistance, finely chipped raw onion. You make the mixture dry and firm. You pat it into little cakes or croquettes between your hands and drop the patties into the smoking deep fat in which the fish have been fried. They brown quickly to the color of winter oak leaves, and you must be sure to have your coffee and any other trifles ready, for when the hush-puppies are brown, your meal is ready.

They must be eaten so hot that they burn the fingers that lift them, for the licking of fingers, as with the Chinese genius who discovered roast pig, is the very best of it. Do they sound impossible? I assure you that under the open sky they are so succulent that you do not care whether you have the rest of your dinner or not. The name? It came, old-timers say, from hunting trips of long ago, when the hunters sat or stood around the camp fire and the Negro cooks and helpers sweat over their cooking and the hunters ate lustily. And although the hunting dogs tethered to nearby trees had been fed their evening meal, they smelled the good smells of man's victuals, and tugged at their leashes, and whined for a tid-bit extra. Then cook or helper or huntsman would toss the left-over little corn patties to the dogs, calling, "Hush, puppies!" and the dogs bolted the toothsome morsels and hushed, in their great content.

The hot biscuit runs a poor second to cornbread, but is considered of higher social caste. We abrogate and deprecate cornbread when we have guests, but we should consider ourselves deficient in hospitality if we served a company meal without hot biscuits. We cannot conceive of a guest's not relishing them, and a tale is told of a visitor to the South who never got to taste a hot biscuit, solely from his hostess' zeal in trying to provide them hot. It seems that the visitor was a great conversationalist, and as the hot biscuits were passed him by the maid, he would take one, butter it, and delve into talk. He would pause, reach for his biscuit, and the hostess would say, "Oh, but that one is cold. You must have a hot one." She would ring for fresh biscuits, the guest would take one and butter it, make conversation, and again, his biscuit would be snatched from him as he was about to eat it. The story goes that he left the South without ever having tasted a hot southern biscuit. It sounds like one of Irvin Cobb's yarns, but it is more than plausible. We do not have here the beaten biscuit of Kentucky, but we make our biscuits much shorter than northern biscuits, and while I sometimes think longingly of my mother's and grandmother's biscuits, light, flaky, falling apart in layers, I bite into a Florida biscuit, crisp as Scotch shortbread, and no longer recall my ancestry. The sorriest Negress, who can turn out nothing else fit to eat, can make hot biscuits that would have melted the hard heart of Sherman.

We have a wonderful recipe in these parts for ice-box rolls, whose yeast-rising dough may be prepared in advance, kept in the icebox, and brought out to be raised and baked when needed. It is perhaps exceptional or local only in that we bake it by preference in a Dutch oven with live coals for heat. Cast iron is so superior for cooking utensils to our modern aluminum that I not only cannot grieve for the pioneer hardship of cooking in iron over the hearth, but shall retire if necessary to the back yard with my two Dutch ovens, turning over all my aluminum cookers for airplanes with a secret delight. The Parker House in its hey-day could not have made rolls as good as those we make on camps in the Dutch oven. I make the rolls a trifle larger than is usual and tuck them in tightly in their buttered iron nest. I put on the heavy cover and set the oven with its three short legs either within faint warming distance of the camp fire, or out in the sun. The heat for baking, when they have risen and are ready in an hour or so, must be handled as carefully as a munitions plant handles its powder. Too little heat in baking means pale wan doughy rolls, and too much means rolls of charcoal. Only experience teaches the number and depth of hot glowing oak coals both under the oven and on the lid. When properly done, the rolls are light as feathers, done to a great flakiness, hazel-nut brown, and of a flavor achieved under no other circumstances.

My most successful Dutch oven rolls were prepared in the middle of the St. John's River. The doctor and his wife Dessie and I were on a fishing trip on a warm winter day down the Ocklawaha River to its junction with the St. John's, through little Lake George, to the mouth of Salt Springs Run, where we planned to cook supper and camp for the night. I had brought along my large Dutch oven and a big bowl of dough for my rolls. We fished late into the afternoon and it was plain that by the time we reached our camping place, it would be too late to set my dough to rise. There would be time enough for the baking, for the fish must be cleaned and fried. We estimated the time to the landing, and an hour and a quarter beforehand, I brought out my bowl of dough, my extra flour, my butter and my Dutch oven from under a seat of the rowboat, and while spray from the wind-swept river dashed into my face, I mixed the dough in the bowl in my lap, shaped my rolls and placed them tenderly in the Dutch oven. I put the oven far forward where the late afternoon sun would rest on the lid, and by the time we reached Salt Springs Run and the camp fire was built, the rolls had risen and were ready for the baking. They had never been so delicious. Supper was superb, the fresh-caught bass white and sweet and firm, the coffee strong and good as it can only be in the open.

We were on a little promontory at the mouth of the run, with great live oaks around us, and palms tall against the aquamarine evening sky. A full moon rose in front of us and we felt ourselves favored of all mortals. After so much delight, we might have expected to pay the piper. The night was hideous. Because the time was winter, we had assumed there would be no mosquitoes. But because the winter was warm, they had hatched, and as we lay on blankets on the sand, they descended in swarms. We built up the camp fire to make smoke to drive them away and the smoke was more annoying than the mosquitoes. Hoot owls settled in the oaks over our heads and cried jeeringly all night. Wood roaches came in and awakened us from our spasms of slumber with their sharp nibbling on our ears. When we arose at dawn, the doctor said, "You know, the only thing that kept me going through the night was remembering those rolls."

Florida vegetables are all found, I think, in northern markets, but many of them are never cooked properly there, for the reason that the Yankee does not understand the benign uses of white bacon. When you say "meat" in the north, you mean beef or lamb or something of the sort. "Meat" in Florida is one thing—white bacon. We call it white bacon to distinguish it from breakfast bacon, or side meat, and it is, simply, salt pork, or, to the army, sow belly. If it is under-rated in the north and by the military, it is perhaps over-rated in Florida, for it is the staple meat. Affluent rural families serve it three times a day, no matter what other meats may be on the table, poor families have it as often as they can afford it, and town families of rural antecedents serve it when the nostalgic hunger becomes too great. The other evening I found my colored maid Idella laughing to herself in the kitchen. I inquired the source of her mirth.

"Guess what I had for my supper," she said.

I could not guess.

"Well, I had cornpone and white bacon. When we were growing up and there were so many of us in the family, all we had most of the time was cornpone and white bacon, and we had to eat it or go hungry. I thought I'd like to see how it tasted when I didn't have to eat it."

It tasted very good indeed, she reported.

White bacon is cooked everywhere in about the same fashion. It is usually soaked a little while in warm water or in milk, squeezed dry, dipped in flour and fried to a crisp golden brown. The large amount of grease that fries from it is poured into a bowl and this to the backwoodsman is "gravy." It is solid grease, and it is poured over grits, over sweet potatoes, over cornbread or soda biscuits, and how country stomachs survive ten hundred and ninety-five servings of this a year is a mystery past my solving.

But the bacon itself is very tasty and is a requirement in cooking many vegetables. I cannot conceive of cow-peas without a few thin slices boiled along with them, and even string beans, which here we call green beans or wax beans according to color, now seem insipid to me when cooked with butter or even with cream. "Greens" probably save more backwoods lives than the doctors, for they are the one vegetable, aside from cow-peas, for which country folk have a passion. Spinach as a green is unheard of, although it is raised for the northern market. Beet greens are not relished. But turnip greens, mustard greens and above all, collard greens, cooked with white bacon, with cornbread on the side, make an occasion. Pot liquor and cornbread have their adherents and have even entered into southern politics, a man addicted to the combination being able to claim himself a man of the people.

Mustard greens are strong and hot and are best used sparingly along with turnip greens. Wherever mustard has been planted, it goes wild and spreads, so that today, ten years after my last planting, I can still go down toward the lake under the old seedling pecan trees and pick a good mess in season. Collard greens are my favorite of the three. They have a sweet nutty flavor. An unhappy combination is collard greens and hog chitlings. Rural Florida is divided into chitling and anti-chitling camps and feeling sometimes runs high. Man stands against wife and mother against child. Fred Tompkins solved the dissension over them between himself and his wife in a practical way.

The Old Hen's a fool for chitlin's," he said, "and I don't believe in deprivin' another of anything they call pleasure. So when she cooks 'em, I just sell out and leave home for a day or two."

Pokeweed flourishes here and in late winter or early spring the broad-leaved green shoots spring up all over the grove. Others at the Creek use the leaves for "poke salat," or cook them like any other greens. I hunt through the grove after a spring rain, basket in hand, for the most tender shoots, cutting those from six to eight inches in length. I trim off the leaves and thin skin and cook the shoots exactly as I do asparagus, serving them on buttered toast with a rich cream sauce poured over, and strips of crisp breakfast bacon around them. The flavor is delicate and delicious, with a faint taste of iron.

Longing for asparagus, I imported a quantity of the roots and made a deep rich bed according to instructions. The asparagus grew and thrived, but the year-round blandness of temperature here, with no long dormant period, excited it so violently that it grew twelve months of the year, sending up long neurotic shoots every night, no larger than a bridge pencil. It grew so fast that there was never a moment of that crisp succulence in which to cut it. By noon the thin sprigs had burst into ferny leaf. I was discouraged, but I think the asparagus was not, for after generations of offering damp heads to a cold northern April sky, here were sun and heat all day long, and the asparagus went wild with joy.

Okra is a Cinderella among vegetables. It lives a lowly life, stewed stickily with tomatoes, or lost of identity in a Creole gumbo. I do not know whether the magic wand with which I wave it into something finer than mere edibility is original, but I know no other cook who serves it as I do. To bring it to its glamorous fulfillment, only the very small tender young pods must be used. These are left with the stem end uncut and are cooked exactly seven minutes in rapidly boiling salted water. I serve them arranged like the spokes of a wheel on individual small plates, with individual bowls of Hollandaise sauce set in the center. The okra is lifted by the stem end as one lifts unhulled strawberries, dipped in the Hollandaise and eaten much more daintily than is possible with asparagus. The flavor is unique. The Hollandaise, it goes without saying, must be perfect; just holding its shape; velvety in texture; properly acid. I use the yolk

Marjorie Kinnan Rawlings

226

of one egg, the juice of half a lemon, and a quarter of a pound of Dora's butter per person. The only other place I have eaten Hollandaise as good as mine is at the Ritz-Carlton, and even theirs does not have quite enough lemon juice to suit me. And of course, for the price of one serving of broccoli or asparagus à la Hollandaise at the Ritz, I can buy a whole hamper of okra and feed Dora for a week.

The Ritz and the Waldorf and such haunts also serve our most exotic vegetable. They call it hearts of palm, but to us at the Creek it is, simply, swamp cabbage. I serve it seldom, for it is truly the heart of a palm tree and the epicure's feast means the death of a palmetto. I am so enamored of the tall swaying palms that I cut one only on special occasions, although it makes one of my favorite dishes. You cannot have your palm tree and eat it too. Only the young palms have edible hearts. The proper height is about six or eight feet. It is a yeoman's job to cut down the tough fibrous trunk and split off the overlapping tight outer layers. I do not see how any one gets the white inner cylinder trimmed down correctly, wasting none of the sweet portion but cutting away all that will be strong and bitter, without Martha's assistance. If she is within hailing distance, she comes to do the job for me. Greed snares me when I try it, for I can never give up the final layer, in the fond hope that it will prove edible. A trace of bitterness spoils the dish. The tenderest core of the wax-white cylinder may be sliced very thin, soaked in ice water, drained and served as a salad with tart mayonnaise or French dressing. It has the crisp sweetness of chestnuts. We usually parboil our swamp cabbage in a very little water, then put it on to cook again in still less water, with thin slices of white bacon. It melts in your mouth when cooked with butter until tender and dry, then moistened and heated with heavy cream. Its flavor is a cross between oyster plant and boiled French chestnuts, but as superior to either as angel food to hard tack.

We raise here successfully an ethereal relation of the squash family, the choyote. The fruitlike vegetable grows on a luxurious vine that has been known to cover an acre. I used it through a hot summer for shade over my Mallard duck pen. The choyote is the shape of a blunt, enormous pear, pale jade-green in color. Peeled, sliced, parboiled and tapered off au gratin in the oven with a dense cream sauce and a nicely calculated quantity of grated cheese, it provides so delicate a dish that I should consider it suitable only for Boston Brahmins, if it were not that Boston Brahmins have a rank and plebeian taste for baked beans, coarse brown bread and odorous fish cakes.

I am reminded of the fabled Britisher who ate a breakfast, which included codfish cakes, at the old Parker House in Boston.

"All the dishes served me," he said to the waiter, "have been exceptionally palatable. But will you kindly remove these little patties? Something seems to have died in them."

Perhaps the delicacy of the choyote is after all most suited to the sub-tropics, where we do everything in so leisurely a manner that we roll a taste on our tongues and savor any subtle flavor with the long view of time.

Here at the Creek we do not have our full quota of Florida fruits, for we are above the frost line, as far north, actually, as citrus may be raised commercially. The two large lakes, Orange and Lochloosa, between which our lands lie, protect us from a greater cold damage. We cannot raise here the avocado, the papaya or the mango, and when I buy them in market I must pay almost as much as in New York City. A hundred miles south all three are raised, though for the fine big Haydn mango one must go south of Miami and to the Florida Keys. I once planted three avocados, or alligator pears, as the Chamber of Commerce wishes us to call them, in pots. They grew into handsome seedlings with large bronzed leaves and I set them out between the pump stand and the pantry window, where the southern exposure would protect them. They grew higher than the house and just as I had dreams of grafting them with cuttings of the edible avocado, a freeze cut them to the ground. They put out hopeful shoots for the next two years, but last winter's cold finished them and there are three black stumps to mark the site of my hopes for my own salads.

The papaya is not properly appreciated away from home, for the reason that it is seldom served ripe enough. It must look completely rotten, black and yellow, with the skin peeling from it in apparent decay, before it is sweet and mellow and ready, and it would not occur to any one out of the tropics to wait for such disintegration. There should also be a minor law compelling its dressing with lime juice. The fruit alone is on the insipid side. The only recommendation for the over-sweetened canned papaya juices is their vitamins and their digestive action on proteins.

Better men than I have written lyrically about the mango. They have also written, to my notion, abusively, for they insist that the only way to eat a mango is in a bathing suit by the side of the ocean or in the bathtub. This maligns the mango. It is necessary only to tie a towel around one's neck and lean far forward. If it could be had in no other way, it would be worth while to stand on one's head to eat it or to hang from the limb of a tree. I have known the best of northern apples in my grandfather's orchard, the Ben Davis, the sheep's nose, the banana apple, the little pink-stained snow apple, sweet as honey. I have known the New York State Elberta peach and the Georgia peach, the West Virginia sickle pear and the Wisconsin Bartlett. I know the Indian River orange and its close rival, the pineapple orange of my own section; our choice grapefruit and tangerines. I would swap them all for the season's Haydn mangoes. There is a smaller mango, fibrous and acrid, that we call the turpentine mango from its strange flavor. This should be avoided unless one is desperate for any taste of mango. The Haydn is born generously with several different flavors, and we choose from the strawberry mango, the pineapple mango and the peach mango.

Tastes and odors can never be described unless they are comparable with known tastes and odors and the mango is unique and completely superior. It may be peeled and eaten out of hand, gnawing at last on the great pit; it may be cut daintily and served just so, or with sugar and cream; or it may be made, with the help of a Jersey cow, into ice cream fit for the gods. Do not desecrate it, do not commit sacrilege, by making ice cream of the mango with ordinary city cream, not even the double whip. If you do not own a Jersey cow or have no friend who owns a Jersey cow, eat your mango plain and forget the Olympus beyond your reach. But if you can lay hold of cream as yellow as June butter, so thick you must dip it from bowl or pitcher with a spoon, then crush your mangoes, add a little lemon juice and a little sugar, stir in the cream, freeze it, not in the electric icebox but in a hand churn, and be prepared to have life afterward, without mango ice cream, a trifle dull.

I recall the time when I was in the hospital on a bland, or nonfibrous, diet. My own doctor, who had committed me to the diet, knew that I shared his passion for mangoes. About eight o'clock at night, when the day nurses had gone and the night nurses were busy, he would slip into my room with a sack of mangoes. He would close the door stealthily, bring me a towel and basin, and peel a mango for me, then peel one for himself over the lavatory. We ate mango for mango, and if there was an odd number, he divided the extra one mathematically between us. I would try to sift out between my teeth as much of the fiber as possible.

"Anything this good," he would whisper over his shoulder, fearful of the nurses whom he had impressed with the exigencies of my diet, "couldn't possibly hurt any one."

To compensate a little for not being able to raise our own mangoes at the Creek, we have guava bushes along almost every fence row. Guavas have the rankness of odor of the tropics, deathly sweet and pungent, and the uncouth say that a self-respecting cat will bury a guava. The flavor, however, like that of many malodorous cheeses, is delicate. The bushes grow sometimes as high as a one-storied house and the fruit is borne in round golden balls the size of small peaches. There are two layers of solid meat, interspersed with countless small, hard, yellow seeds like bleached buckshot. True guava addicts eat seeds and all, and the sound of two or three of them at it is like the clashing of worn gears. The Florida stores carry Florida-canned guavas, but these have the seeds left in. The Cubans can the seeded layers of large choice guavas in a heavy syrup, so whenever I am in Tampa I go down into the crowded Cuban quarter, redolent of scorching coffee beans and the long sweet sticks of Cuban bread, and buy canned guavas there. I serve them with cream, or with crackers and cream cheese. For making guava jelly, I have a line of Cattley guava bushes along the edge of my back porch. The bushes are as ornamental as ligustrum and the tiny red fruits, as inedible as wild crabapples, as full of pectin and tartness, make a ruby-red jelly much superior in taste and texture to the commercial guava jelly. A glass of Cattley guava jelly works miracles in a wine and raisin sauce for baked ham, in a mince pie, and in a certain rum and brandy Christmas punch.

I tried futilely to make jelly of our passion fruit, which sprawls its exquisite lacy vines all over the east grove through the late summer. Among the truncated leaves the passion flower opens pale lavender rosettes, fringed and marked at the center with the stigmata, and with stamens indicating the number of the apostles. There is even visible the crown of thorns. The fruit resembles a little the May apple, but is of an open, fibrous texture. There is a passion fruit liqueur that is the primary ingredient, after the varied rums, of that marvelous and deadly drink, the Zombie, and I was sure I had heard of passion fruit jelly. My own vines in the grove had been destroyed by the last mowing, and I walked two miles to Big Hammock where the vines grew along the roadside. I gathered a skirtfull of the fruit and went home to my experiment. Perhaps I should have eliminated the skin or the seeds, but at any rate the exotic jelly on which I had set my heart did not materialize. The mixture jellied, but it tasted like a mediaeval poison, acrid and strange, and I threw it out with horror. There are several tropical edibles that are poisonous when improperly treated, notably the coontie palm root and the cassava. Both must be soaked and pounded to get rid of the poisonous element. The coontie palm root when treated makes a starchy flour for bread, and the reason the Seminole Indians were able to hold out against us, was their use of the root. The treated cassava root makes a delicious pudding, amber in color, translucent, delicately sweet.

There are two jellies here, however, rare and ethereal, that, like the wines of some provinces, may be found only in their own habitat and are not on any market. One is the roselle, rosy-pink, tasting like candied rose petals. The roselle belongs to the okra and cotton and hollyhock family, and when the flowers, which we raise for ornaments, are just past full bloom, we make the jelly of the seed pods that have begun to form, seed pods that resemble rose hips. The other is may-haw or hawthorn jelly, as delicate as its name. I first tasted it, incongruously, on a bear hunt near the St. John's River. Marsh Harper brought it, of his wife's making, as part of his contribution to the hunt's food supplies. It is necessary to pick the may-haws at the immediate moment of proper ripeness, for if unripe they are bitter, and if over-ripe they will not "jell."

Of the wild fruits, the large single wild Florida grape and the wild plum, or hog plum, make the finest of tart jellies, and I make these to serve through the winter with game. But I am obliged to watch the development of the fruits closely and pick them a trifle green, for the 'coons and 'possums and jay-birds are likely to be ahead of me. I feel sometimes in gathering them that I am stealing from the needy, for the jelly is a luxury for me and the fruit a necessity for the small animals. I take no more than I am sure I shall use. As for the pawpaws, which bloom like miniature white orchids late in February, the banana-like fruit is gone down the gullets of the varmints long before I have had a chance at it, and with pawpaws covering our woods, I have never tasted one.

Martha said to me, "Only a nigger young un kin beat the varmints to the pawpaws."

Thinking of the small hungry creature faces, prowling for food of nights, I have never picked a spray of pawpaw bloom, for all its loveliness, but once, and that was to take to my artist friend Robert for his enchantment. I wrote this verse once, after I had held my hand:

> I did not break the may-haw bough,
> Nor pull the flowering plum,
> For ripe fruit follows April's plow
> And falls when locusts drum,
> And windy summer nights I know
> New-weaned raccoons will come.
>
> I left the fox the pawpaw bud
> To ripen near his lair—

But brambleberries strewed the wood,
And they had bloom to spare.
I picked a thorny spray and stood
And tucked it in my hair.

I am the sole admirer of my verse, but I felt a great nobility during its composition.

The Scuppernong grape is not a Florida native, but cuttings from old Carolina and Georgia vines have been brought in with many a covered wagon and on many an ox-cart. The vine thrives here in the dry sandy soil, and on many abandoned clearings, where even the brick chimneys have fallen into dust, a huge Scuppernong will stand, seeming to support the rotten lattice work rather than to be sustained by it, an echo of some dead and gone family struggle for existence. The purple Scuppernong is rich and fat and unexceptional, but the white Scuppernong, in the hands of loving and expert care, makes a vintage white wine that can stand with the best Sauterne.

When Zelma and I were taking the census, we came on an old man far off in the piney-woods who gave us cups of white Scuppernong wine so dry, so fine, that I could not believe my palate. He gave us the recipe, and I took it down as he dictated:

"Now don't look to this not to fail you if you don't do like I tell you. And when I've done told you all I know, then you still got to have a sort o' feelin' about it, and if you ain't got that feelin', you just as good go buy your wine some'eres, for you cain't make it.

"Now you mash your Scuppernongs the very same day you pick 'em. Don't you go pickin' 'em of an evenin' when the sun's low and the day's coolin', and then you go traipsin' off some'eres, sayin', 'I'll start my wine come mornin'.' You pick 'em fust off in the mornin', with the dew on 'em, and you mash 'em with a bread roller.

Put 'em in a deep crock. A keg? Well, yes, I've used a keg, but a crock's better. Now you sprinkle sugar or honey over 'em. How much? Now I cain't no more tell you that than why a bird sings. Just sort of kiver 'em light-like, and honey's the best. I'd say flat-woods honey. Palmeeter honey is a mite too dark. Now you let 'em stand three to seven days. I cain't tell you which, nor what day in betweenst. They git a certain look.

"Now some folks, when that time comes, skim off the pummies. That ain't my way, and you kin do as you please. When that time comes, I put 'em in a flour sack and I squeezes hell outen 'em. Then I put the juice back in the crock and I add sugar slow, powerful slow, stirrin' all the time. How much sugar? Now if you like your wine sweet, you put the sugar to the juice until a egg'll float. I don't fancy it that sweet. I like wine to lay cool and not sickly on my tongue. I put in sugar to where a egg don't quite float, to where it sort o' bobbles around, and mebbe just raises itself oncet almost to the top.

"Now some folks leaves it lay in the crock. I don't. I put it right now in the bottles, without no tops on. I keep some back in the crock. I kiver the bottles with a cloth. The wine'll work, and it'll shrink down, and ever' mornin' come sun-up I'll add some from what I've helt back in the crock. I do this until it quits workin'. Then I cork it tight and lay it down on its side in a dark place. Now that ain't the way of a heap o' folks, but it's my way."

I have never tried his recipe, because I have never had enough white Scuppernongs at any one time to work with.

When the winter at the Creek has not been too cold, we have our own bananas. Martha fries the coarse horse-banana and calls it edible, but it has singularly little flavor. The tiny lady-finger bananas are almost as sweet as the commercial sort and in the rare years when a banana blossom appears, I nurse and watch it through the summer. My plants make a man-high cluster beside the wash-bench and the black women are grateful for the shade of the broad leaves. The blossom is exotic past description, so that only Georgia O'Keefe could do it justice with her brush and palette. It is a ruddy maroon in color, yellow-tipped, and a hundred fingerlike flowerets are the forerunners of the long upside-down bunch of fruit. It is necessary to cut the spray before the bananas are quite mature and to hang it in a dark place. The fruit ripens and yellows slowly in the store-room back of my kitchen.

It grieves me that we are too far north to raise the truly tropical plantain, blood-brother to the banana. In late summer I haunt the fruit stores, watching for the stalks of fruit that must be as black as a bat before it is ready to use. The plantain is peeled like a banana, sliced lengthwise very thinly, and fried in butter, sugar being sprinkled over the slices as they are turned in the skillet. It is suitably served with, say, fried chicken, or alone as a dessert.

All my life the pomegranate has held for me a magical connotation, for the story of Proserpine, daughter of Ceres, had enchanted me as a child. No explanation of the seasons has since seemed as plausible as the tale that told of the swallowing of the forbidden pomegranate seeds by the child of Mother Earth, condemned to spend, for every seed, a month in the underworld while the earth sorrowed. When a neighbor gave me a thin rooted twig of the bush, it was as though an ancient wand had been put in my hand. I nursed the small thing until it grew lean and feathery and as tall as the sloping roof by the kitchen door. In its fourth spring it blossomed. The flowers are carved jewels, strangely solid of calyx, made of polished carnelian that opens out, not into petals, but a bright fluted mouth. The fruit are ripe in September and vary in size from an orange to a small grapefruit. This year they are so heavy that the roof-high slender boughs are bent to the ground. Set in the fibrous, acrid pulp is a nest of rubies, blood-red and transparent. These are the seeds and it is their crisp casing that is edible. One's teeth crack into it and it seems to splinter and melt away on the tongue in a brief acid coolness. I scatter the bright shining things across a pale fruit salad. I should not care to run the risk of swallowing one, though probably the gods pay no attention to us modern mortals and I could do so with impunity.

It is the meats that I prepare at the Creek that are the most exotic of my dishes. I take no credit for some of them, for they are old in local culinary lore. Alligator steaks, for instance. It is no doubt absurd to balk at rattlesnake steaks and enthuse over alligator, for the saurians are not much removed from the reptiles. Drawing a line between dangerous rattlers and harmless alligators is as though a cannibal said he would eat a friend but would not eat an enemy. But surely we may all be allowed our prejudices, and I have none against steaks from the tail of an alligator. I can say dispassionately that properly cooked it is a great delicacy. The meat is pink and clean, like veal, and is similar in flavor. The first time I cooked it, I fried it too long, and it was tough and dry. I discovered that it is like veal cutlets or liver, in that it must be fried quickly, or simmered a long time. It is best, pounded, drenched with flour and fried rapidly in butter. Otherwise, it may be smother-fried, browned in the fat, hot water and lemon juice added, covered, and allowed to simmer until tender.

I am especially enthusiastic about our turtles, especially the soft-shell cooter. We have four turtles, the gopher, or land tortoise, which the Minorcans hunted for some unknown purpose, perhaps medicinal; the hard-shell cooter; the soft-shell; and the alligator cooter. At the Creek we have nothing to do with the gopher, a hole-digger, an underminer of land, a provider of refuge to the rattlesnake. As far as we know, he is not edible. We are partial to the hard-shell cooter and I can never be in too big a hurry on my way to town to stop the car and get out and capture one to take home to Martha, with the proviso that she save me some of the eggs, if it is a female, and a portion of the meat. I learned to love the soft-shell cooter from Ed Hopkins. Ed is gone from the earth he loved so well, but in his life he was a country gentleman with the tastes and instincts of an Indian. He announced that he would gather us a dinner directly from the land, and we set out from the Creek one Sunday morning in early summer.

"The Lord will provide," he said.

Rain threatened, and the turtles were crawling. They lay their eggs ahead of a rain, so that no trace will be left to catch the bright eyes of skunk or raccoon. We followed fresh trails and came on our cooters in the act of laying. We took two sizeable ones and part of the eggs, leaving the rest buried for seed. Our entree then was to be turtle eggs, the turtle itself our meat course. We cut a swamp cabbage, or palmetto, for one vegetable and wild mustard greens for another. We gathered poke leaves for a salad, to be dressed with the juice of wild oranges. We roamed across a gallberry flat and found blueberry bushes waist high, and picked our dessert into our hats.

"The Lord will provide," Ed repeated.

We made cornpone of our own meal, ground at the old watermill at Hawthorn. Dinner was cooked outdoors over the open fire. It was a feast. For drink we had a pale dry yellow wine made of wild elderberry blossoms.

The soft-shell cooter is cooked in the same manner as the hard-shell, but more of it is edible. The preparation is the most difficult part, as the separating of the meat from the shell requires strength, patience and several implements. The meat is then cut in small pieces, parboiled in salted water until tender, then dipped in an egg batter and fried in deep sizzling fat. I prefer it to fried chicken. The soft-shell cooter is a flat fellow, like a flounder, an enormous brown pancake. The outer rim of his shell is a soft gristle, and when prepared like the meat itself, cooks to the texture of gum drops, and is of a flavor to make you eat until you are weak and faint from surfeit.

The alligator cooter is the most highly prized of all inland turtle meats. He is very dangerous, a virulent fighter encased in a ridged, scaly shell from which he takes his name, with a fierce hooked beak at the end of his head and long neck that can make mincemeat of an enemy. While other turtles attempt to scramble away, the alligator cooter lunges at you with incredible swiftness, and when you have finally taken one, you have won a small battle. The meat is whiter than that of the other turtles, perhaps because of a difference in feeding habits, and is of a less gamey taste and an even greater sweetness.

Turtle eggs, like chitlings, divide friend from friend, but to my notion they are a major delicacy. Ed Hopkins proposed the riddle, "Why does a hard-shelled cooter lay a soft-shelled egg, and a soft-shelled cooter lay a hard-shelled egg?" I do not know the answer, but the fact is there. The eggs taste exactly the same, and also exactly like the larger eggs of the huge sea-turtles that come to lay in summer on the Florida beaches. I watched one of these monsters lay one night in front of my beach cottage. She had already dug her deep, incurving nest and had begun to lay when Norton and I discovered her. She heaved up and down rhythmically. After an hour or more she was done, and packed the sand hard with her back flippers. She turned her great body laboriously and began a slow trek back to the ocean. She seemed in no fear of us, and in the glow of our flashlight, looked at us sadly, as though for sympathy, tears rolling from her eyes. I am certain that they expressed no emotion, but only exhaustion. We took turns riding her down to the water, then for all her bulk, at least four feet each way, and weighing several hundred pounds, felt that she must be too tired to carry any burden. We lifted her hind legs and walked her wheelbarrow fashion, and she seemed grateful for the assistance and took on a little burst of speed. She lay for some minutes in the shallow water, recuperating; then we saw the great dark form lift in the surf and head for the open seas.

There were a hundred and thirty-five eggs in the nest, the size of golf balls. The custom here also is to leave half of them buried. In all three types of turtle eggs, the yolk is the delicacy, the white being of a consistency that never hardens, no matter how long the eggs are boiled in salted water. There is one set way of eating turtle eggs, Ed Hopkins said, and an important rite is connected with it. First you tear or break off the top of the egg, holding it in your left hand as you operate with the right. You add salt, pepper and a lump of butter. You pop the yolk of the egg inside your mouth, and as you pop it is required that you say solemnly, like a grace, "This is the most delicious morsel God ever gave to man."

It was Ed too who taught me to make a fish chowder that makes a poor thing of any New England chowder. Ed's was a virginal chowder, uncorrupted by such alien elements as peas, corn and tomatoes. I weaken now and then and serve large baked sea-bass or red snapper with a Spanish sauce, but for fish chowder of a pristine quality, I follow Ed's recipe. The fish of course may be bought, but is immensely better when you have caught it yourself. Any fish will do that is large enough to be boned and filleted. Ed and I always preferred the big-mouthed bass of local waters. In a Dutch oven by preference, or a deep iron skillet by second choice, place a layer of finely cut white bacon or breakfast bacon. On top of that lay gently a layer of boned fish. Place above that a layer of thinly sliced raw peeled Irish potatoes and a layer of thinly sliced raw white onion, and lastly, a layer of soda crackers. Dot with butter and salt and pepper. Repeat the layers in the same order until the cooking pot is filled. Add water halfway to the height of the vessel, cover, and simmer slowly until fish, onions and potatoes are tender. The liquid must cook entirely away, so that the bottom layer of bacon bits and fish is well browned. Add cream to cover, heat to boiling, and serve immediately. You are not quite certain of what the dish consists, for fish, onion and buttered cream are lost in a cosmic delicacy. You know only that something almost too good for common man is before you. And that reminds me of Ed's experience with lump sugar when he was a little boy. Among the grocery stores patronized by his family was one run by a Negro. Little Ed was prowling about among the barrels of crackers, the cheeses, the strings of smoked mullet, the hams, and came across a sack of lump sugar.

He asked, "What's this, Uncle Ben?"

The Negro adjusted his spectacles.

"That, son," he said, "is a kind of sugar, used by a few white folks and no niggers a-tall."

The expression has become a shibboleth among Ed's friends, and we say of something special, like the chowder, "That's used by a few white folks, and no niggers a-tall."

Under this classification comes one of our food items, so choice that it should have straws drawn for it by the gourmet elite of a very few white folks. Off in the scrub country there appears from nowhere a clear, bubbling, underground spring. The spring pours forth such a flood of water as to make a stream, or run, that flows into the St. John's River. In this spring and down this run are found enormous blue crabs. They are of the ocean variety, but I have never known any salt water crabs to equal them in size or flavor.

Robert and Cecil and Norton and I go crabbing of a dark night. We drift down the run in a small boat after night has fallen. The experts wear focussing flashlights on their foreheads, or have a passenger focus an ordinary flashlight over the side of the boat. The light shines through the dark water and picks out the great crabs, feeding on the bottom. The expert lowers cautiously a pair of crab-claws—open-springed iron jaws at the end of a twelve-foot pole—and strikes the crab dexterously. The iron jaws snap shut and the live crab is hauled aboard and dropped in the fish-box in the boat. As with all hunting, the surroundings are a great part of the delight. The moving flashlight picks out a moss-hung cypress there, a swamp maple here, and hoot-owls as big as eagles sit on low boughs, blinded by the light, and shift their feet and stare big-eyed at us. Fireflies flicker along the banks and mullet leap in the darkness. We prefer to crab-hunt on a night when the moon rises late. We work in darkness down to the mouth of the run, where the water hyacinths mass against the current, then paddle upstream with our catch in the moonlight.

We boil the crabs immediately, twenty minutes in salted water. We like best to eat them just-so, with homemade mayonnaise and Cuban bread and cold bitter ale. The meat comes from the shells in enormous flakes, snow-white and incredibly sweet and flavorsome. There are two schools of crab-eaters. Some like to eat as fast as they pick. I find this an infuriating process, for one works for an hour or more, getting a small mouthful at a time, and is never satisfied. I take the long view and patiently pick out the meat from my share of the crabs until I have built up a fine mound to be eaten in luxury. There is considerable risk in this procedure, for the still famished piecemeal pickers eye my luscious pile greedily and have been known to saunter past my place at table and one by one snatch a forkful from my plate in selfish jealousy, all because of their own improvidence.

When we have crab meat to spare, I make a crab Newburg so superlative that I myself taste it in wonder, thinking, "Can it be I who has brought this noble thing into the world?"

It is impossible to give proportions, for I never twice have the same amount of crab meat to work with, and here indeed I have no mother, but only instinct, to guide me. In an iron skillet over a low fire I place a certain amount of Dora's butter. As it melts, I stir in the flaked crab meat, lightly, tenderly. The flakes must not become disintegrated; they must not brown. I add lemon juice, possibly a tablespoonful for each cup of crab meat. I add salt and pepper frugally, paprika more generously, and a dash of powdered clove so temporal that the flavor in the finished Newburg is only as though the mixture had been whisked through a spice grove. I add Dora's golden cream. I do not know the exact quantity. It must be generous, but the delicate crab meat must never become deluged with any other element. The mixture bubbles for a few moments. I stir in dry sherry, the quantity again unestimable. Something must be left to genius. I stir in well beaten eggs, perhaps an egg, perhaps two, for every cup of flakes. The mixture must now no more than be turned over on itself and removed in a great sweep from the fire. I stir in a tablespoonful, or two, of the finest brandy, and turn the Newburg into a piping hot covered serving dish. I serve it on toast points and garnish superfluously with parsley, and a Chablis or white Rhine wine is recommended as an accompaniment. Angels sing softly in the distance.

We do not desecrate the dish by serving any other, neither salad nor dessert. We just eat crab Newburg. My friends rise from the table, wring my hand with deep feeling, and slip quietly and reverently away. I sit alone and weep for the misery of a world that does not have blue crabs and a Jersey cow.

I speak with some trepidation of my blackbird pie, for it might have brought down on me Federal dishonor, or roughly speaking, jail. I began the shooting of the blackbirds and the making of the pies in a spirit of innocent experimentalism. I sat in a blind on Orange Lake on my first duck hunt. Around and beyond me the good shots were bringing down their ducks. I had not touched a feather. Nearby, hundreds of red-winged blackbirds were stirring in the tussocks. I thought of the four and twenty blackbirds baked in a pie and wondered if these grain and seed eating birds might not be the edible ones of the rhymed fable. I slipped No. 10 shells into my shotgun, and two shots brought down a dozen birds. I made the dozen very secretly into a pie. It was utterly delicious. For the next few years, when game was scarce, or I had not been to market for meats, I relied on blackbirds to make a tasty dish. I dressed the birds whole, but skinned, dipped them in flour and browned them in butter, along with tiny whole onions and tiny whole carrots. I covered them with hot water, seasoned them with salt, pepper, a bay leaf or two, sometimes a little of the Greek herb originon, and simmered until tender. I added small whole new potatoes, chopped parsley and sherry, placed them in a baking dish and covered them with a thick rich pastry crust, and finished the dish in the oven. The blackbirds were exquisite morsels of sweet and tender dark meat. Then I began to be ashamed of shooting the cheerful chirruping things that were so ornamental in the marshes. I decided I would do no more of it. And then I discovered that they were listed on my hunting license, by a name I had not recognized, among the birds protected by Federal game laws and forbidden to the hunter. I wondered what I should have done if the game warden had walked in on one of my blackbird pies. I decided that there would have been nothing to do but follow in Fred Tompkins' ways. He and his wife, the Old Hen, and I were dining at his house one day. She went to the door and returned nervously.

"Honey," she said to him, "there's a carful of law at the gate."

"Why, if it's the law," he said, "invite 'em in and give 'em a snort."

It was in the Big Scrub that I had roasted limpkin. The Ocklawaha River is one of the two or three remaining haunts of the strange brown crane who cries before a rain. I lived above the river with my friend Leonard and his mother Piety, and often slipped down the high bluff to the swamp along the river, to see what I might see. I walked there one summer day and beyond me saw a slow, long-legged bird with a mottled breast and long bill, feeding on crayfish. It could only be a limpkin, the old timers had spoken of its flavor, and Piety's kitchen would welcome it. I crept closer in the swamp, among the cypress knees, and shot with my .22 rifle. The bird dropped in the water, and only then I realized that it was out of reach. I believe in killing game only for one's needs and it distresses me to leave dead or wounded game unfound. I waded toward the floating limpkin, above my ankles, above my knees, at last waist-deep. A moccasin swam in spirals in front of me. I found myself at the edge of a deep slough. I reached forward with the rifle and drew the limpkin in to me. Leonard and his mother rejoiced, and we parboiled the bird and stuffed it and roasted it in the wood range, and I have never eaten a more delectable fowl. I shot another while I was there, and then I heard of their vanishing history, and would not shoot another.

Mistress Piety would have cooked anything I suggested. Leonard caught a raccoon in a trap, and though I had heard that " 'coon has a foolish kind of taste," I knew that it was eaten and set to work. I parboiled it, as I had done the limpkin, then roasted it, and it was so inedible that one by one the three of us were obliged to head for the open door. I found later that the raccoon has a musk-sack that must be removed before cooking.

Leonard said, "We hadn't never been hard put to it enough to try to put down one of them jessies, but we wouldn't leave you to try it alone."

I am of a divided mind about 'possums. Zelma's mother had one waiting for our supper when we came in one night from the census taking. It was roasted with sage stuffing, with sweet potatoes roasted around it, and it was more delicious than any roast pork. Then I baked one myself at the Creek, and it was completely inedible. I found, again too late, that 'possums are scavengers and must be penned and fed clean food for a week or two before they are fit to eat. It explained why Martha rejoiced whenever I captured a 'possum alive on the road at night, but silently buried it when my car had hit and killed it.

Bear meat is good according to the condition of the bear and the manner in which it is cooked. A male in the mating season is almost inedible, like a boar hog. If mast has been scarce and the late fall and winter have offered poor forage, bear meat is lean and inclined to stringiness in the early spring. But under proper conditions, a Florida bear may be fat and sweet at the end of winter. The Florida bear goes very late into hibernation, emerges early and the hibernation is never absolute. If acorn mast and palmetto berries have been plentiful and he has fed late, piling on layer after layer of fat; if the winter is warm and feed still abundant, he comes out often, lazily, feeds close to his den, sleeps again, rouses to stuff in a few mouthfuls of feed, and goes back to sleep. Under these already favorable conditions of established avoirdupois, sleep, continued feeding and no ranging, early spring may turn him out in plump condition.

The finest bear meat I have eaten was at a church meeting at Eureka. One of the village inhabitants had shot a bear along the Ocklawaha River a few days before and an enormous roast had been hung in the smokehouse just long enough to be tendered and aged in time for the church dinner. It had been cooked as a pot roast, browned in its own fat, simmered half a day in an iron pot on a wood range. It was served in cold slices and was the first dish on the long loaded plank tables to melt away. The flavor was that of the choicest prime beef, with an added rich gaminess. I gave thought to a second slice, but so many little Eurekans were holding up their plates for it that I retired.

I heard a mother say to a small overalled boy, "Now son, you savor this good. This here's bear meat, and what with things changin' outen the old ways, and the bears goin', you're like not to never get to taste it again."

Leonard's mother cooked it equally well. She also sometimes cut very thin slices from the rib steaks, dipped them in flour and fried them in deep hot bear fat. They were crisp and brown and tender. The steaks I ate came from a very large fat bear that Leonard's bride noticed lumbering down the scrub road. She called him casually to its despatching. The meat, some fried and put down in its own fat, some smoked lightly, lasted the family for many weeks. The golden liquid fat filled two lard tubs and provided a sweet nutty cooking fat for whole summer. The bear was the one creature for which Bartram did not have a kind word. Although he developed "gratitude and mercy" toward the rattlesnake, and regretted the killing of a young wolf, he protested in 1773 that there were "still far too many bears in Florida." He would find them very nearly gone today.

My elderly friend Cal Long, a famous hunter, told me that wild-cat liver was a tasty dish, especially in lieu of anything better by the campfire.

But Leonard said, "I don't want anything to eat my old hound won't eat. I tried him on a piece of wild-cat liver once, and he spit it out and just looked at me."

But Cal had old-fashioned tastes in general, and had even given up hope of curing his rheumatism, since panther oil was no longer available. All his way of life in the last of his nearly eighty years irked him. This was especially because a Federal game refuge had been established in the scrub, taking in his clearing. He was no longer allowed—he was no longer ostensibly allowed—to kill deer on his own land. But I noticed that venison continued a staple meat on his table.

"The law says I cain't shoot a buck in my own potato patch!" he raged. "The law says I cain't kill me a wild turkey scratchin' up my cowpeas. The law this, the law that! Why," he snorted, "I'm too old a man to begin obeyin' the law!"

I have a glass jar of venison in my icebox, of Cal Long's killing. After it is gone, I think I shall eat no more of it, for I have lost stomach for the meat of animals that I once studied, to use for an emotional purpose in a book. I have never killed a deer, holding my shot several times in wonder at their beauty and fluid grace of movement. Long ago Leonard and I hunted deer together in the swamp below his clearing on the Ocklawaha. He put me on a stand on a narrow island, to which the deer came, sometimes to feed, sometimes to rest before crossing the river when pursued.

I stood shielded behind a clump of ash trees, where I might watch and cover the crossing. Leonard's Indian-soft steps faded and I strained my hearing for other steps. There was no sound for a long time but the wind in the cypresses and the rushing of river current on both sides of the island. In the distance I heard a light pounding, then running steps so rapid that the two creatures were breaking cover in front of me before I understood that they were deer. They hesitated on the bank for an instant that was only a break in a musical rhythm, a change of beat, then plunged smoothly into the swift arm of river between mainland and island. They passed so close to me that I might have tossed the pointed ash leaves on the beautiful tawny bodies. I do not know whether they saw or scented me. The great liquid brown eyes turned anxiously, for the fear of man, the great killer of all killer animals, is always on them in the hunting season. They emerged from the water, bounded up the bank of the island, lifted their white scuts and were gone like ghosts of deer into the cypresses. As they went, I remembered Piety's waiting cook-pot and the empty smokehouse. I lifted my gun and fired half-heartedly far behind the deer, afraid on the instant that by accident I might not have missed them. In a few minutes Leonard crashed through the bushes and jumped to the island.

"I missed," I said, and did not tell my story.

He bent down to examine the tracks.

"Just as good you did, I reckon," he said. "They was an old doe and a maiden doe."

He led the way back soberly.

"We'll cut us a swamp cabbage up the trail a ways," he said, "so's not to go home to Ma empty-handed."

Many a hardened hunter has told me that he is done with his deer killing. When a clean kill is made, he takes pleasure in the sport, but when the fallen deer is yet alive when he comes up to it, and he must cut its throat, he cannot face the big eyes turned on him with a stricken wonder. Such use as Leonard and Piety make of game is an ancient and honorable and necessary thing. The meat is needed and none of it is wasted. It is eaten gratefully. The sportsman often comes to feel that he might better buy a roast of beef at the butcher's. Venison is seldom as good as beef.

I am still torn on the matter of bird-shooting. I dread the day when conscience shall triumph over palate. There is no more delicious food than quail or dove, the one meat white, the other dark. I dress them whole, and they must be picked, never skinned. I stuff them with buttered crumbs and pecans, dip them in flour and brown them in butter. I place them then in a casserole, pour over them the browned butter to which a little hot water has been added, add an eighth of a cup of sherry for every bird, cover and bake slowly until meltingly tender. I prefer as accompaniments a Chablis or even a Sauterne for quail, and Burgundy for doves. I like to serve with them soft-cooked grits, small crisp biscuits, wild grape or wild plum jelly, whole baby beets warmed in orange juice and butter with grated orange peel, carrot souffle, a tomato aspic salad, and tangerine sherbet for a dessert. I make the tangerine sherbet by any good orange sherbet recipe, substituting tangerine juice for orange juice, and using more lemon juice and less sugar syrup. I cannot recommend the dessert, delicate as it is, unless one has one's own tangerine trees. It takes two large water buckets of tangerines to make sherbet for eight.

In the matter of cooking ducks, I am in violent opposition to the pretendedly Epicurean school of raw bloody duck whisked through a duck press. The advice to "run your duck through a very hot oven" leaves me shuddering. I prefer my thoroughly done, moist, crumbling duck to any dripping, rubbery slices, fit only for the jaws of a dinosaur. When my flock of Mallards has an unusually successful season, so that I am fairly over-run with ducks, and the feed-bill equals that of four mules, I am sometimes obliged to decimate their numbers. My friends hint the year around that I have too many ducks. When I give in to them and announce a duck dinner, I find myself unable to eat, and must have a poached egg on the side. But on these sad occasions, I am certain of the age of the ducks, and I roast the young ones quickly. When I am uncertain, as one must be, with wild killed ducks, I take no chances, and steam them until tender, then proceed with the roasting, basting often with butter if the wild ducks have little or no fat. The rest of the menu is: claret; fried finger-strips of grits; sweet potato orange baskets; small whole white onions, braised; hot sherried grapefruit; tiny hot cornmeal muffins; a tossed salad of endive dressed with finely chopped chives, marjoram, basil, thyme and French dressing made with tarragon vinegar; for dessert, grape-juice ice cream.

To make the sweet potato orange baskets, I mash peeled boiled sweet potatoes, add beaten eggs, butter, cream, salt, a few spoonfuls of orange blossom honey and a little grated orange peel. I cut oranges in half, scoop out the contents, serrate the edges so that the half-shells look as though a large and accurate fox had bitten them; fill the shells with the potato mixture, dot with butter, and place in a hot oven to brown. A handle of orange peel may be added, but this is only elegance and gets in the way. The hot sherried grapefruit that I serve with the duck makes also an excellent first course on a cold night, or a dessert when something light is needed. I prepare grapefruit halves as for breakfast serving, turning them upside down to drain off the excess juice. I sprinkle the fleshy part with brown sugar, powdered clove and dots of butter, and fill the centers with sherry. I brown them in the oven or under the broiler and serve them piping hot. The grape-juice ice cream is pleasantly acid after the rich duck. To a pint of grape juice I add the juice of one lemon, half a cup to a cup of sugar, and a pint or so of heavy cream, and freeze. This meal sounds simple and well-balanced, but somehow it is deadly. I have very nearly killed people with it. I keep hoping that it will teach them not to hint for my ducks.

The pilau is almost a sacred Florida dish, and for making a small amount of meat feed a large number, it has no equal. A Florida church supper is unheard of without it. Bartram found the dish here those many years ago, and called it "pillo," and once, "pilloe." We pronounce the word purr-loo. Almost any meat, but preferably chicken or fresh pork, is cut in pieces and simmered in a generous amount of water until tender. When it falls from the bones, as much rice is added as is needed for the number to be fed, and cooked to a moist flakiness. The flavor of meat and gravy permeates the last grain of rice. Fred Tompkins once cooked a coot liver and gizzard pilau at the Creek. It was very good, and the only time I have been able to down coot in any form. The rest of the Creek considers coots almost as edible as ducks. I have followed Martha's directions faithfully, soaking the coots overnight in vinegar-water and parboiling with soda before roasting, but they still taste rankly of the marsh mud on which they have fed.

We are all in complete agreement on squirrel meat. Fried, smother-fried with a rich gravy, or made into a pilau, we esteem it highly. There are, however, strong differences of opinion on the edibility of the head. I saw this disagreement flare up violently at the doings at Anthony.

Word came that Fatty Blake, a snuff and tobacco salesman, and Anthony's richest citizen—wealth at Anthony, as elsewhere, is relative—was having a big doings on a certain Thursday night. The world was invited. Fatty himself stopped at the village store to verify the invitation. He was inviting two counties to his doings, and all was free. There would be squirrel pilau and Brunswick stew. Fatty couldn't likker folks, as he would like to do, but if you brought your own 'shine and were quiet about it, why, he'd meet you at the gate for a drink, and God bless you.

"I got boys in the woods from can't-see to can't-see," he said, "getting me squirrels for that pilau. I got a nigger coming to stir that pot of rice all day long. And my wife, God bless her, is walking the county, getting what she needs for Brunswick stew, the kind her mammy made ahead of her in Brunswick, Georgia."

Cars and wagons and lone horses and mules began coming in to Anthony long before dark. They brought women in homemade silks and in ginghams, men in mail-order store clothes with stiff collars and men in the blue pin-checks of the day's work. Children screamed and played all over the swept sand about Fatty's two-story house. The wives of Anthony bustled up and down a forty-foot pine-board table. Each had brought her contribution, of potato salad made by stirring cut onion and hard-boiled eggs into cold mashed potatoes, of soda biscuits and pepper relish, of pound cake and blueberry pie.

Back of the house a Negro stirred rice in a forty-gallon iron kettle with a paddle as big as an oar. It grew dark and the crowd was hungry.

At seven o'clock Mrs. Jim Butler played three solo hymns on the Blakes' parlor organ, moved out to the front porch for the occasion. Then she lifted her shrill soprano voice in the opening strains of "I know Salvation's free," and the crowd joined in with quavering pleasure. At seven-thirty the Methodist preacher rose to his feet beside the organ. He lauded Fatty Blake as a Christian citizen. He prayed. Here and there a devout old woman cried "Amen!" And then the parson asked that any one so minded contribute his mite to help Brother Blake defray the expense of this great free feast.

"Will Brother Buxton pass the hat?"

The hat was passed, and as the pennies and nickels clinked into it, Fatty Blake made his address of welcome.

"I've done brought all you folks together," he shouted, "in the name of brotherly love. I want to tell you, all at one great free table, to love one another.

"Don't just stick to your own church," he pleaded. "If you're a Baptist, go to the Methodist church when the Methodists have preaching Sunday. If you're a Methodist, go help the Baptists when their preacher comes to town.

"Now I want to tell you this meal is free and I had no idea of getting my money back, but as long as our good parson here has mentioned it, I'll say just do what your pocket and your feelings tell you to, and if you feel you want to do your share in this big community feed, why, God bless you.

"Now, folks, we've all enjoyed the entertainment, and I know you're going to enjoy the rations just as much. There's all you can eat and eat your fill. Don't hold back for nobody. Get your share of everything. I've had a nigger stirring the pilau since sun-up and it smells the best of any pilau I've ever smelt. It's got forty squirrels in it, folks, forty squirrels and a big fat hen. And my wife herself made that Brunswick stew, just like she learned it at her mother's knee in Brunswick, Georgia. Now go to it, folks, but don't rush!"

The crowd packed tight around the table, weaving and milling. The pilau and stew were passed around in paper dishes. The passing hat reached a lean, venerable farmer just as he had completed a tour of exploration through his pilau.

"No!" he shrilled, with the lustiness of an old man with a grievance.

"No, I ain't goin' to give him nothin'! This here was advertised as a free meal and 'tain't nothin' but a dogged Georgia prayer-meetin'. Get a man here on promises and then go to pickin' his pocket. This food ain't fitten to eat, dogged Georgia rations, Brunswick stew and all. And he's done cooked the squirrel heads in the pilau, and that suits a damned Georgia Cracker but it don't suit me.

"I was born and raised in Floridy, and I'm pertickler. I don't want no squirrel eyes lookin' at me out o' my rations!"

18. Spring at the Creek

*H*ere in Florida the seasons move in and out like nuns in soft clothing, making no rustle in their passing. It is common for me at least to fall on a certain kind of sunny day into a sort of amnesia. I think with a start, "What is the time of year? Where was I yesterday? And is this May or October?"

Because time frightens me, and I seek, like a lonely child, the maternal solace of timelessness, I plant only the evergreen shrubs and have no more than can be helped of the deciduous trees around me. All year the orange grove is luminous. The oleanders glisten. The palm trees shed the cold as blandly as the rain. Unless severe frost has struck them, the Turk's-cap and hibiscus bear red lanterns day in, day out, to light the timid before the dark face of time. Only the pecan trees scattered through the grove shed their leaves in November and stand stripped and shivering until April. Strangers ask in winter, "What are the dead trees in the orange grove?" I bear with the sight of them for the sake of the harvest. When in spring the first feathery leaves appear and the gaunt grayness is misted with green, I draw a secret breath of relief, as though a danger were now over.

Yesterday when I stood under the large pecan tree by the barn gate, the amnesia came over me. I had not expected a crop this year, for the trees bore heavily last season, and are almost completely biennial in their bearing. But as I reached absently to pull down a bough, I saw that slender green nuts were forming at the growth-ends of all the branches. The sight was unexpected, and I was suddenly lost in a wave of timelessness. I thought for an instant that I was back in the May of a year ago. Then it seemed to me that I had skipped this present season and had been precipitated into the coming year. The pecan tree was bearing again, and where was I in time and space? And the old comfort came, in the recurrence, and on the heels of the comfort, despair, that there was no end to seasons, but an end to me.

A knowledge brushed me as briefly as though a bird had flown past me from the tree. Lives are only one with living. How dare we, in our egos, claim catastrophe in the rise and fall of the individual entity? There is only Life, and we are beads strung on its strong and endless thread.

The bird was gone. I remembered that the rationalists call this consciousness mysticism. I did not think that by any name it was shameful. The season was May of this year. I withdrew into the turtle shell of my mortality. It was good to know there would be pecans, unexpectedly, this November. I turned away and left them to their maturing.

There is a beauty of the strange and a beauty of the familiar. The traveller to far places is enchanted because what he sees is new. If he found himself obliged to live forever in some quaint hamlet, the picturesqueness that intrigued him with its novelty would be likely to become his prison. The test of beauty is whether it can survive close knowledge. This is as true of persons as of places. The dancer, dazzling behind the footlights, may in ordinary living be so dull, so unkind, so fractious, that her smooth limbs and lovely face are lost in the immediacy of her spiritual unloveliness. On the other hand, a very plain woman or an ugly man may receive a deep devotion, because the known qualities of mind and spirit are beautiful, and this familiar beauty lies like a soft veil over any physical inadequacies.

I wonder what spring would mean to one who was encountering it, if such a thing were conceivable, for the first time. My notion is that it would mean nothing. Spring is beautiful because it is familiar. Its implications are stirring because we understand them. We know the cold that precedes it and the hot sun that will follow it. It is generally believed that the northern spring is more portentous than the tropical or sub-tropical spring, because the contrast between cold and warmth, between frozen sterility and hot fertility is more apparent. This is not true when, as in the sub-tropics at Cross Creek, spring is so well known that its coming is as important as a smile across a beloved face. A very clever poet, Wallace Stevens, ended a poem with saying, "But there is no spring in Florida." He did not know Florida. He came as a stranger, a traveller, to Florida, and the lushness of spring was to him only lushness. He could not differentiate among the shades of green, which at Cross Creek tell us when to plant and when to fertilize and when to cultivate. He did not know when the red-bird begins to sing again, and when the cypress bursts from gray bareness into a dress of soft needles and the swamp maple puts out young passionate red leaves.

At the Creek, spring is as definite and as exciting as in Greenland. We have not had snow behind us, but we have had an ungrowing period, as have they, and life now stirs and sap rises and the creatures mate and the snakes come out of their winter's lethargy. Because it is familiar and beloved, we watch every gradation. It is

dear to us because knowledge of it is necessary to recognize its varia-
tions. There is no sign of spring, but several spontaneous burstings.
At the moment of the cypresses' needled sprouting and the swamp
maples' glory of color, there bloom the yellow jessamine and the red-
bud. If anything comes first, it is the jessamine. Along the fence rows,
through the hammocks, slim dry vines are suddenly a mass of golden
bloom, so fragrant that the initiate all but swoons. Like many tropical flowers, the jessamine is most potent in the night time. I have
been on Orange Lake by night and had the scent of the jessamine
come so strongly from the far shores that it seemed an immense perfume flask had been spilled from the stars. There is a cousin of the
yellow jessamine, the night-blooming jasmine, whose odor is so
sweet and strong that invalids cannot endure it in their rooms or outside their windows.

Martha says, "It really tears loose after nightfall."

The jessamine is at its height, spilling waterfalls of gold from
high in the tallest trees, when the major miracle occurs. One evening
there is the jessamine in the sunset, alone in a world of arrested color.
The next morning there is a tinge of green across the gray Spanish
moss, and infinitesimal rosy blossoms may be discovered along its
strands, the distant hammock is emerald, and on the soft air floats a
fragrance for which we have hungered the whole year through. The
first orange blossoms have opened. For a month or six weeks we shall
be giddy by day with them and at night drown in a sea of perfume.
When the orange blossoms are almost done, the grapefruit blooms
and then the tangerines, and these have a sharp spiciness of odor, so
that after having lived with them for a few years, one knows blind-
folded which citrus fruit is flowering and what month it is. For the
seasons at the Creek are marked, not by the calendar, but by fruits
and flowers and birds.

When the oranges bloom, it is time for the spring fertilizing and the first spring cultivating. After a warm winter, the jessamine blooms in late January and the orange trees in early February. After an average winter, the jessamine blooms in early February and the oranges in the middle of the month. After a long winter with protracted cold, as this year, the jessamine waits wisely until the frost is over. While the orange trees are more injudicious and come into bud at what should be the proper time, regardless of temperature, they too understand that they have thrust their small white noses into an unfriendly world, and hold up the full blossoming until the atmosphere is propitious.

The wild iris is as stubborn as the orange bloom is impatient. Norton and I make useless trips every spring to the River Styx, to find the buds ready but tight-shut week after week. The iris knows what it wants in the way of April weather and waits for precisely the acceptable conjunction of rain and warmth. Then acre on acre bursts open on the same sunny morning, and the swamp bordering the Styx is blue from the edge of the narrow sand road to the farthest rim of cypresses. We must wade knee-deep to gather the flowers, going cautiously through the leaf-brown water for fear of roots or sharp cypress knees or moccasins. The egrets are nesting when the iris blooms and fly up from their feeding like bursts of white spray as our splashing disturbs them. They light close by their nests in the cypresses and wait, preening the lacy tail feathers of the mating and nesting season, for us to finish our swamp business. The wild iris does not have the fragrance of the fleur-de-lis of cultivated gardens, but its color is a more exquisite and a lighter blue. And where the gardener's iris may be only politely looked at, the wild iris grows in such a wanton profusion that our armfuls, taken home to the house, leave no break in the blue sheet beside the Styx.

We say at the Creek, "When the first whippoorwill calls it's time for the corn to be in the ground."

The first whippoorwill may call in late February or in March. I cannot guarantee his accuracy as a weather prophet, but I have never known frost to come after that first plaintive, heart-tearing cry. If the corn is not already planted, we hurry to get it in. Our Florida whippoorwill is not the same bird that stirred me as a child on my father's Maryland farm. The bird here is the chuck-will's-widow and the call is not so melodious as that of the more northern bird. It is as though the northern call were harshened and syncopated, like the modern swing versions of Mozart and Bach. Martha told me that the bird is crying, "Chip hell out of the red oak! Chip hell out of the red oak!" The phonetics are accurate. Martha spoiled the romance of the whippoorwill's call for me, for now I cannot hear it without repeating her belligerent and unbeautiful words.

But there was a spring night, before I knew that the whippoorwill was actually the chuck-will's widow and that it was insisting, "Chip hell out of the red oak!" when the spell of the cry brought me from my bed. There was a full moon and the scent of orange blossoms was heavy across the night, and a whippoorwill was calling, only a little distance away. I went out into the grove and my dog went with me, and we played and danced in the moonlight under the flowering orange trees. Old Jib came wobbling to join us and the dog and cat and I romped together until nearly dawn. The whippoorwill came closer and closer until he was sitting within sight of us on the fence, as though he were pleased to have dancers for his music. It is as well that no late frog-hunter passed by while we were at our frolic, or it would surely have been told as proved fact that those who live at the Creek are fey.

The robins, who bring spring to the north, have for us here no connection with the season. They come to my grove in vast flocks to feed and wait for the mysterious signal that sends them on. But they are tourists, interested in passing matters, and they stop with us only long enough to rest and feed and go on again. Before they reach their nesting places in the north they have made half a dozen such stops of varying duration and it is impossible to estimate their arrival in New York, for instance, by the date of their dallying at the Creek. I do not know what feed it is they find, but they go to the same grounds used by the turtle doves and I suppose the same seedpods appeal to both. The robins darken the pecan trees across the road, they cover my yard, not singing the song that I used to know, but emitting meaningless chirps. Their breasts at this time are not ruddy. They are restless, and feed with their usual bobbing run, then for no reason all fly at once. On windy mornings I hear, not a casual flying, but a storm of wings. They are here in such numbers that I am sometimes tempted to try them out in a robin pot-pie, but I recall my own days in the north and cannot annihilate any symbol of spring for folk in a more unfortunate clime.

Our bird-hunting season ends toward the end of February, when mating begins, and the quail and doves have their mystic calendar marked with the date as plainly as our own. During the hunting season they are wise and wary. Within a few days after the guns have stopped firing, the quail feed in plain sight along the roadways and the doves, the wildest of all birds, I think, except the wild turkey, fly into my yard. This spring one dove came ahead of time and flew inside my gate before the season ended. The laws of hospitality and refuge forbade my disturbing him and he took the overflow from the red-birds' feed basket unmolested. I am hypocrite enough in any case not to shoot at birds who live on my place. A covey of quail lives the year around in my grove and I think of them as co-inhabitants. The human ego is a fearful thing and we consider those things, friends, relatives, stock, that touch our lives, to be somehow different because they are close to us.

The mating season is not at the Creek quite as markedly a thing of spring as farther north. My wild Mallard ducks breed all winter and calves and pigs may be born at any time. Yet there is a resurgence of the life sap, no matter how subtle, for the creatures and birds as well as for the trees. The red-birds sing all through the winter and I have awakened to delirious duets on a morning when icicles hung from the water-tower and the oranges were frozen solid. The red-birds' song has to do with their mating, for it is the males who proclaim in season the delights of love and the glory of the world. Yet the first of the year's two hatchings of young arrives in our spring.

In late February or early March I hear pitiful cries about the feed basket in the crepe myrtle, and the two pairs of red-birds who have shared my life at the Creek as long as I have been here, are introducing their young to cracked corn and grains of wheat. The young are almost as large as the parents at this time, and while they can fly quite well and are entirely capable of picking up the feed for themselves, they flutter with a false helplessness, sit in the very middle of the feed basket, and allow the devoted father and mother to pick up the grains and drop them in their perfectly able maws. I once saw a mocking-bird mother go into a rage at her offspring's insistence on a prolonged adolescence. Food was at the young bird's feet, but he cried lamentably and ruffled his feathers and opened his mouth for the manna to be dropped into it. The mother patiently picked up the feed and dropped it and picked it up again, to show her child the manner in which it was done. He opened his bill the wider. Suddenly she flew at him in a fury, pecked him several times, and flew away. He must shift for himself. He looked over his shoulder disconsolately, then went to work and fed himself with complete efficiency.

My Mallards theoretically should show signs of restlessness in the spring, even though they are not penned. All their kind are flying north. Night and day the V-formations pass over the grove. But my ducks are as enthusiastic about our mutual life as I, have no intention of changing its security for the unknown, and the wild instinct seems in them completely stultified. It is altogether too easy to attribute human characteristics to animals. It is perhaps logical, if unfortunate, for man to create God in his own image, but it is taking advantage of the creatures' dumbness to assign our complicated emotions to their simpler natures. Nature writers who turn foxes into little men and women are somehow embarrassing. Yet in the face of my own prejudice, I am obliged to insist that my domesticated wild Mallards possess to the highest degree of any creatures I know, animal or human, an acutely conscious *joie de vivre*. A dog knows when he is having a good time. But his fun derives from a definite objective, a walk, a ride, a hunt, a swim. The Mallards awaken with the first tinge of light, shake their wings, and give voice to their delight as plainly as though they shouted, "Hah! Another day of good living!"

It was when I began to understand their capacity for enjoyment that I turned my first flock loose from their pen. A gift of a dozen eggs from a Carolina marsh had been set under a hen. Eight of the eggs hatched into golden ducklings, self-sufficient from the first breath. I allowed them to wean themselves from the puzzled foster mother as soon as they were ready, and put them to live in a generous enclosure, screened overhead as well as on all sides.

I was told by every one, "Once they are out of the pen, you have seen the last of your ducks."

We watched the gate carefully, going in and out to feed them, to change the water in the syrup kettle I had sunk in the ground for a swimming pool. We pictured them slipping past us to escape at the first opportunity. They grew, thrived and lived, a year and a half, as wild as birds could possibly be. When any of us entered the pen, they shrieked and huddled at the farthest corner. They could not be starved into coming to any one to take feed. They seemed to live in suspended animation—waiting. Yet I began to be aware of the delight with which they greeted the day, the conversations they had among themselves, the sudden bursts of playfulness in which they flew back and forth in the pen. One day I could not endure it any longer. I opened the pen door and went away.

"Your freedom," I said over my shoulder, "with my compliments and apologies."

I expected them to rise in a great sweep and take off for the adjacent marsh. I hoped only that they would migrate out of reach of the hunters' guns before the season should open. An hour later I saw them investigating the barn. When the chickens were fed that evening, the Mallards joined them. At sundown they walked in single file into their pen. I heard them talking amiably all night. In the morning they filed out again. They took possession of the grove as of a rightful heritage. In the four years since then they have never once gone out of sight of it. For sport, they fly back and forth through the grove and sometimes over the house. Their wings are unclipped, they are strong and able, Orange Lake is within a few seconds' flight. Yet the grove holds all they ask. Freedom, it would seem, can lie in the smallest area. It is necessary only to know that there are no bars. I rejoice in the day when I set them free, and watch them for hours at a time, almost, sometimes, in envy of their patent excitement in living.

Food is a constant adventure. They clamor for the morning scattering of the scratch feed. Then, stuffed, they waddle about in search of choice items for dessert; grasshoppers, small insects and worms, and something they find, or perpetually hope to find, under grass roots. When one comes on that rare delicacy, a small green tree frog, there is a commotion and a chase of the flock after the finder that seems more of a game than a threat, for finders seem to be keepers, and I have never seen the prey snatched away. The lucky duck stands and swallows his frog and the others stand in a circle and admire his cleverness. They cock their heads, their bright beady eyes shine in the sun. Then the whole flock suddenly flies across the yard in a burst of enthusiasm. Their landings always alarm me. I am forever expecting them to break a leg. Accustomed in a wild state to landing on water, they soar down on the hard sand with apparently no attempt to soften the bump. Their expressions show a mild surprise each time, as though the pitch forward, on landing, were something on which they had not calculated.

In the late morning and again in mid-afternoon they take a siesta. They cluster in the shade of an orange tree in the front yard, or under the tangerine tree in the side yard where the old cat lies already in the coolest spot, tuck their heads under their wings and drowse. Then the game is on again, and there is a swim in the syrup kettle, with a terrific splashing and a standing on heads after the under-water growth that should be at the bottom of the kettle if the place were a proper pond. At evening, they shriek again for scratch feed. They eat quickly but sparingly, merely making sure that the game chickens have not been given a superior feed to theirs, then waddle single file into their pen where they eat again at their leisure. They prefer to be shut up at night. It is amazing to find so strong a home instinct in wild and migratory birds. Most of them were born in the pen, and when the sun goes down, the pen is where they choose to be. If there is a delay in the farce of driving them in and closing the door, they stand inside near the entrance and demand the service. Until dark they make a pleased and pleasant clacking. Now and then in the night they burst into an uproar and I know that some small animal trespasser is going by. Sometimes the commotion, I know, comes when one of the drakes is having a nocturnal amorous moment.

It is the ducks, the females, who have the loud voices. It is an as-

tonishing contrast to their sprightly gentleness. The drakes, shame-
less and brutal and lusty fellows, are doomed to the faintest of sibilant whispers. There must have been a prehistoric mix-up in
assigning voices to ducks and drakes. In the breeding season, from
late fall through winter and spring, until June or July, the drakes in-
furiate me so that I swear I shall eat them all. Their love life is mer-
ciless, public and continuous. The chickens mate so casually, a mere
duty to be done, that the onlooker thinks nothing of it. The drakes
are Rabelaisian, they are Turks, they are Huns. The ducks go for
months with pecked heads and lamed legs. They must feed surrepti-
tiously by night, for it does not seem as though the drakes give them
time by day. In odd moments the drakes fight one another. There is
always one outcast drake among them whom they have evidently
agreed shall not have a chance to produce his pariah's progeny. Such
a one comes as close as a drake can to unhappiness, lean for lack of
love, his neck picked clean of feathers. He lives slyly and shrewdly,
appealing, I believe, to the ducks' maternal instinct, for I sometimes
see things made easy for him when the head men are busy chasing a
butterfly.

Yet during the months when Mars and Venus are rampant, the
drakes are so handsome that it is a joy to see them. They are jet-black
and purple, with doeskin-colored wing patches, and iridescent as
opals in the sunlight. I let the fall go by, and the winter, furious at
them and doting on them. Then the new clutches are safely raised
and join the parent flock and one day in summer it is suddenly almost
impossible to tell the drakes from the hens. They have lost all their
fine color, and with it, their arrogance. They live decently and amiably, are thoroughly charming and ingratiating, and I am glad that I
spared them.

Raising the young each year is a difficult business. The first season was good. The original eight became forty, and ate more scratch

feed than at the time I could afford. Visualizing the same rate of increase each year, that winter I let my friends devour half of them. Then lean times came for ducklings, for I think word spread through the hammock that there were new delicacies in the orange grove. Chicken snakes, rats, skunks and 'possums made nightly calls. The older ducks still choose to lay their eggs and brood their nests inside the family pen, which is reasonably safe, but the young matrons, who will not, I suppose, listen to what their elders tell them, have a trick of stealing their nests under my ornamental shrubbery and along the fence-rows, where the first prowling varmint or snake cleans them out.

The birth of a fresh clutch is a grand moment. From under the dark patient wings of the mother pops a small fluffy yellow head with a pair of black shoe buttons set in it. If the event takes place in the pen, the other ducks announce it. The drakes are displeased and suspicious. The childless ducks make a great to-do, much upset that they themselves have nothing. We drive the adults, male and female, from the pen, and shut the door against them. They file around and around, raucous with interest. The first duckling slips out and darts around like a wind-blown shuttlecock. Another follows. Then, terrified, they rush back to their mother and climb on her back to wait for what is now to them the tedious business of the rest of the hatching. Sundown usually sees the last out of the shell, and duck and ducklings are moved to the safe small pen where they will live until the young get their tail feathers. At this time they develop as well the oil sack with which they protect themselves against a rain. Before, they cannot survive a thorough drenching. Casualties, too, were high in the big syrup kettle until I found what was wrong. They could swim, of course, from the moment they broke the shell. But they swam themselves literally to death, for if the kettle was not filled to the brim, they could not climb out again.

Now life is as safe as I can make it until they are ready to shift for themselves. The last batch has been given its freedom. I went to the small pen door and threw it open.

"Come out," I said, "and see the world."

Snow stood behind me.

"It ain't much of a world to come out to right now," he said, "but I reckon a duck's one thing that won't know the difference."

The blue-jays bring their young to the feed-basket and the bird-bath for a week or two in the spring. Ordinarily the jays are almost as sociable as the mocking-birds and like to live near people and houses. They drive off other birds and many bird-lovers have difficulty in keeping them away in order to have the song-birds about. My blue-jays live most of the year in the hammock. I believe they are kept away by one most belligerent male red-bird, who has set up an arbitrary order of feeding for all other birds who come to what he considers his own boarding house. He stands guard while his lady feeds and if there are young he feeds them tenderly. He drives off any other birds fiercely until he and his family are replete and bathed. The quarrelsome jays retreat before the small ruffled bunch of red feathers, and I am constantly amazed at the potency of a bluff.

He is more tolerant of the tiny West Indian ground doves who nest in the orange trees, perhaps because of their size. He allows them to bathe with him, but if one takes up the desirable center of the bath, he drives it to one side. He is recognizable among the other red-birds, being a trifle larger, quite the reddest of them all, and with a crest that seems higher, perhaps only because it is constantly erected, thanks to his choleric nature. He likes to sing loudly from the pecan tree by the kitchen, and continues his singing when I walk directly under the tree. I call up to him to thank him, and he pauses, cocks his head at me, flicks his tail, and breaks into a fresh tune. He is a devoted husband and last summer I saw him make patient efforts to induce his lady to share with him a sunflower. It grew by accident outside the kitchen window and came early into seed. I saw him come again and again, peck out one or two seeds, then fly away. He had gone to tell his mate of the feast he had found. At last he persuaded her to follow him. She sat in the tangerine tree a few feet away and was plainly bored and unconvinced. He perched on the sunflower, pecked and lifted his bill with a recognizable delight. He chirped to her, and when she turned indifferently to preening her feathers, he flew to her with a sunflower seed in his beak and fed it to her lovingly. She followed him then to the sunflower, took another seed, but still was not impressed. She flew away and I never saw him make another attempt to share the flower with her. He came every day and finished it alone.

The little West Indian ground doves are enchanting. They are of the softest gray, with ashes of roses breasts, rosy beaks and tiny pink feet that make a lacy pattern in the sand. They walk rapidly with a bobbing motion, and fly in small explosive bursts, like a milkweed pod popping open. They are amorous, as doves should be, and mate several times a year. I once saw a pair consummate their union on the tip of a crepe myrtle bough, most precariously, and other pairs have mated at the edge of the bird-bath. The male makes a pretence of ferocity, and after having crooned softly for hours to his mate, suddenly ruffles his feathers and pursues her with what would pass for viciousness if she were not so easily and happily caught. I think of them as giving their throbbing call the year around, but I am sure it is a concomitant of the mating, and since the breeding is so frequent, it is only now and then that I realize I have not been hearing the sweet sad cry from the roof-tree.

One spring in the mating season two pairs were fluttering into the palm tree by my gate. The long grooved stems of the large palm fronds leave the trunk at a downward sloping angle. I saw first one dove and then another bob to the top of a stem and slide down it, sailing off into the air at the tip of the frond like ski-jumpers. A few minutes later either the same pair or the other pair, I could not tell which, slid down the same palm stem and across the frond. This could easily have been a coincidence and an accident, yet it had every appearance of a blithe game, as though the doves were honeymooners at their palm tree Coney Island.

I have difficulty in distinguishing the cry of the ground dove from that of the mourning, or turtle dove. It is only when both varieties are calling that the difference is clear. The cry of the ground dove is softer and sweeter. That of the larger mourning dove is fuller and richer and infinitely more sad, a lament rather than a croon. The cry of the mourning dove comes also in their mating season in late February and early March, but to the Negroes it is the cry of death and they shudder when they hear it. Martha told me that the mourning dove is the Biblical dove, the turtle dove whose cry is heard in the land, and the dove liberated by Noah in search of signs of land. Noah, Martha says, promised the dove to pay him if he would bring a tangible portent. The dove believed him, flew far and wide, found land emerging from the flood waters, plucked an olive branch with great difficulty and flew back with it, exhausted, to Noah. The patriarch refused to pay him.

And since then, Martha says, the words the sad dove cries are, "No-ah, *pay* me! *Pay* me!"

I am familiar only with the lives of the birds who live close around me at the Creek and come to the grove. There has been so much to do, so many creatures to watch and study, that I do not know the ways of the Louisiana heron, the great white heron, the small white heron, or egret, the cranes and all the other birds who fly over and are gone to their secret haunts. I see them pass, I hear the calls of those that are articulate, such as the great bittern and the curlew, but I know from books only a few details of their living. When my own life shall not be so crowded, when Cross Creek itself quiets down, if that is possible, and things stop happening, I mean to learn more of these other neighbors. I know that the eagles nest in spring, for a vast ragged nest stood until a few years ago high in a cypress across the Creek, and I saw the pair at the nest, and then awkward young sitting on adjacent limbs, and have had the female sweep low over me as I stood, damning with harsh scoldings my busybody staring. The tree blew down in a great storm and the pair moved several miles away, between the Creek and the village. My friend Moe said that the ruined nest had stood across the Creek for forty years, to his knowledge. These are the bald-headed eagles, the true American eagle.

The egrets are coming back into their proper numbers, thanks to Federal protection and to women's vanity taking another turn than the wearing of their feathers. They nest and feed around little lily-filled ponds all along the Creek road. The great American heron is here in smaller numbers. This is a solitary bird and he lives usually alone except in the mating season. One year we had only one of the birds with us. He seemed to begin to feel his loneliness and took to wandering from across the Creek and coming to our gates. He made the rounds of each house and bent his beautiful white head on its long neck to pick up the crumbs we put out for him. He was so tame that one day he flew into my yard and walked nobly and unafraid under the orange trees. We all tried to approach him, but the only human he would allow to come quite close was Sissie's little black boy. The great white heron would take food from the black child's hand, and the two stood looking at each other in a strange primitive communion.

I wrote Doctor Gilbert Pearson of the Audubon Society that I had heard a pair of whooping cranes on the Lochloosa side of my grove. He wrote me that unfortunately that was impossible, as the whooping crane was almost extinct and certainly would not now be found in my section. The birds I had heard, whose harsh cries had sounded like a rusty pump, were great American bitterns. But later I did see a pair of whooping cranes in the Everglades, and my hunting companion the Major, a trustworthy ornithologist, is certain that he saw a pair fly over Orange Lake. The whooping crane was once shot for food and very nearly annihilated, but he too is coming back again. I wrote of their mysterious dance in a book, and while the account came from hearsay, it was reliable, the witnesses being two old men who had known the birds in their youth.

An exotic visitor came several years in June to my grove, and I was mad with excitement. I believed it to be an ivory-billed woodpecker, considered probably extinct, or very nearly so. The woodpecker was enormous. Swooping from trunk to trunk of the orange trees, he appeared the size of a half-grown turkey. He was brilliant in black and red and white, and gave a loud clapper-like cry. I discovered that he was almost certain to be, not the ivory-billed, but the large pileated woodpecker. There is one distinguishing mark between the two, and for two Junes I have had my Audubon bird book ready to open to the two portraits, to identify definitely my visitor, but he has never come again. At the Creek the pileated woodpecker is known as the Lord-God.

Of the small animals that frequent the Creek, the skunks, 'coons, 'possums and an occasional wild-cat, I also know too little. I shall know them better some day. But the habits of the domestic animals are there for all to see, and spring brings us an ever-fresh crop of such things as biddies and calves. I keep game chickens and the hens are half-wild and steal their nests. They come in from their hidden settings in the grove or fly down from the hayloft, proud and maternal, trailed by enormous hatchings of fluffy yellow and black balls.

I keep cows through no love of having them about, but for frank culinary purposes. A country kitchen has no excuse for existence without pans of yellow milk, inch deep in cream, pounds of fresh-churned butter and foaming buttermilk. But calves are charming and their birth is a part of the spring quickening of life. I remember the early April when Dora had her first baby. I had no man on the place, but my friend Ivey had come out from the village to give me a hand with some odd jobs. I had known Ivey as a great dancer and the best caller for square dances in three counties. He is tall and lean and kicks up his heels in the figures like a young colt. He makes excuses to do work for me, for he is enamored of the Creek and hopes some day to have his own farm here. Meantime, the next best thing is pruning in my grove, or setting out bougainvillea vines and hibiscus bushes. He begs cuttings from his mother to plant at my place. He came to me with big eyes from his work in a misty rain.

"Dora's just had her calf in the hammock," he said. "It's going to rain hard in a little bit. Don't you think we ought to get them in the barn?"

We went to the hammock among the blackberry vines in bloom and found the new-born calf beside the mother. Dora lowed to us in greeting. She licked her calf's small face, to call our attention to its charm. The birth-nest was nearby and she had tried to draw the wobbly calf for shelter from the rain under a patch of sparkleberry bushes. She seemed to understand when Ivey picked up the calf in his arms and she followed us lowing but without anxiety. Ivey's young face was luminous. He carried the calf tenderly and spoke reassuringly to the mother. At the barn he pitched down fresh hay and made a good thick bed for both of them. He fed and watered Dora and stroked the calf. His voice trembled.

"This is a wonderful experience," he whispered, "for all of us."

Unfortunately, the spring birthings also mean pigs. Hordes of them are born to torment me. In a no-fence county, stock is free to roam as it wills, and the landowner must fence against them if he does not wish to be over-run. My fences are good, but smart pigs are better, and I have always an assortment of Creek hogs making free of my pasture. It is particularly easy for them to come in when the pigs' owners slip in by night and cut my fences. The owners reason, I suppose, that I have acrorn and pine mast going to waste, but do not take into account that while their pigs would be welcome to feed on the mast, it is not desirable from my point of view that they also root up all the grass in my cows' pasture.

There are two sets of hogs in the pasture at the moment. One set belongs to Mr. Sam Turner, who lives fourteen miles away, and it does not seem likely that he would travel so far to cut my fence. The other set belongs to a neighbor. Neither seems likely to have appropriated my pasture. An alternative suggested itself to me lately. I wished to go down to the lake edge and determine for myself the fence cutting, reported by Little Will. Martha dissuaded me. The lake was too high, the approach to the fence was too boggy for me to attempt it. I should put on boots and breeches, then. Martha drew a lurid picture of the pitfalls. The suspicion came to me that perhaps Little Will had an interest in the invading stock; that the fences were not cut at all; that if they were cut, perhaps a third party with whom the Mickens family might not be on good terms, had done it, and the Mickenses knew that on my arraignment of my neighbor and Mr. Sam Turner, the guilty party would come to light, yet the Mickenses would not bear the onus of having accused him. It came to me, too, that we have been peaceful at the Creek for an unnaturally long time. The Mickenses love nothing better than for me to take the war-path, and, tired of the quiet, may have cooked up the whole story for the fun of seeing me start a fight.

Even when the neighbors' hogs are not inducted into my pasture, they disturb me. Last year Bert Ergles turned a drove of them loose at the Creek, on the strength of having rented one of Joe Mackay's fields for raising squash. Bert's hogs developed a passion for my front yard fence line. They dug nests under my oleanders, they rooted under my spider lilies, they made a shambles of my coral honeysuckle. I decided this time to settle the matter legally. I bought all the hogs at above the market price, sold them at a loss, and thought the matter ended. This year, Bert has hogs on the road again. I feel a certain sumpathy for them. They must feed wherever they are turned loose to feed, and if the pickings are poor, they must make the best of it. They breed, produce young, and are lucky to survive. This spring I looked out from the veranda and saw an unhappy sight. A lean sow was being serviced by a boar. The young of her previous litter seized the moment of her immobility to nurse. I spoke of it to Norton, mentioning that the sow had a thoughtful aspect.

"Of course she was thoughtful," he said. "She was thinking, 'This is just a vicious circle.'"

With all the trees and fence-posts at the Creek to rub against, the migrant hogs run squealing to use the rickety post that holds my rural mail-box. They take turns, crowding and pushing, and the post teeters precariously. I am the Miss Betsy Trotwood of Cross Creek, and as the mail-box rocks and sways, I cry, "Pigs! Pigs! Pigs!" My dog Pat leaps the cattle-gap to harry them, Little Will comes running with his hoe, and sometimes Martha comes with great dignity and waves her apron at them.

"Martha," I said, "why do they choose my mail-box post to rub against? Why must they root under my oleanders and lilies? Why are they so sure the rooting is better on the wrong side of the fence?"

"Sugar," she said, "that is a hog."

The rambling range cows on the road are intrusive, too, but

only on occasions, and these are invariably in the spring, when new grass excites them more intensely, I think, than their mating. Love comes and goes, and a casual bull will appear at the proper moment, but the first tender spring grass is a vital matter. The cows, thin from the winter's poor forage, eye my yard, bright green still with its winter rye, gather together their clumsy bodies and sail over my fence. My own cattle have given me quite as much trouble as those of the neighbors. I have had a varying succession of cows, calves and heifers and all have been troublesome. I did not help the situation when I accepted a male Jersey calf from a friend who owns a dairy. The calf was engaging when young, like all young things. His first solid food after he was weaned was a mouthful of allamanda bloom, so of course I named him Ferdinand. He came daily to the kitchen door for a bit of brown sugar. He was great friends with Old Jib the cat, and washed the cat's enraptured face with his rough tongue. Then overnight, it seemed, the calf had disappeared and Ferdinand was a very large bull of ferocious tendencies. He came of breeding age and I told Little Will that I wished the two cows, Dora and Lady, to be bred at intervals, so that I should have milk and cream and butter through the year, and not all at once in a useless superfluity. Will saw the wisdom of the arrangement. When Dora and Lady came in season simultaneously, and it was time for one to be bred and the other shut up, Little Will was beyond wisdom.

Will and Dora and Lady had all chosen Saturday afternoon for their respective flings. Little Will was gone and out of reach. Ferdinand and his amours were at my doorstep. The first I knew of it, Dora had coyly leaped the pasture fence and was eating asparagus fern from in front of the veranda. I went on with my work, meaning to drive her back a little later. I looked up from the typewriter to see Ferdinand charging into the yard. I was appalled by his size. I had not been close to him since he was a yearling. He had then taken grass as usual from my fingers, chewed it a moment, rolled his eye, pawed the earth, given a low bellow, and made for me.

"He don't like womens no more," Little Will said. "Jes' cowwomens."

I had left Ferdinand strictly alone, keeping up what I had hoped were superficially friendly relations by speaking to him cordially whenever I walked past his gate. He had not reciprocated. Now he was a mammoth thing, peering at me from the veranda steps a foot away. I recalled that a sportsman's magazine had taken a poll on the most dangerous animals in the country, and the Jersey bull was at the head of the list. I saw a cluster of Creek children coming down the road with their buckets for milk. I called to them that Ferdinand was loose in the yard and to go home. Martha came from the back of the house to tell me that she was afraid we need not look for Little Will back before morning. I warned her to return to the tenant house through the back of the grove. Ferdinand crashed through the blue plumbago along the front of the house and chased Dora around the bird-bath.

"Ferdinand so mannish," Martha said proudly.

He seemed only to be doing his duty by Dora. He was much more interested in the coral honeysuckle and the orange blossoms. He fed greedily. The honeysuckle vines would have no more bloom this spring. Suddenly he took care of Dora and marched away, bored both with domesticity and the honeysuckle, toward the barn. It occurred to me that he was remembering his young days of being fed there. It occurred to me too that if ever a bull was likely to be in a quiet mood, it would be at this moment. It was necessary that the cows be milked. Their calves were only two months old, and the cows were in full milk, their bags bursting. Lady saved me time by coming through the gap Ferdinand had made in the fence, and joining the family. The two calves, Chrissy and Cissy, galloped after her from the grove where they were allowed to run free. I was tempted to let the calves do the milking, but there were gallons more than they could drain. I opened the gate of the milking lot and Ferdinand filed in haughtily, his harem trailing behind him.

I dashed to the feed barrels in the barn and brought out two brimming bucketfuls. Ferdinand took one as his mannish right and I divided the other between Dora and Lady. I tried to drive Chrissy and Cissy into their own stall, but they were excited by the family gathering and would not be driven. I was working against time and I dragged their trough into the lot and filled it. They fed happily side by side, their small tails twitching. By the time I had them settled, Ferdinand had finished his bucket and was pawing a warning cloud of earth. I brought him another. Dora and Lady had now finished theirs.

Martha and Idella came cautiously outside the lot and I commissioned them to bring feed in relays and hand it over the fence to me. I milked literally in circles. We milled about together in the small lot, Ferdinand, Dora, Lady, the two calves, the feed and I. I milked first on one cow and then the other, according to the convenience and practicability of their positions, especially in relation to Ferdinand. A quart was as much as I could get at a time, when it was necessary to rush to the fence for a bucket of feed. I made no pretense of stripping them. I decided that if my getaway proved embarrassing, I should fling the milk bucket over the fence and follow it. I heard a groan behind me. Ferdinand, his great belly bulging, had dropped to his knees to rest. I was able to make a dignified exit through the gate. I looked back to see Dora and Lady licking Ferdinand's face, consoling him for the head-of-the-household efforts that had so exhausted him.

Martha made fierce African threats against the missing Will. If only, I said, we did not have to go through the same thing again in the morning. The next morning the red-birds sang, the game cock crew and the Mallards quacked cheerfully in the bright spring sunshine. There was no song in my heart and Martha muttered direly. We walked cautiously toward the lot. It was plain that Ferdinand was now past female handling.

Martha said, "Praise the Lord!"

I looked where she pointed.

Down the road came a figure. Little Will was coming home.

"Sugar," Martha said, "if that was our President comin' down the Creek road, he couldn't look no better."

*f*olk who have never known a tropical summer have never luxuriated in indolence, while the world around them burst out of its sheath in a mad exuberance of growth. It is at the Creek as though Nature said to us, "You have toiled for me, now rest quietly in the shade, and the sun and rain and I will do all that is needed." The bees have slowed from their orgy in the orange blossoms and the pale gold honey is ready for gathering. They work leisurely, dipping into the long heavy sprays of the palmetto bloom, stabbing carelessly the pink tarflowers, the gallberries, the andromeda, and what may be left over of flowers in the garden. They know there will be long months of sweetness and there is no longer any hurry. Once I cut a spray of late stock with a gold and black fellow so lazy in it that he allowed himself to be brought into the house with the bouquet. The swarm of wild bees in a dead sweet gum at the edge of the lakeside hammock flies slowly back and forth, for their pantry is already full. The crepe myrtle beside the bird-bath explodes into Roman candles of bloom and showers of rosy blossoms fall hour after hour into the water, so that the red-birds and doves and mockingbirds emerge covered with flowers from their bathing. The scarlet hibiscus and the yellow allamanda bloom side by side, gaudy but not dissonant, and butterflies of the same colors flutter in to drink from them. The yellow lotus blooms on Micanopy marsh and a small black boy will wade out bare-legged and gather an armful for a dime. I have lain on my veranda and asked no more of the summer day than to watch, one by one, the lotus petals falling.

The humming-birds come in, to stand on their heads in the red hibiscus cups, to sit like minute bright twigs on the tips of orange boughs, to poise, motionless except for the vibrating wings, outside the screen and stare at me. One day I selfishly picked all the hibiscus blossoms and put them in a bowl on the veranda table. A humming-bird tried to dart through the screen to come at them. His needle-bill caught in the wire and I loosened it gently. He flew away and perched on the fence and shook himself and tried to adjust his mind to invisible barriers. Martha calls them the June birds. The baby lizards are born from the eggs under the steps and emerge violently, one inch of body and one inch of tail, all youthful energy, not having learned with their parents that there is no hurry, and all things come to lizards who wait.

We have little advance news of summer. One day it is spring, with the air cool and the buds still opening. The next, it is summer, and the sun is very close to the earth, and the redbirds lift their wings and open their bills to cool themselves. They seem to discover newly the bird-bath and instead of taking a casual wetting, splash themselves all over for minutes at a time. They are angry when the water has not been changed and is too warm, and fly back and forth across the yard, scolding human thoughtlessness. When fresh cool water is put in the bath, the word goes out, and a dozen are there, scattering the water for yards around.

I leave the oranges unpicked on the trees in the yard around the house, to have them for ornaments through the summer. They are dead ripe and over-sweet and the woodpeckers come to them. They drill through the golden rinds and feed briefly on the nectar, then fly a few feet away to puncture a fresh orange. The bees and wasps cluster at the neat small holes and in a day or two these oranges drop to the ground. They fall with a heavy thud, bursting open, and the game rooster runs to the feast and calls his hens and the hens in turn cluck to their biddies. Nothing is left but the rind and within a week it has been absorbed into the soil. Nothing is wasted.

We do some work, for the ravens cannot be counted on to drop food in our mouths. But even the Negroes, who spend the summer hoeing and pruning, work as slowly and rhythmically as the bees, pulling the hoe toward them with an even, easy motion, cutting out the dead orange wood with long-spaced snips of the pruning shears. They wear Prussian blue work shirts and the shirts are the same color as the sky. In other seasons they may buy ready-made cigarettes, but in the summer they roll their own, for the rolling takes many minutes, and while they are doing it they lean against the orange trees and rest themselves with long breaths of the same cadence as the breathing of the fertile earth. They take a long siesta at noon, and it would be a cruel white man who would rise from his own to hurry them from where they lie in the shade, hats over their eyes, immobile as only the primitive can be.

The corn is rank, the cowpeas are knee-high, the peanuts are forming small nodules under the earth, and only a light working is needed for all of these, the mule moving in a dream down the rows, the Negro behind him guiding the plow deep in the same lethargy.

At night there is singing in the Mickens house, for the slow time is
the time for song, and Little Will's guitar is strummed softly, the
sound as soft as the summer air. The whippoorwills go mad, and in
the moonlight, the mocking-bird, who has been silent all day in the
sun, tears his throat apart to make a melody. One night he imitates
the red-bird, another he makes up a new tune all his own. Edward
Bok imported English nightingales for the bird sanctuary at Bok
Tower. The caretaker told me that the nightingales died, for lack of
the proper food or perhaps for homesickness, but meantime the
mocking-birds had learned their song. It was even lovelier, he said,
than that of the nightingales.

There is time in summer to lie idly on the veranda and observe
a thousand minute things that through the busier part of the year
have gone unnoticed. There is time to study such things as the motion of birds and I found that I could identify various birds at a great
height or distance by their flight alone. The soaring of the buzzard is
unmistakable and the wheeling of an eagle is almost identical. Yet
when a bald-headed eagle is so high in the sky that the distinguishing
mark of the white head is invisible, one who has watched both birds
can identify them each from the other. Something about the eagle's
circling is more purposeful than that of the buzzard. The great wings
lie in a straighter line on the air, without so much of uptilted curve.
He is no more graceful than the buzzard but the hallmark of the
fighting aristocrat is on the flight of one and that of the lazy scav-
enger on the other.

Too far down the fence row of coral honeysuckle to distinguish
whether I am seeing a bird or a dragon-fly, the humming-bird reveals
himself by his swinging arcs. It is as though he were suspended on an
invisible wire and swung only to its limits. The woodpeckers, too,
seem to be motivated by puppets' strings and drop jerkily a few feet
down a tree-trunk, only to be jerked back up again. When they fly,

they open and close their wings and propel themselves like a boy with one foot on a scooter.

The little ground doves fly as though uncertain of themselves, like apprentice birds learning the business. The take off with a "whirring of tiny rose-lined wings, achieving the safety of the crepe myrtle with a spasmodic effort. I perpetually expect them to miss the bough they have aimed for and topple indignantly to the ground, for they flutter nervously as they land. The large turtle doves on the contrary fly with such speed and directness that they seem like gray bullets shot from a long-range gun. They are hurled across space and when they light in the pecan trees it is as though the limbs had halted them abruptly and they are only caught and tangled there. A covey of quail explodes like a pan of popcorn popping and I can recognize the spasmic scattering far across the grove.

The great blue heron often flies at great heights and labels himself plainly with his slow flapping. The ibis, known at the Creek as the curlew, flies almost as slowly but his head is carried higher and the wing-beat is more frequent. It is a rare sight to see a flock of perhaps twenty circling in the sky. I suppose this community uncertainty is an indication of a mass migration to new feeding or roosting grounds. I have seen a flock wheel for hours in an endless circle over the grove, like a merry-go-round that cannot be halted.

The most engaging of bird flights to my notion is that of the red-birds. They seem to take life very lightly and in motion they give an effect of haphazard gayety. They seem not to fly of their own volition, but, scatterbrained, to be tossed from tree to tree like wind-blown leaves.

When summer comes, our garden flowers are largely done for, except the roses. These bloom themselves literally to death, almost the year around, and we usually replace the bushes every two years, having had more dozens of blooms from them than is quite reasonable. The wild flowers burst open to fill the breach, and if any house at the Creek has no bouquet, it is either because the householder is too comfortably idle to go to the roadside to gather it or has, merely, a preference for seeing it in its natural state. The phlox grows maudlin everywhere, red and pink and lavender and white and yellow, and the small darkies carry handfuls for their own pleasure as they stroll by my gate. One season I had an early spring bean crop in the sixteen-acre field. It was heavily fertilized. When the wild phlox appeared a few weeks later, it had drawn up the foreign nourishment avidly and I had acres of phlox as large and fine as any cultivated variety.

The stretch of flats between the Creek and the village is pink all summer, first with gallberry and blueberry bloom, then fetterbush and andromeda, and lastly the showy tarflower. The individual tarflowers are shell-pink, much the shape of the large marsh pink, and impregnated with a sticky substance that gives them their name. The young Negro girls wear them for earrings, pressing the mucilaginous calyxes against the dark lobes of their ears.

The Cherokee bean puts up brilliant scarlet spikes from poor soil. It is always a marvel to me that some of the handsomest wild flowers grow profusely in the barest places. The magnificent yellow-fringed orchis bloom in August in damp flat-woods where even the scrub range cattle can find no pasturage. The yellow false foxglove grows like a cultivated plant in wild parts of the open scrub. The wild allamanda is a cloth of gold in late July near the Creek fences, where only myrtle and scrub oak have been before. With the summer rains come the pink mallows in the ditches and meadow beauty is riotous in all low wet places. In late August the red wood lily flames across open pine woods and is as handsome as the new exotic rubrum lily imported from Africa. The wild hibiscus, or blazing star, lines the banks of streams and rivers.

Summer is established at the peak of its lushness when the bay tree blooms. The blossom is a miniature magnolia, with the fragrance of a rare perfume. A few sprays are immensely ornamental in the house. There is a mile of bay trees, forming what we call a bayhead, just before the Creek is reached from the village. I drive or walk slowly past them, for they are flung tangibly from out a dream.

May is the dividing line, when there is one, between spring and summer. In June, in a normal year, the rains begin. With the new moisture, the orange trees remember the spring again and put out a second burst of blossoms that we call June bloom. If cold has nipped the spring flowering, the June bloom is heavy, and perhaps our only crop of fruit will come from this. The fruit of June bloom is coarse-skinned and knotted, more like the wild oranges. It matures late and seldom loses all its green of color, and is never the best of citrus.

The rains last usually until mid-August. We wait for them anxiously, for in the last weeks the elements seem stationary. The sun seems to stand all day in one steady blazing. May is sometimes the hottest month of the year. One day in June a cloud passes over the sun in the late afternoon. The cloud spreads until all the sky is gray. The air is so still that even the restless Spanish moss hangs motionless. Although the sun is hidden the atmosphere is stifling. Then an impalpable breath stirs. The tallest palms in the east grove bend their heads, the moss in the hammock lifts as though a silent hand moved through a gray beard. There is a sibilant sound in the pecan trees, the grayness thickens, and rain marches visibly across palms and orange trees and comes in at the gate. Sometimes it is a gentle shower, sometimes a rushing flood. After it has passed, the air is as fresh and clean as April and the night will be cool for sleeping. The sun strikes through the wetness, there is likely to be a rainbow, and the palms are rosy in the evening light. The Mallards are vociferous, waddling through the puddles.

The atmosphere is ominous before the rain. I recall a day last summer, when Adrenna was low in her mind at her failure to find us a man, and clouds darker than those in the sky rolled across us. The day was sultry from its dawning. The sky was a sheet of zinc, against which the sun beat hot and furious hands. The seedling zinnias and marigolds drooped and finally lay bent against the earth, sapped and exhausted. At three o'clock in the afternoon the temperature on the veranda, with the dark slat blinds drawn, was ninety-eight. The redbirds dabbled indolently in the warm water of the bird-bath and did not sing. Pat the pointer dug a futile hole under the guava bushes and lay on his side, puzzled by his discomfort. Adrenna did not go to the tenant house, but lingered.

She said, "I aimed to wash me out a few pieces, but seems like my backbone is melted in the middle."

I said, "Try to rest. No one can work in heat like this."

She said, " 'T'ain't exactly the heat. It's something in the air, suckin'."

"Perhaps we'll have a rain and things will be better."

She burst out, "You know I been tryin' to make out by myself, so's not to leave you. God knows I don't want to leave you."

"I know."

"I been aimin' to tell you. They was tracks around my house yestiddy. A woman's tracks, with sharp heels."

"They were your own tracks. I haven't been to your house in weeks. No one has been there."

"There's what I'm feered of. But the tracks is there."

"I don't believe in things like that, Adrenna."

"No'm. I don't believe in such things, neither. But I wisht I could find me a good root man, to find out is something buried under my house."

"A cunjur bag."

"Yessum. I been aimin' to tell you. Last night it cooled off in the night and I got up and put a quilt over me. This morning something had drug the quilt off me and dropped it in a heap by the door."

"You threw it off yourself, in your sleep."

"Yessum. And for three nights now, something been runnin' through the house at night. And I heered a pistol shot. I turned up the lamp and when I turned it down again, the pistol shot in the other corner."

"That was the tin roof crackling when it cooled off. If a pistol had been shot, I'd have heard it."

"Maybe 'twasn't for your ears to hear."

"Adrenna, nothing like that can harm you."

"No'm, for I ain't et nothing from nobody's hand. But I wisht I could find me a good root man. I burned sulphur around the house night before last. But I must of left a gap."

In the west a white cloud rolled itself together and turned gray. Thunder boomed across the lake. The sound was muffled, as though the detonation came from under the water. Lightning flickered like a tongue, then went, tasting the south.

I said, "You'd better milk early. I think we will have rain."

"Yessum."

I heard her at the pasture gate, calling the cows. Glisson's bull was bellowing by the lake edge. The cows were stubborn and took a long time to come. The gray cloud spread as though it were a great maw, feeding on the sky. It swallowed the last morsel of blue in the north and the thunder crashed across the swamp. It was the longest day in the year, but by five o'clock the world was dark. I heard Adrenna go into the kitchen with the bucket of evening's milk. On the veranda I walked up and down. Pat whined at the door and I let him in. Lightning sizzled over the young grove across the road. I had expected friends that afternoon but they did not come, kept away perhaps by the ominous skies. City folk are afraid of the country in a storm. And I, too, was afraid. At first it annoyed me and I shrugged it off. The thunder beat closer its invisible drums. I went back to the kitchen to ask for an early supper. Adrenna sat crouched in a chair, her arms folded over her face.

She said, "I ain't afeered. But I wisht I knowed is the sperrits after me."

The spirits were after me, too. I returned to the veranda and paced up and down, up and down. Adrenna brought my tray and looked at me.

She said, "Oh, you sick. I kin tell by your face, you sick."

I was ashamed, for if I failed her, there was no other bulwark left.

I said. "I'm all right."

She cried out, "I know. You sick at heart. Don't I know. But please don't cry, else I be in the same fix."

I said, "The rain will be here any moment. You'd better get to your house before it comes."

I gave her Pat to take with her for company, for her need was greater than mine. Suddenly the palms rattled their fronds, the pecan trees bent before a nameless pressure, and the wind and rain roared in. The rain fell in a flood. I thought of the mother duck on her nest under the allamanda, where the eaves of the veranda made only a partial shelter. Her clutch of blue-white eggs was soft under the thick down of her breast, but her dark head must be bowed under the force of the torrent. The rain pounded on the shingled roof and poured in sluiceways at the house corners. The thunder and lightning were the attacking cavalry of the enemy. The rain fell for an hour. Then a cosmic broom swept it away as swiftly as it had come, and there was the sound only of spent water dripping from the eaves. The thunder and lightning were routed, and the clouds that held them rolled away

into the north, like dark driven horses. Unbearable, heavy hands released their pressure from my shoulders. I went out to the clean
washed road and walked a long way along it, and turned to walk back
home again in company with the sunset.

The sun itself was trivial. It sank humbly into a modest bed of
subdued gold. But in the north, the east, the south, cloud piled on
cloud, arrogant with color, luminous with lemon yellow, with saffron
and with rose. Three bands of opal blue lifted suddenly from the sun.
The west took over its own. The unseemly magnificence of north
and east and south faded. The sun at the horizon came into its full
glory and the west was copper, then blood-red, blazing into an orgy
of salmon and red and brass and a soft blush-yellow the color of ripe
guavas. Northeast and south faded instantly to gray, timid at having
usurped the flame of the sunset. Then suddenly the west dimmed, as
though a bonfire charred and died. There was only a bar of copper.
All the sky, to every point of the compass, became a soft blue and the
clouds were white powder, so that in the end it was tenderness that
triumphed. I went home to sound, cool sleep.

The next morning the world was fresh and bland. The sun
shone benignly, without virulence. Pat romped with Old Jib and the
red-birds trilled from the feed basket. The mother duck came quack-
ing from her nest for a little corn. A light breeze ruffled the allamanda.

I said to Adrenna, "What a lovely day!"

She said, "Sho be's fine. I got me a misery in my stomach, but I
feels a whole heap better in my mind. Don't you fret. Ain't no sperrits goin' to scare me off into leavin' you."

The extraordinary becomes in summer the accepted. Snow and
Little Will kill casually the rattlesnakes in the path of the mowing machine and only think to mention it if the snake is large and fine and
they inquire whether I shall want the skin. Foxes as big as small dogs

flicker along the fence by night. Raccoons stop their frog-hunting in the ditches to lift their masked faces to the car's headlights. An alligator lumbers across the road, crossing from one lake to the other. A bull 'gator sounds his vibrating roar from Orange Lake. The hoot owls quaver all night and a rabbit squeals like a puppy as a varmint pounces on him in the darkness.

The convict road gangs come through, clearing the weed-choked ditches and cutting and trimming the right of way. Up the road I hear the swishing of scythes and the swinging of lazy-boy weed cutters, then a burst of song. I hear the Negroes sing "I want to hear my mother—*swish-swish*—pray—*swish*—again," and they punctuate the song so rhythmically with the sweep of their cutters that a set of light percussion instruments seems to be playing with them along the highway. They work evenly and not too rapidly and the white guards dawdle among and behind them. The transport and water wagons follow the gang and in the last wagon sits an enormous bloodhound. He is surrounded by Negroes idle for the moment and one or two of them always have their arms lovingly across his great neck. He is very much *en rapport* with those whom he is supposed to track down if the occasion should arise. I am certain they have a complete understanding and that nothing would induce him to bring one of his good friends to bay.

One summer day Fred Tompkins and I drove into the scrub and our car sank hopelessly in hub-deep fine sand. We were not within fifteen miles of any habitation. We sat a while and estimated our chances of having a truck drive by. Behind us we heard in the distance a tumult that resolved itself into a convict road gang on its way to a new location. The cavalcade of men and mules and machines came to a stop while the overseer studied our position. He gave a sign and a swarm of gray-striped black men climbed down and surrounded us.

"Boys," the overseer said in a quiet conversational tone, "I want you to take hold of this car and lift Hell out of it."

It was a shocking thing somehow to sit in a large machine and feel it lifted from the ground and moved forward by man power, with men's backs and shoulders under it. It was too primitive to be decent. Yet it was a natural thing. It is fitting in a pioneer country that men who have offended society should be at the service of society, which needs so many things done; roads built, trees hewn, rivers bridged and travellers helped through impassable trails. Organized labor protests such a use of the offenders, as an encroachment on legitimate employment. But the alternative is for men to languish sullen in their cells; and surely, if we were not so stupid as economic organizers, there would be work enough for all.

That afternoon we passed the gang at work on the grade. Each man was driving a span of mules, standing on a small dirt cart or on a sled that levelled the sand as it moved. The black men drove like African emperors in chariots. Heads were high, long whips cracked, and an ebony giant with a blue bandana knotted about his head broke boastfully into thundering song. Three stations down the grade another man picked up the irregular melody. The seething mass of convicts chanted a spasmodic chorus. Harness clanked, golden dust clouded up behind the scuffling feet of the mules, black men and their beasts sweat in the heavy summer air. Songs of love, songs of death, songs of the spirit's hope and the spirit's despair, overlaid the labors of strong black men "working for the County." Here and there a white man hobbled along with chains about his ankles. These were the dangerous characters, men who had tried to kill their guards or a fellow convict. We shared our cigarettes, and the dangerous men were as courteous in their acceptance as the others. So slight a weight in the balance of character makes a man "good" or "bad."

That night we had supper at the convict camp; boiled beans, white bacon, soda biscuits, turnip greens, chicory, and syrup to pour over the biscuits for dessert. A convict named " 'Possum" waited on us. Small fires flickered here and there in the camp. Lanterns swung under the gray hanging moss. Before we had finished our supper, the camp was deep in sleep. The men had finished the day's work and the day's song. None of it seemed unnatural.

I remember the time I buried my gold, and so preposterous an accident as came about could only have happened in the summer. In the spring I knew that I should have the manuscript of a book completed by August. I wanted to take it myself to New York to consult over it with my editor. I had a hundred dollars with which to make the trip. I knew that if I did not put the hundred dollars in a place more difficult of access than a bank, August would find it gone. I converted it into five twenty-dollar gold pieces—this was before even the government began to bury gold—and I went furtively along the fence toward the lakeside hammock in search of a hiding place. Under a fence post seemed a proper spot. I lined up one of the posts with a cedar tree, a palm and a pecan tree and dug deep. I put the gold in a covered jelly glass and the glass in a covered coffee tin. I filled in the hole, patted down the earth, scattered grass over the top, and went away as contented as a dog who has done an especially good job with a choice bone.

The summer passed, the manuscript was finished, I was ready to go. I was to be driven in the grove truck to the village to catch my train. Somehow, things went wrong that morning, and I was busy until dangerously late. I decided to bathe and dress, then make a quick dash to dig up my buried treasure. The day was hot and steaming. The sun beat down mercilessly and the sand gnats swarmed and stung. I thrust my spade deep beside the fence post that lined up with a cedar tree, a palm and a pecan. I dug deeper. There was nothing there. I backed off and studied the terrain. Five posts lined up with a cedar tree, a palm and a pecan. I excavated all five in a frenzy. There was no coffee tin, there was no jelly glass, there was no gold. I stood dripping and frustrated in my best clothes. Then I began digging all over again, three times as deep as I had remembered doing the burying. Under a fence post that did not appear to line up with anything at all, my spade struck the disintegrated coffee tin and the jelly glass, full of water and tarnished gold pieces. I swung on the train at the last possible instant and paid for my ticket with money that to all appearances had been buried during the Civil War, held tightly in a grimy paw. I was wet, dirty and dishevelled, and neat passengers stared at me.

I longed to say haughtily, "My good people, you have no conception of the difficulties I have encountered in being here at all."

I remember, too, a summer when peace and war battled for possession of the Creek and for all of Florida. The conflict was grave for us. The enemy was the Mediterranean fruit fly. I remember that I walked to the sixteen-acre field in search of wild flowers and stopped at the edge to stare at the wild grape vines in the hammock around the clearing. The wild grape is a perfect host for the tropical devastator that had just invaded its last unconquered continent by way of Florida. If anything could ruin this peninsula appended to the United States, it seemed that it would be the Mediterranean fruit fly, the insect of the agricultural scientists' nightmares, a pest more destructive to fruits and vegetables than the boll-weevil, the Japanese beetle, the cotton moth and half a dozen others combined. Florida has survived the West Indian hurricanes that brush our coast. It has survived the madness of "the boom." It has maintained against all enemies its beauty, and at such places as the Creek, its privacy.

The orange industry has fought and defeated the white fly, the citrus canker and the periodic freezes. For every abandoned grove, frozen to the ground in 1895, there are a hundred new ones, incredibly neat and geometrical. My own grove has survived the freezes of early vintages, due to its sheltered location between Orange Lake and Lochloosa. It is supposed to be among the last to go when the mercury drops into the perilous twenties. My acres are part of the Arredonda grant, a grant from the crown of Spain to Don Fernandez de la Maza Arredonda and Son, and it is said that any land that is part of an original Spanish grant is good orange land. The Spaniards knew how to choose it, for soil and protection, out of the unfamiliar hammock.

Indians, Seminoles or mound builders, Spaniards in search of fabulous riches or still more fabulous youth, fugitives from justice from the Carolinas, Georgia Crackers seeping slowly over the border, Yankees with axes to grind, or seeking the sharp blade of beauty—all the intruders have seen Florida's calamities threaten them and come and go. Now a small gauzy fly imperilled the life of the state, and with it, the agriculture of all the southern states. Florida was a battleground, a Belgium, a Poland. Four and a half of federal millions and the keenest brains in modern entomology set in to do battle against the insidious visitor come without passport from the infested tropics, none knew how or when, save that the invasion was recent. Military quarantine was thrown around the infested areas. There were Zones 1, 2 and 3, with corresponding stringency of regulation. In Zone 1, vegetation was stripped down to the unfruiting plants. My place seemed safely in Zone 3, but we pulled up by the roots, and burned, the top-of-the-market crop of bell peppers and of eggplant, perfect fly hosts. I dared not juggle the safety of my citrus crop and that of Old Boss against the mere amenity of a summer's income.

Not a ripe orange, grapefruit or tangerine was left that summer on the trees. The clean-up crew went through half a dozen times.

When we went swimming a few miles away in Cow Pen Pond, we crossed from Zone 3 into Zone 2, and coming and going a military guard stopped us at the boundary line. The car was inspected for fruits and vegetables and thoroughly sprayed. Inspectors net-worked the state in search of fresh infestations. Doctor Newell of the University shut himself in his office in Orlando and studied charts, reports and laboratory findings. Research scientists worked over-time feverishly, cramming a year's experimentation into a week, hoping to say "Such and such will control the Mediterranean fruit fly." If the fly could be starved out during the summer, Florida would be safe again, and all the south-eastern agriculture. But deep in the jungles, out of reach over the fence lines, were hanging the wild grapes. They were turning rosy in the summer sun. Wild grapes, the perfect host. Wild grapes running riot in hundreds of miles of all but impassable jungle.

> "Good God, with a bounty
> Look down on Alachua County,
> For the soil is so po' and so awful rooty, too,
> I don't know what to God the po' folks gonna do."

My friend Fred will not eat a meal, at table, in the woods, or by the water, without pronouncing this grace. I suggested to Fred that he amend his prayer, for it seemed for a time that only God with a bounty could spare Alachua County from the fruit fly. If the fly reached us, we faced ruin, with the actual menace for the poorest, of starvation. In Zones 1 and 2, pitiful small crops were torn up and destroyed. Gray-bearded backwoodsmen with shotguns threatened Plant Board inspectors, but the necessary destruction of fields of beans and eggplant and peppers went on; peaches and citrus and guavas and figs continued to be stripped from the bushes. The Plant Board was ruthless. But so is the fly. Many small homes and farms in

Zones 1 and 2 were deserted. Negroes migrated north in search of work.

Doctor Berger of the Plant Board said, "Only a miracle can save us. If the fly is not yet in the wild fruit—if it has not reached the wild guavas, the grapes, the wild oranges, the paw-paws and persimmons out in the jungle hammock lands, there is a chance—a chance—that we can exterminate it. Otherwise—"

Only the bulletin of the Department of Agriculture, issued long before on the Mediterranean Fruit Fly in Hawaii, could picture coldly and dispassionately enough the devastation of that "otherwise." I read the page-long list of host fruits and vegetables whose ripe or ripening crop is totally destroyed within a short space by this light-winged devourer, this prodigious layer of larva-making eggs, and thought, "But there are no other fruits and vegetables left!" The inexorable bulletin summed it up:

"The fruit fly . . . is an insect pest of the first importance in horticultural development. Practically every fruit crop of value to man is subject to its attack. No effort . . . is too great to combat it."

The horticultural development of Hawaii almost entirely ended after 1910. Florida without agriculture! Without tomatoes, beans, peppers, eggplant, peas, squash; without its golden-headed glory of citrus! Georgia without its peaches! For Georgia across the border quarantined against us and shivered with fear.

The war raged all summer. The next season proved that it was won, for the fly was never seen again. The first bitter cold night came in, blessedly cold, for now the incubation would be halted. We shivered in the icy wind.

"Well," Zelma said, "a Mediterranean fruit fly'd be a fool to lay an egg tonight."

It seemed strange to us at the Creek that any one should think the Florida summer oppressive as to temperature. Our battles are the age-old ones against the vagaries of nature, but the season itself is usually clement. The wind blows all summer from the Atlantic on the east or the Gulf of Mexico on the west, cooling itself across either of the great bodies of water, and moves beneficently across the narrow Florida peninsula. The Florida summer climate in general is the most delightful I have known. Of the thirteen summers I have lived at the Creek, two have been unbearable, two on the uncomfortable side, and the other nine have been perfection. We look forward to summer, we swim, we fish, and we fox hunt.

Fox hunting with us is not the elegant northern or English matter of red-coated masters of fox hounds, expensive mounts and the serious intent on bringing in the brush. We fox hunt as we do everything else in the summer, leisurely and comfortably. We are interested in the chase and in the fox hounds, in the beauty of the night, and we hope always that the fox will get away so that we may run him another night. For we fox hunt in Florida of nights, and added to the delights of the hunt we have the tropical moonlight.

My friend Nettie Martin introduced me to fox hunting. She is a curly-headed person, so tiny that she must buy her boots and breeches in the children's department, and so ardent a lover of horses and hounds that although she owns neither, she has been an officer of the state fox hunters' association. She has broken countless bones, following the hounds on a behemoth of a stallion, but she is on a horse again as soon as the cast is off. When I reported seeing foxes near Big Hammock, she induced John Clardy to bring out his hounds.

The summer moonlight was so bright that we could distinguish the colors of the markings on the fox hounds. They arrived in a cage in the back of a truck, their long tails waving for delight in the nearness of the chase. Hounds are sad, soulful beasts, their lives darkened by the fact that there is not a fox chase every night. John let down the door of the cage and they trooped out decorously, snuffing the earth and waiting patiently for the "Hie away!" Nettie spoke to each by name; Big Belle, Flora, Sugar Boy, Black Sam, and on down the line. They acknowledged her greeting with a dignified eye and an extra swish of the tail. It is not considered etiquette to make pets of sporting dogs, but now and then one would brush her as though by accident and her hand rested for an instant on a lean, loose-hided neck. John examined the sand for fox tracks, found them and gave the dogs the signal.

They were away like bullets, voiceless as ghost dogs in the moonlight. They cut to the north, across scrub palmettos, and silence followed on the rustling and the soft padding of big feet. The hunters on horseback lit cigarettes, talked together, then took the same direction as the dogs, leisurely. I did not see how any one might hope to see or hear anything of the chase. My own broken neck was too recent for me to relish the idea of trotting through the dense growth, treacherous with gopher holes, where a false step sends horse and rider pitching. I stayed with the truck and with others cautious like myself. As time passed, and only the hoot owls sounded, it seemed to me that if the night were not so beautiful, fox hunting would be the most stupid of all sports. Then in the distance an old hound gave tongue. I had thought that talk of the hounds' "voices" and "music" was nonsense. Old Belle's cry was a deep-toned bell ringing across the palmettos. A younger dog with a high-pitched voice, known to the adepts as a "fine" voice, sounded above the lower pitch, and then the whole pack was in full cry. The harmony was like that of a Negro choir, the basses deep and rich, the intermediate tones a solid background, and the one high silver voice like that of a Negro soprano soaring above the others. The hoot owls hushed in wonder. The riders crashed back to the road.

Nettie called, "They're headed for the gallberry flats. Follow."

The truck started and we were plowing across land I should have considered impossible to cross in any car. But there were cattle trails and here and there a dim old woods road and we bounced along. Big Hammock lifted to the right and the sharp scent of orange leaves came to us on the night air. We heard the hounds and riders pass near us in the hammock. The hunt doubled back, and we were abandoned, and the cries faded.

The hunter at the wheel of the truck said casually, "They'll come back this way. We'll wait here."

It seemed to me then, and on subsequent hunts has still seemed, a complete miracle that a man should know when and where a fox would run, and the dogs after. But the great joy to the hunters lies in this intimate knowledge, and in hearing the hounds do the proper and clever things, and in following the voices of their favorites among the dogs. We waited a long time. Very late in the night we heard the hounds come closer. The moon was high overhead, the gallberry bloom was recognizably pink in the brightness, and the sweetness of bay blossoms came to us from the thicket. The hunter driver straightened from his lounging.

"Here he comes," he said.

I had heard no sound of small sharp-pointed feet on the sand, no rustling even among the harsh leaves of the gallberries. But a gray fox slipped past us, so close we might have touched his back. He was going slowly and his brush was dragging. It seemed to me that he was done for and I sickened at thought of the kill. But the dogs were tired, too. They came through on the trail a moment later, the riders followed, there was a great commotion at the edge of a bay-head, shouts and then silence. Hounds and riders came back to the truck.

"He treed," John said. "He's a good fox. We'll run him again."

The hounds threw themselves on the ground to rest. This is the time when a roaring camp-fire is built, allowed to die down to coals, and coffee made and steaks broiled. The hunters smoke and the bottle is passed and the camp food is nectar and ambrosia. There is long heated talk of the performance of the hounds and each man praises one and damns another, until all agree at last that whatever the merits and voices of the rest, there is no beating Old Belle. Toward dawn on this night a light fog settled down over the hammock, the gallberry flats, the bay-heads and the palmettos. The world was veiled with silver-gray and the moon struck through it wanly. I went home to sleep. Now and then I awakened to the music of the pack, for the true fox hunters were back at the chase, and Old Belle had struck a fresh trail.

The fog of the night was one of our phenomena. We have fog at two seasons, the heart of winter and the peak of summer. Both come from the sharp night-cooling of the sun-warmed earth. The humidity of Florida, surrounded on three sides by water, is precipitated into fog by the shock of the quick cooling. Spring and fall seldom produce fog, for the variance of temperature then is slight. The fog is a combination of beauty and nightmare. One's personal reaction depends on whether it has proved friendly or inimical. Summer fog will always be a nightmare to me. Even in maturity we are conditioned by our experiences, and one sharp enough leaves an imprint, no less indelible for being understood. I am not easily frightened, but I was truly afraid the night I fell asleep at the wheel of my car when a bear hunt was over, and I drove home afterward to Cross Creek in a summer fog.

Uncle Barney, whose tales I added to those of old Cal Long for much of my hunting material in *The Yearling*, invited me to join him and Hubert for a bear hunt. Hubert had brought us together in the first place, and the wonderful old man and I were fast friends. If his favorite name for me was "Old Ugly," he said it with a twinkle and an affectionate undertone. An invitation to a hunt with him was a command. The bear hunt was to be west of the St. John's River and I was to meet the two men at the river "just before day." I had a fifty-mile drive ahead of me from the Creek, and figuring "day" in summer at five o'clock, I set my alarm for three in the morning. I distrusted the alarm, which had sometimes failed me, and did not sleep all night, listening and waiting. I was up ahead of the alarm. I brewed a cup of coffee, gathered my duffle and set out. The drive was dark at first, then acquired luminosity as I became accustomed to the stars. I drove up to the bridge at Astor a few minutes ahead of Hubert's car. Uncle Barney came on foot across the bridge from his house on the river.

We met other hunters from the neighborhood, with dogs, near Juniper Creek at sunrise. The bear we were after had been making depredations on nearby stock. We tracked and trailed all morning through swamp and low hammock, and later I used the details for a bear hunt in *The Yearling*. The trail disappeared across Juniper Run and we gave it up. At least, the neighborhood hunters gave it up. Uncle Barney did not give up so easily. After our noon dinner, a baked ham from me, bread and may-haw jelly from Marsh Harper, coffee from Hubert, cold baked sweet potatoes from Uncle Barney, the Harpers took their dogs and went away.

Uncle Barney said, "That was a cold trail we were following on that bear. We'll find us a fresh one."

He found the fresh trail, and I lamented years of comparatively easy living, following him. He was seventy-six years old, and he whipped me down. He understood my unvoiced distress and gallantly assigned me to a futile stand while he and Hubert went on. There was a twinkle in his old blue eyes when he said, "Now, girl, don't let that bear trip over you while you're asleep." I did not sleep, but I stretched out my aching booted feet and hoped he would not return too soon. In late afternoon the two men returned. Uncle

Barney said, "I believe he'll head back this way this evening." We climbed into Hubert's car and drove back to Juniper Creek. Uncle Barney studied days-old tracks.

"Now, girl," he said, "you go off into that bay-head to the south and climb a tree and sit there and wait. You're likely to have that black rascal come out snorting and puffing and feeding right under your feet."

They left me and I pushed my way through dense undergrowth to the bay-head. There was a half-fallen pine tree there, inclining at an angle, and I climbed up it and took my stand some twenty feet above the terrain. The perch was comfortable. The sun was setting. Under me was a tight thicket. A light rain fell, like a gauze veil between me and the sun. A redbird and two bluebirds flew to the bay tree beside me and preened their feathers among the bay blossoms in the mist. I sat very still. The birds cocked bright eyes at me and went on with their toilets. The thin shower ended and a rainbow arched across the sky. The birds flew leisurely a little distance away. The bay blossoms were nacre, with diamond drops at their centers. I hoped the bear would not come, not in fear, for he would be too easy a shot. I decided that if he came I should shoot high over him and simply face Uncle Barney with the news that I had missed. The last red and orange faded from the sky, the rainbow and the birds were gone, and when it was dark, Uncle Barney and Hubert called me from the far road.

That night was moonlit and we drove all night through the scrub. Night hunting is illegal, properly so.

Uncle Barney said, "I wouldn't hunt deer at night. But if one was to attack me, I'd have to protect myself."

We saw no deer. We saw no bear. Hubert and Uncle Barney did not know that I was passionately willing the creatures, "Don't come!" We drove Uncle Barney home across the river, and Hubert and I got into our separate cars. It was three o'clock in the morning. I had been without sleep more than forty hours. All day I had fought my way behind Uncle Barney through swamp and hammock, bay-heads and oak thickets, through horse briers and bull briers. With no special consciousness of fatigue, I suddenly fell dead asleep behind the wheel of my car. I awoke with a jolt, headed at a high speed for the ditch. I swung the car sharply, bounded toward the opposite ditch, swung back again, and cleared the four-foot ditch to the left so clean that there was never any mark of the tires to show that I had crossed it. If I had not quail-hunted with Fred Tompkins in his Ford across black-jack and pine-woods, mowing down small trees, dodging gopher holes, I think it would not have occurred to me to try to steer my way through the forest in which I found myself. I dodged the larger trees and crashed across the smaller. I dared not put on the brakes. I ripped past large pines and flattened down saplings. I came to a stop across a ten-foot palmetto.

I climbed out to investigate the damage. The left side of my car was crushed. The motor was still running, but the left front fender was jammed in over the wheel so that I had no play and could not move the car. I turned on my parking lights so that I could find the car again and walked back to the highway. There was no traffic at that hour of the morning. I had walked two miles back toward the Ocklawaha River when a car passed and I flagged it down with my flashlight. The driver took me back. My car lights were ominous, deep in the woods. When we could find no marks where the car had leaped the ditch, the stranger suspected a trap and was reluctant to go in with me. When I pointed out the first pine tree past which I had ripped my way, he knew I had told the truth. I had an axe in my car and with it he cut down a sapling to use as a prize-pole to lift the damaged fender a little away from the wheel. Between us we freed the wheel enough so that I could drive the car.

I was obliged to drive home to the Creek at no more than ten miles an hour. After the shock it seemed to me that it would be impossible ever to sleep again. Yet as I turned from the village down the four-mile stretch to the Creek, the deadly fatigue overtook me and it was all I could manage, talking to myself, singing, to keep my eyes open. Then I met the fog. It was a soporific enemy. It lay over the hollows like a ghostly trap. I drowsed. I stirred. The fog lay no higher than the car, but it was a morass. Again and again I dropped into exhaustion, and roused out of it with a fearful rushing feeling. The fog was about me and I was plunging blindly into it, and imaginary trees closed in on me, and the road ended, and I was doomed, and I got a grip on myself and there was still open road, smothered with the fog. I minded especially the rushing feeling—a drowning man would feel so. I reached Cross Creek and went to bed. And all that night, and for weeks after, a road swam ahead of me and suddenly ended, and the trees poured in on me, and I was damned in the fog. I still dream sometimes of rushing to destruction through the mist, and I think that for me summer fog will forever be a nightmare.

I was struck, with Harper's bear dogs on the hunt, as with John Clardy's fox hounds, by the sharp line drawn between house dogs and work dogs. Florida hunters believe that any dog allowed the run of the house cannot be made a good sporting or working dog. I cannot agree. I make companions of my pointers and take them with me in my car. It seems to me that my Mad Pat, for instance, hunts with even greater enthusiasm and earnestness than kennel dogs I have known, through his delight in sharing the hunt with me and his desire to please me. Discipline of course must be strict and businesslike and must begin with the puppy. Because of this, I did once a cruel thing to a work dog whose path crossed mine.

The dog and I first met on a warm June evening. I was walking east along the Creek road, a little later than usual. The sun had set. I remember feeling lonely. I was a little uneasy, as well, for the moccasins and rattlers cross the road in the twilight. A ramshackle car came out from the lane that leads to Cow Hammock and turned toward the village. A dog followed it. He ran with the dejection of the forsaken. He was not noticed. A half-mile ahead he stopped disconsolately and began to trot back toward home. I saw that he was of a tawny yellow. He had something of the build of the Belgian police dog. As he came closer, I became aware of his mixed breeding. A black and alien smudge ran down his nose, and his long tail was ignominiously curled, revealing the mongrel. He trotted with a wolflike purpose.

I called to him with some uncertainty as to his nature. The yellow dog stopped. He came to me. I held out my hand and he snuffed it. I touched his rough coat. I pulled one ear. He rubbed his nose briefly against me in a gesture of acceptance. A feeling of friendliness passed over us in the dusk.

I said, "Come, boy," and he turned and walked with me.

It was good, after long months without a dog of my own, to have him beside me. He left me in a few minutes and went ahead, but the link between us was unbroken. Now and then he stopped and looked back, to be sure that I was following. Once he came to me to be touched; to be reassured that we were, truly, together. Studying him, I saw that he was a working dog; the catch-dog, it proved, of my new neighbor in Cow Hammock, who used him to round up his vagrant hogs. The business dog has his own ear marks. He is self-contained. He expects no luxuries of life, no graciousness. He possesses usually a simple integrity. He does his work faithfully and well and takes his pan of cornbread and an occasional bone, not with gratitude, but with the dignity of one who knows he has earned, that day, his keep. His gratitude is reserved for the rare expression of friendliness such as I had given him. That first night he ran well ahead of me and up his home lane, not taking too much for granted the closeness of our relation.

The next day I set out up the road in the late afternoon. I passed the entrance to Cow Hammock.

I called, "Here, boy! Here!"

I expected no response and there was none. I was halfway to Big Hammock when a clicking sound on the gravel road caught my ear. The yellow catch-dog was running to overtake me as though his life depended on it. I waited for him and he bounded about me with the joy of the alien who comes at last to his own. I was as glad as he. We walked that evening in a great content and that time he did not turn up his lane until I passed it with him. After that he waited for me with a faithful regularity. If I went early, I might have to call. Invariably he heard and joined me as soon as he could leave his business. If I went late, he was waiting at the lane. A few strokings of his head and he was satisfied. He went ahead, not far, looking back often over his curled and shameful tail.

Sometimes we romped together. We enjoyed most the game with the bull-bats. We stalked them together. They have a trick of sitting bright-eyed in the road, waiting for the approach. At the last instant they take off, circling to swoop low over their pursuer's head. It is a good game of tag. The yellow dog beat me at it. Often, a bull-bat too sure of himself all but lost his tail feathers. When this happened, the catch-dog raced joyfully around and around, or chased a quite imaginary rabbit.

One evening we loitered, for the approaching night was hot and sultry. As we turned west again, the last red stain of sunset faded from the sky and the road was dark. The catch-dog walked slowly beside me. Suddenly he stiffened. He made a sound, half growl, half moan, deep in his throat. Then he backed against me. I became aware that he was pushing me with his strong hindquarters, moving me away as deliberately as though he possessed an arm with which to do so. I backed with him to the far side of the road. On the gray gravel what had been a wide shadow resolved itself into a large rattlesnake that slid now into the grass. The catch-dog and I quivered, for the blood curdles instinctively at such an encounter in the dark. We hurried the rest of the way. Then and afterward we were joined by the closeness of those who, together, have escaped a danger.

One night I heard him being beaten for having gone away when he was wanted. Once he failed me, when an outlaw boar was being cornered. I heard the shrill squealings of the hog and knew that the catch-dog was at his work. He came later to my gate, as though to show me that his failure to join me was not of his intention. He did this sometimes, too, when circumstances kept me from my walking. Otherwise he did not intrude on my life of which, he recognized, he was not a part.

Some weeks after we began our jaunts together I was given the high-bred pointer puppy for which I had been waiting. The puppy was captivating. I devoted myself at once to his care and training. I wanted to raise the handsome young fellow as a companion, so that I was especially anxious to discipline him firmly from the beginning. I ended my evening walks down the highway, going about the grove instead. The puppy was not yet broken to go to heel and I could not risk the distraction of the catch-dog, a rabbit chaser, to disturb his training. Two or three days later the yellow dog came to my gate, wagging his tail. I ignored him and he went away.

A week later I took my young pointer on a leash. We passed the entrance to Cow Hammock. Passing, the catch-dog must have scented us, for some distance on he came after us on the gallop. He was insane with joy. He jumped against me, he went taut proudly, introducing himself to the puppy. He dropped his forelegs to the ground and shook his head, inviting the new dog to play. The puppy barked shrilly and tugged at the leash. Discipline was hopeless. There was nothing for it but to drive the catch-dog away. I made a menacing gesture. He looked at me unbelieving and did not stir. I picked up a handful of light gravel and threw it in his direction and went on, dragging the puppy behind me. The catch-dog followed. He watched me with bewildered eyes.

I shouted with as much as I could manage to bring from a sick heart, "Get back!" and he stopped and made no further effort to go with us. On the way home, we passed him, lying at the Cow Hammock entrance, his head on his paws. He fluttered his tail a little, as though in hope that I did not, could not, mean my rejection of him. The pointer and I hurried by.

Now we pass as though we were strangers. I am ashamed to face him, having used him in my loneliness, and then betrayed him. He shows no signs of recognition. His tail curves over his back. He trots with a high head, looking straight ahead. He is a work dog, and he must be about his business.

20. *Fall*

Somehow "autumn" does not seem properly used of Florida. There is a connotation in the word of flaming color, of sharp change, of hoar frost heavy on cornfields, of all of northern harvest. The subtropical fall is so impalpable, so much a protraction of summer, pendulous before the time of winter fruiting, that we might almost say that we have no such season. As with spring, we change our habits not so much in relation to a calendar month, as according to the storms, which are only relatively equinoctial. Our summer temperatures are seldom extreme, never reaching the 100's and above as elsewhere in the country. But when the summer rains have ended, we sometimes have a temperature maintained in the 80's for many weeks, and the steadiness, through August and perhaps all of September and even into October, becomes wearing, like the ancient torture of the dropping of water on the head.

The sky is a glaring blue, too blue and cloudless, the redbirds no longer sing, the rank summer vegetation turns sere, and the sun goes down in a burning ball. The sand is powder and a fine dust rises from it and coats the roadside bushes. In a temperate climate, this would be a part of summer. Here, it means summer's end. Even the sturdy zinnias curl and shrivel. The pecan trees, water-loving, draw up within themselves and their pointed leaves are crisp. At this time, flocks of diminutive drab birds sift into the pecan trees, and cling there like dead leaves blown by a dry wind. The palm fronds are without luster. The doves mourn plaintively and the sound is tiresome.

The second week in September I gamble on the season and plant most of my seed-beds. The broccoli will probably survive in any case, but if the storms with their rain do not come soon, the parsley and lettuce will never germinate, nor can I bring through my seedling flowers, African daisy, gypsophilia, forget-me-not, schizanthus, stock, larkspur, calendula and the rest, for my well water is harsh and the delicate plants resent it. At the Creek we all watch for signs of change. When the dog fennel blooms, we count that it will be forty days until frost. When the curlews wheel, high in the sky, we are despondent, for they are called the dry-weather birds, and the circling flocks indicate that the rains are a long time away. The golden rod is no help to us, for it is not a fall flower here, but blooms in August or even in July. We listen hopefully for the big bull alligator in Orange Lake, prophesying change, and watch for the poor-Joe flying, for the bird is the best of weather prophets. We eye the Spanish moss for the direction of the wind, for as long as the wind is from the east there will be no rain. One fall when the storms were late and a long drought was holding up the fall planting of truck crops, the village held a meeting to pray for rain.

One of the town patriarchs arose to say, "You-all jest as good to pray for the heathen, or pray Jim Wilkins'll git sober, or ary thing but rain. You know good and well hit ain't a-goin' to rain until the wind changes."

The Negroes are depressed and pass the blues on to me, and I begin to put stock in Martha's voodoo. She comes for long mournful conferences and tells of the friend who vomited up a snake, and the one whose husband was tolled away from her, and had to be tolled back by getting some hairs from his head and burying them with other items under the house. She tells me how to make a cunjur bag, and how difficult it is to get all the ingredients together. The principal one is the right bone from a black cat. The cat must be black all over, without the faintest trace of white. It must be boiled alive in an iron pot until the meat falls from the bones. The bones must be thrown into a running stream, and the bone that floats upstream is the one that holds the magic. I spilled some potassium of permanganate crystals and Martha threw up her hands in horror when she saw them, and inquired if I were making fumble-dust. I came across the word "fombé" in the book on Haitian voodoo by the Florida Negress, Zora Neale Hurston, and it seemed to me that the Haitian "fombé" must surely be Martha's fumble-dust.

I listen to Martha now, not overriding her, when she refuses to clean out the fireplaces on a Friday. Through the summer guests have thrown matches and cigarettes untidily into the fireplaces, but if Martha says that Friday is an unlucky day for removing them, I agree, for a sense of ill luck hangs over us.

"Us was maybe born to good luck," she says gloomily, "but bad luck done overtakened us."

We are careful to throw onion peelings into the wood range, and not to throw peanut hulls out of the door, to prevent the quarrelling that could so easily arise in the tenseness. We do not sweep anything out of the door after sunset, to avoid catastrophe. Who is there to object? Who could be standing outside the door after the sun goes down, to mind being swept on? Yes, but who couldn't be? I thought I heard feet going down the porch steps in the early morning.

Martha said, "That was the night-folks goin' away."

It is probably the night-folks who don't like to be swept on. If I were a night-folk, I should hate it.

There is an unexpected treat of jellied chicken in the icebox. It was made, with no need at the moment of jellied chicken, from a fine fat hen. The hen in this evil time was foolish enough to crow on the yard. Martha said we could not have it. Anathema to me, and bad luck to boot, are a whistling woman and a crowing hen. Every one in the tenant house goes down with malaria. The doctor calls it malaria, but Martha knows better. When I built an addition to the tenant house, so that Martha and Old Will could move back here to live for the rest of their lives, I used new lumber. If you add new wood to old, you may as well begin saving up for medicine, for all in the house will be ill. I should have remembered, for I paid for both my bath-rooms, made of shiny new pine against the old weathered house, with trips to the hospital. Martha thinks that I learn very slowly.

Out in the grove hangs a hawk-repeller. It is the spread-eagled body of the last hawk shot, strung between two poles, with a gin bot-tle hung at its neck. It did not have to be a gin bottle. It had to be a bottle, to catch the sun, and I happened to have a gin bottle handy. As Gertrude Stein would say, if it had to be a bottle it had to be a bot-tle and a bottle is a bottle and a gin bottle is a bottle. The macabre af-fair sways and glints in the sun and there has not been a hawk in sight since Martha and I put it up. I could not say how much of a moral lesson the hawks take from it. I doubt whether they associate humans with gin and gin with sin. But the bottle does shine in their eyes and they see a very dead fellow hawk and they think the grove must be a good place to avoid. At any rate, with the rains held up, it is no time for me to quibble.

At the back of the farmhouse a dead chicken snake hangs in the crotch of a grapefruit tree. This is not, as might be supposed, to keep away other chicken snakes. It is for the all-important purpose, late in a dry September, of inducing rain. Very often, it works. I should never dream in a dry time of burying a freshly-killed snake. I hang it in the crotch of a tree and usually it makes rain. It is possible that snakes, like turtles, crawl ahead of a rain, and that it would have rained anyway. Facts are ineffably simpler than explanations. Sometimes we have a false shower in the morning, a few futile drops, and Martha says, "A mornin' rain is like an old woman's dance—soon over."

If a limb breaks from a tree, says Martha, and no wind is stirring, it is a sign of death. This is plausible enough, for it may mean that in the great battle between creation and destruction there comes an instant when the forces of disintegration are strong, and if they can work on a tree, why may they not in the same moment strike at a life? Martha's insistence that if a cow lows in the late hours of the night, that morning you will hear of a death *somewhere*—if somebody doesn't come to tell you, she says, you'll read of it in the paper—is one of those generalized prophecies that cannot fail of fulfillment, for I suppose there has never been a morning paper without an obituary. Death does take an occasional holiday in a small area, being no doubt busy elsewhere, and perhaps Martha meant that in such an instance he would be at work in one's own vicinity, for the Negro world of the body is a small one. It is only their spiritual geography that reaches far, out to the deep rivers and the spaces where the Lord watches the sparrow's fall along with the courses of the stars, and a man, black or white, must climb Jacob's ladder to the streets of gold.

Martha and I went through an evil fall day together. I had obeyed all her dicta, but a sense of the ominous still hung over us. The morning was gray, with a treacherous promise of the healing storm that never came. A false light came instead, and faded and the sky was metallic. I found a praying mantis on the asparagus fern in front of the veranda and put it in a glass jar with a few sprays of the fern. It was angry and restless. It folded and unfolded its green praying hands, and opened and closed its mandibles, more in curse than in prayer. I called Martha to look at it, wondering if she had some special name for it, and some age-old story. But she had never seen the insect before, and recoiled from its spurious reverence. I stood at the foot of the veranda steps as we talked. When I turned away to come in the house again, I looked down and saw a cotton-mouth moccasin lying not two inches from my heel prints in the sand. My negligee must have brushed its coils. I hurried for my gun and shot him. The head struck at me after the shot, and he died with hate in his viper's eyes.

All morning a blue-tailed lizard ran in and out of a crack along the veranda. He switched his tail, sleek and shining and lacquered. A cockroach came out in the daylight, of a breed that usually stirs only by night. The two bird dogs, ordinarily bent on some mischief together, slept all day. Once or twice they lifted their noses, were not pleased with something, and went back to sleep again. I grew feverish in the afternoon and slept a drugged sleep. I awakened and tried to work and could not. I read, but the words had no meaning. At five in the afternoon Snow came to milk the cows and feed the calves and ducks and chickens. He hung the cottonmouth in the crotch of a tree. I fed the dogs. They ate silently and curled up again. Snow went away. I bathed and dressed.

Martha came to the house to tell me that Sissie had come from her cabin by the Creek to say that a suspicious Negro had just come and gone. He had demanded water at Sissie's in a belligerent tone, had walked boldly about the cabin as though estimating the belongings, had said that he would go back across the Creek bridge, and had, instead, doubled back on his tracks and slipped east along the Creek, back of my grove. I remembered that I had read in the paper of a Negro murderer who had escaped and had last been seen coming our way. I drove to the village to report the matter to the deputy sheriff there. He promised to bring men to the Creek for the search. I came home, and was restless and uneasy, and set out to walk along the road. I called the dogs to go with me, and usually exuberant, they let me go alone. The sun must have set, for that is its unbroken habit, but there was only a stain like old blood to make the sunset.

My feet dragged and it took me a long time to cover the return distance to the grove. Lightning flashed but there was no thunder. Dark overtook me before I reached home, seeming to close in like an enemy. There was light enough to determine that the tail of a snake extending into the road was that of a rattler. I hurried by and a screech owl shrilled its wavering lament in the hammock. I opened my gate and a small snake moved ahead of me. I bent close, and I could see that it was the deadly coral snake. I avoided it and when I returned with a gun it was gone.

The deputy sheriff came to report that he and his men had searched all the Creek area back of my grove, but because the earth was so dry, had found no footprints past the wetness of the Creek itself. If the criminal came out, he said, he would certainly try to cut back into the main road. He and his men would wait all night halfway between the Creek and the village to trap him. He went away. I knew that a desperate man would attack a house for food, for money, and above all, for a gun. I brought all my guns to the veranda, loaded a rifle and a shotgun, and waited. I did not dare turn on a light, for then I should be at the mercy of an invader.

I sat in the darkness and heard Martha and Old Will pounding away at the tenant house. They were barricading the doors and I could not blame them. Home was usually a safe and cozy place, but now it was menaced. I sat taut, listening for sly footsteps at the back of the farmhouse. There was no sound but the crickets. They chirped cheerily, hoping, as I, for change. Discouragement took them over and the chirpings ceased. No car passed, no horse and rider, no lowing cow, no dog, no friendly frog hunter on his way to the Creek. The stillness was almost unbearable. At last I lit a candle. It burned steadily for a while, then wavered. There was a rustling in the distance, as though invisible wings passed over marsh and grove and hammock. The palm trees rustled their fronds in the darkness. There came the cleanness, the relief, the beneficence, of wind. It was near midnight, and I knew that if the criminal had not now approached the house to take what he needed, he would not come. I went to bed and slept soundly, and the murmur of boughs stirring softened my sleep. In the morning we heard that the fugitive had been seen walking in the other direction. And on the heels of the wind came the storm. The season had broken, summer was ended, and the healthy fall had come.

Martha remembers a time long ago when the only warning of hurricanes, other than natural portents plain to the wise, was the whistle of the train four miles away at the village. In the hurricane season the engineer gave an agreed signal in announcement, and in winter another to tell of an impending freeze. When the wind is right we can hear the passing of the train itself, and the warning whistle must have come mournfully and distinctly to the Creek. Hurricanes are not a serious menace in the interior, but we get the fringes of the big coastal storms. An ominous green light precedes them, and a great stillness that may hold for twenty-four hours. The green deepens, is infiltrated with a cosmic black ink, and the sky-writing has its meaning plain. Then in the distance we hear a roaring, as though the express passing through the village had left its tracks and were headed for the Creek.

The sound, once heard, can never be forgotten and is always recognizable for what it is. It means that the wind is rushing in with such force and such volume, filling the atmospheric vacuum, that the obstacles of trees tear and shred it in its coming. The roar becomes a booming and the path of the wind is visible far ahead. I have sat on the veranda with the moss on the pecan tree that shades it hanging motionless, and across the grove seen the palm trees flatten halfway to the ground. They toss their heads like tethered lions, fighting to be free of the thing that rips at their bodies and loosens their feet from the safe earth. The fronds are stripped like paper from the trunks, and sail through the air, stabbing into the ground, stem ends down. Live oaks and tall pines crash in the hammock. The wind strikes the farmhouse a physical blow. If any of the old hand-hewn cypress shingles are loose in the lichened roof, this is when they go. The house sighs, but does not rock nor rattle. It has stood through too many storms to be disturbed by this one. Sometimes the wind comes alone, and goes on its way, and leaves a still lower barometer behind it. When it returns again it will have even greater force, and this time the rain will accompany it. The hurricane rains fly always at an acute angle, borne outward by the fierce pressure. They give the appearance of a swinging curtain. Cows and pigs caught up in it are swept along in a panic and must go in the storm's chosen direction. Twice I have been overtaken in the field and it seemed to me that I should never beat my way out of the tidal wave. The great storms may last for three days and these days and nights howl like all the mad dogs in the world loose at once. There is not the coziness of being shut in away from ordinary storms. Too gigantic a force is at large for any sense of safety.

When the September storms are over we have some of our most superb weather. The oranges take on color, the red-birds are delirious, and in the morning and evening long shadows lie under the citrus trees. The skies are the brightest of robin's-egg blue and the air has a translucent quality, as though the storms had washed it with a fine gold dust. The bear grass blooms and we shall use the harsh strips of the leaves for hanging our fall hams and bacons in the smoke-house. The deer tongue, or wild vanilla, blooms in the flat-woods, and when we step on the leaves, crushing them, the scent is spilled perfume on the air.

If they are not planted already, we hurry to put in our fall crops: beans, English peas, squash and cucumbers; our winter crops of cabbage, lettuce, carrots, beets, broccoli, turnips, collards, kohlrabi, cauliflower and celery. The hurry now for the fall market crops is against the first frost. The beans are delicate and must make before the cold has touched them. The crops that have matured through the long summer are ready. Sweet potatoes are dug and mounded for the winter's use, the vines fed to the cows and the nubbins to the hogs. The fields of sugar cane are gold-green, Chinese scarves waving across the tawny sand. It is desirable for a light frost to touch the cane to sweeten it, as persimmons and citrus must be touched, but a heavy frost ruins it, so that the stalks sour where they stand.

The cane is scythed down, the bundles gathered like sheaves of wheat, and drawn with mule and wagon to the grinding. I think the cane mill will survive all mechanization on our remote Florida farms and backwoods clearings, certainly as long as there is any individualistic and agrarian society. Each family has a small plot of sugar cane for its own use and several families use one mill. A mule or horse walks around and around. A boy feeds the cane stalks into the gears of the mill, and the cloudy sweet juice bursts through a spout and into a barrel. We have cane-grindings and syrup-boilings, festive occasions when the children may run and shriek as they please and the old folks come and renew their childhoods. There are experts among the syrup boilers, and when these give a boiling, their followers flock to them. And when the new cane syrup goes in bottles or tins to the rural grocery stores roundabout, the proprietors announce to their

customers that they can now offer Martin's syrup. There is a fine flavor to syrup that you have seen boiling and bubbling in the great kettle, with the fatwood fire blazing under it, the sweet smell of it
cooking, the bees that come even at night to guzzle at the edges, the
skimmed heavy syrup seen poured into a clean hewn cypress trough.

We have peanut boilings in the fall earlier than syrup boilings,
for the peanuts are good for boiling only before they are mature.
They are well washed and boiled in the hull in salted water. The nuts
are gelatinous, with all the peanut sweetness, and quarts may be
eaten without a trace of stomach ache. In Georgia they call peanuts
"goobers" and in Florida we call them "pinders." Pinder-ripening
time is the height of harvest, and the hogs are turned in to the fields
to root up the vines and grow fat and marketable in a week or two on
the rich oily kernels. The doves and quail flock to the fields, for the
greedy hogs chew the peanuts carelessly, and walk from row to row
with broken fragments dropping from their snouts, precisely the
right size for the bills of birds.

One fall, one of my first at the Creek, I had two fine porkers I
had bought for fifty cents each in the wilds near the Ocklawaha
River. I heard that old man Butler, at Orange Lake Station, had fifteen acres of pinders and wanted to fatten hogs on shares. My shoats
had outgrown the table scraps. I loaded them in the truck and drove
off to Butler's in the September twilight. The old man came to the
gate with outstretched hand.

"Now I'm powerful glad to have visitors," he said. "Come right
in, friend."

I had not come to visit, I said, but on the business of fattening
hams.

"Now, friend, you must be a stranger. How come you're in such
a hurry? Ham can wait. Pork always do be sweeter for a mite of time.
You like boiled pinders?"

I confessed to a passion for them.

"Then we'll go pull you some pinders to carry home to boil, and I want you to come back for another visit and tell me they was the best you ever sucked outen the hull. What's your name? Never mind, I'll just call you Friend. Come on now. The moon is high and we can see as good as day."

He was excited, intoxicated with something I could not place. An elderly female figure emerged like a shadow from the cedar-bordered path.

"You come to buy the farm?" she quavered. "You know anybody wants to buy a farm?"

"The farm ain't for sale," old Butler said placidly. "Now sugar-plum, me and my friend here aim to pull pinders. Go fetch us a basin and come with us yonder to the field."

She followed obediently and sadly with an ample pan. The moonlight flooded the peanut field. Hogs came behind us and rooted in our wake, snuffling and grunting.

"Ain't this a fine farm?" Friend Butler demanded. "I was born on this place."

The woman stripped peanuts from the vines mechanically.

"He just says that," she murmured mournfully. "It was some place in the county, but the record's lost and he don't really know."

I understood that there was war between these gentle veterans. It was the age-old conflict between love of the soil and hate of it.

"Ain't this peaceful, friend?" Butler asked. "Ain't it beautiful? I lived in a blasted town for twenty years, and now I'm back again, right on the place where I was born."

The woman did not address him or me directly, but spoke in the manner of a Greek chorus, chanting dismally.

"He acts drunk all the time," she lamented to the moon. "Just runs around plumb crazy, raising hogs and pinders and sweet potatoes. Nobody to talk to, no place to go. No lights at night to look at, nothing but the tormented moon and stars. I got ten kittens, but they ain't real company. Run around near about as bad as him. He talked me into trading good city lots for this. If we could only sell and go back to town. But nobody in their right mind would buy it."

Friend Butler waved his arms, dripping earth and peanuts from the vines he held. He ignored the chorus, as befits a hero of Greek drama.

"Now this is what I enjoy! Pullin' pinders in the moonlight, with a friend to enjoy them with me."

He gave a vast sweep and the peanuts flew wide.

"Independent! That's it, independent!"

He must show me his four acres of orange trees, old time-worn fellows as big as oaks. The moonlight filtered through the arched rows. Friend Butler became speechless with ecstasy. He must give me a drink of icy water from an ancient well with buckets and windlass, and I must understand how sweet and rare it was. My porkers must be ushered gravely into the Elysium of pinders, my basinful of peanuts loaded in the truck. The unhappy quaverings of the woman trailed after me as I drove away. I promised to stay longer when I came next month for the fattened pigs.

I never saw my friend again, sending for my pigs when they were ready. Last month I read in the local paper of his death. I was immensely gratified to read that his address was still Orange Lake Station.

21. *Winter*

*W*e have one fixed seasonal dividing line. While spring and summer and fall merge silently one into the other, we announce winter with the crackling of gun shot. On November 20 our hunting season opens. The day comes close to being a state holiday. Men who hunt at no other time go out "the first day of season." Even Little Will begs off from his morning's work and goes to the hammock for squirrels or to the Creek edge for ducks or coots. We are excited and hilarious, and I think that a part of this is because we are unconsciously returning to the pioneer aspect of the state, when all men took a portion of their living from the hunt. It is the marked end of one thing, too, and the beginning of another, and something in men's minds likes a simple demarcation. Our crops are harvested or reaching their maturity. Ahead of us is the good season, when growth is slowed and a very little hoeing keeps clean the farm fields, the groves and the gardens. It is the tidy time. The lush exuberance of summer is forgotten and the hurricanes of the fall. All is neat and ordered.

My own flower and vegetable gardens are thriving, if they will thrive at all, and my citrus crop will not be ready for picking before Christmas. I do most of my writing in the summer, when there are no interruptions, and I have hurried to finish such work. I have a space of freedom and I am ready to go into the woods and the fields with my friends. Fred Tompkins and I open the hunting season together. He has long been my favorite hunting and fishing companion. He brings to the sport a great gaiety of spirit and any eye for all the beauty of the open. The hunt with him is a comfortable affair and I love him for his frequent stops to sit on a pine log and smoke a cigarette.

"No use to kill ourselves havin' a good time," he says.

My only grievance against Fred is that he has never been entirely convinced that I am not a Yankee. I should not hold this against him, for he judges Yankees, after more than fifty years at it, as he would judge any one else. If they are good sports, like to fish and hunt, and are always ready for a laugh, they will do for friends. The first time he came to see me in my first February here, he brought me a strange bouquet. It was of holly berries and orange blossoms.

He said, "I studied what would please a Yankee lady, and I figured it'd be new to her to have winter and summer all in one bouquet."

I murmured, in the same breath with my thanks, words to the effect that I did not consider myself a Yankee. He accepted the thanks and passed lightly over my protests. I had arrived from New York state, and I should have hard work of it proving any contradictory antecedents. He tried me grievously in our early friendship. It was late in my first spring at the Creek. An affluent New York car drew up at my gate. A middle-aged man and woman came to my door and greeted me warmly.

"Mr. Tompkins sent us to you," they said. "He said just to tell you that Fred sent us."

They were friends of Fred and that was good enough. I invited them into the living room and we sat, attempting conversation. I wondered why Fred had sent them and I offered a highball. They refused stiffly.

The woman said, "You have very good fishing on Orange Lake, Mr. Tompkins tells us."

"Oh, yes. Orange Lake is famous for its big-mouthed bass."

"We are fishing fanatics. We have fished all over Florida. You fish, Mr. Tompkins says."

"Yes, indeed. I'm not much good yet at casting, and I have no outboard motor, but I go when any one will take me."

Brightly, "We have our outboard motor with us."

"How convenient!" I said.

Conversation languished. The woman looked at her husband and he looked at her. At last she took the plunge.

"We're very anxious to fish in this part of Florida. Mr. Tompkins said he was sure you would take us in."

"Take you in?"

"Yes. So that we can fish on Orange Lake. We'll be glad to pay anything within reason."

"There must be some mistake. I don't run a boarding house. I don't take people in."

The woman said desperately, "Mr. Tompkins said for us to offer pay, but he was sure you would refuse it." She looked despairingly at her husband. "He said that if you took a notion to us, he was sure you would invite us to spend the month with you."

I wondered if friendship in Florida meant that one offered hospitality for a month to friends of a friend. It seemed too much, even for the vaunted Southern hospitality. But if I was cold now, and I was becoming colder every moment, these good people, friends of my friend, would think that I had not taken a notion to them, I fumbled for an excuse.

I said, "Ordinarily, of course, I should love to have you. But we have a large crop of beans and are picking now and have extra helpers and I have no room in the house, none at all. I'm so sorry. Please tell our mutual friend Fred that I'm very sorry."

"Oh, we won't see Mr. Tompkins again. We've never seen him before. We just met him at the garage in Citra. We asked about fishing and the garage man called Mr. Tompkins over and said he could tell us more than any one else. Mr. Tompkins told us about Orange Lake, and said he knew you would invite us to stay for the month—if you liked us."

"I do like you, of course. I can see you're charming people. But you understand about the lack of room. I guess Fred didn't know about my not having any room."

They left puzzled and reluctant. The first time I saw Fred I questioned him.

"Why on earth did you send those perfect strangers out to me? Why did you tell them I would take them in?"

"Well," he said, "they come through, Yankees and strangers. I studied, how would I feel if I was living up in New York and folks from Florida come through? I'd be so proud to have home folks, I'd put 'em up for as long as they'd stay. So I figured, you being a Yankee, and them being Yankees, it'd be a big treat for you to have 'em visit you."

I said, "I came to Florida just to get away from Yankees."

Fred laughed heartily over my facetiousness and is entirely convinced that I just did not take a notion to the strangers. Fred is an amazing person. I do not know his age, but he was a sergeant in the regular army in the Spanish war, so he is no lad. Something about him is timeless, and when he was young he must have looked much as he does now and will always look. His wife says that he was handsome in his youth.

"He had them sparklin' brown eyes," she said to me, "and he had a gold tooth, and he come to court me drivin' two black horses drove tandem. I hadn't never see a gold tooth nor horses drove tandem, and my heart turned to water in me."

Her heart is still water within her, but her devotion does not prevent her from quarrelling steadily and hopelessly with him over his habits. Because of her motherly and uneasy fluttering, he calls her the Old Hen. My sympathies are of course with her, for I know that the most ingratiating friend can be the most exasperating husband.

"He's just different," I say to her. "You're a domestic fowl and he's a wild fowl. You want him to stay home and he just doesn't want to stay home."

"I know," she says, "but honey, wouldn't you think he'd want to stay home nights once in a while? All he wants to do is prowl and ramble. Just like a varmint. He's worst moonlight nights. There's no keepin' him home after the moon comes up."

The Old Hen favors me with her friendship, and I think this is because, whenever Fred and I hunt together, I try to bring her home a fox-squirrel.

"The Old Hen's a slave to fox-squirrel," Fred says.

Our first-day-of-season hunt is a glorified combination lighthearted search after deer, squirrel and quail. We set out for the big scrub about four o'clock in the morning. Sometimes I oversleep and we are a little late, leaving at five.

Fred says comfortably, "Maybe day'll hold off 'til we get there."

We have always beaten the sunrise to the river. We cross the hand ferry at Orange Springs in the grayness and the Ocklawaha

River boils darkly under us. We turn south on the narrow scrub sand road and then west to the river bank at Ingram's field. Fred's Ford goes unerringly through shoulder-high grasses, bumps over gopher holes and comes like a homing pigeon to a cluster of hickory trees at the edge of the rushing water. We leave the car, leave the bird dog comfortably asleep in it, and go on foot along the river trail in the darkness. The theory is that we will come on a deer, and that day will break at that moment, so that our shots will coincide with the technical instant of sunrise, at which hunting legally begins. We have crowded day every time, and only the fact that we have never seen a deer on these occasions has kept us out of the hands of the law.

We know the river trail by heart, but each time it is as though we moved silently into the dark core of a dream. There is no sound but the rushing of the swift river current. Sometimes a buck rabbit thumps or whistles, or a hoot owl cries through the forest. It is an hour at which the small night creatures seem to have finished their night's feeding and the day creatures have not yet come from their sleep. Bamboo vines brush us as we go. We can only distinguish one tree from another by the feel of the bark as our hands touch it in passing. There is no greater darkness than this high wood by night. The river bank steepens and we turn up it, away from the river. The black curtain through which we have been pushing thins to the gray velvet of dawn. The trees at the top of the slope are spaced more widely. A dust pink glow seeps into the tops of the tall oaks and hickories and magnolias. I learned here that what I had considered the fiction of Cabell's mystic hour between daylight and sunrise is a magical fact.

In this hour we abandon our deer hunting and find soft places on the bank to sit and wait for squirrels. I have no compunction here about killing them, for our breakfast depends on it. They make themselves known a long way off. Where the river bank levels off at the top into the broad stretch of thick low-growing scrub, there is a swaying of scrub oak boughs, as though a sudden breeze swept through them. There is a rustling, a scurrying, and as though the rising sun released minute squeaking springs, a shrill and rusty chattering. The squirrels are coming in to feed. The gray bodies whisk up and down the hickory trunks. I hear Fred's gun from his distant stand, and there is a great commotion for an instant, until the squirrels decide the menace is remote. We shoot no more than we shall need, and according to whether other hunters are to join us for breakfast. The signal to meet comes from Fred, who has gauged the number of our shots, and knows when we have enough meat. He gives the bob-white call, and since I cannot whistle in return, I work my way back toward his calls.

We put our bag together and move back along the trail. The scrub is a mass of green and gold, the jorees are calling in the underbrush, and the swift river runs copper under the early sun. At times, if the morning has been cold or windy, we have only a squirrel or two, but cut into small pieces and simmered in the Dutch oven they seem to multiply like the loaves and fishes and there is always enough. We are famished, and the smother-fried browned squirrel, the rich gravy made with river water, the bread and camp coffee, are all we want of a feast under the shining hickories. We eat leisurely and let the bird dog out to run and we talk of where we shall hunt quail the rest of the day.

The dew is still heavy on the grasses and the quail have not fed far from their night's bed. The scent is strong. The pines cast long shadows and the air is sweet and cool. Some of my hunting companions, such as the Major, seek out the most inaccessible hunting grounds, but Fred and I avoid the swamps, the bay-heads and too heavy a growth of palmettos.

"No use to kill us nor the dog neither," Fred says.

We hunt from the car, which the Major considered effete. The custom antedates automobiles, going back to the days of the hunting wagon. Then men piled their dogs, their camping supplies and themselves into an open buckboard and set forth for the day or the weekend or the week, independent and free. Hunting dogs love to ride, especially in the company of humans. They hang over the side of truck or wagon, or from the window of a car, their long ears flapping in the breeze, their noses keen and lifted for the great unrolling ribbon of smell.

Hunting from a car is no vicarious business. It means only that great distances can be covered, moving from one good territory to another without wasting hours in unlikely places. Once in bird territory, Fred puts my Pat out. The dog works both sides of the road, seldom ranging out of sight. A whistle and a wave of the hand turn him in the desired direction. Fred drives slowly, often in second gear, and when Pat's tail begins to vibrate with a new tenseness, we leave the car and follow wherever the scent may lead, for the dog is definitely on birds. The point is a beautiful thing. Pat stands staunch and true, a sturdy pattern in black and white, his nose on a line with his back, one forepaw lifted daintily, his tail rigid, curving upward a little at the end.

Fred takes Pat in the car at frequent intervals so that the dog is always fresh. He gives him water from a shell box or finds a clear pool in a sinkhole for him. We take with us a Dutch oven, cooking fat, flour, bread and coffee. When the sun is high overhead and the quail are nooning and dusting themselves in the warm sand, we build a fire with fatwood chips and oak twigs, dress what birds we have shot and fry them whole in deep sizzling fat. We make strong coffee and stretch out our feet to rest them while the birds brown and the coffee boils. We eat the birds in our fingers and dip our slices of bread in the brown gravy in the Dutch oven. Pat gets the bones and what is left over of bread and gravy.

"Some folks say a dog can't smell good with gravy on his nose," Fred says, "but a dog ain't goin' to leave no gravy on his nose." He wipes the Dutch oven clean with the last slice of bread and holds it for Pat. "I have a good time on a bird hunt and I aim to have the dog have just as good a time as I do."

Game birds have an added flavor when you have shot them yourself, or have at least been on the shoot. I am a poor shot, and hypocritically have little true desire to do better. What makes the sport is the magnificent country and the stirring performance of good dogs. Good companions lift it into high adventure, and while there are solitary souls who rove the fields alone with dog and gun, it is one of the pastimes that I, who can do with much solitude and like to walk alone, prefer to share. But the birds I have downed would not make a respectable covey. Some day I shall lay down my arms entirely.

I had a worse struggle over the kill with my Aunt Wilmer than with my own conscience. Our line descends from Wesleyan Methodist preachers and the flame burns fiercely, if fitfully, in Wilmer. Fred and I took her with us on a quail hunt one winter when she visited me, I dubiously, Fred full of mischief. At his most conservative he drives with an utter disregard of the terrain. Now, with a wide-eyed school teacher to terrify if possible, he plowed with his Ford straight across the piney woods. We hit gopher holes at forty-five miles an hour. The bird dog braced himself stiff-legged on the back seat. We rushed at pine saplings much larger than Fred usually attacked, sometimes hanging in mid-air as the sapling resisted, then dropping over it like a roller-coaster. When we left the car and the dog began to find birds, I blundered along with my shooting as usual but Fred was on his mettle. Every time he swung his gun to his shoulder, a brown ball of feathers dropped to earth. Each time Wilmer ran forward with a little wounded cry and retrieved the bird, nestling it to her.

Fred said, "Now if you can keep your auntie here, we got no use for a bird dog."

The dog was puzzled and a trifle resentful at having the retrieving taken out of his control. He began going like an arrow to the dead bird to get there ahead of Wilmer.

"The darlings," she murmured, stroking the bird feathers. "How awful! This is awful!"

Left to myself, I, too, often feel that it is an unwarranted slaughter, but Wilmer's moans made me perversely take the opposite stand.

"It's really not so frightful to shoot them," I told her, "for if a covey isn't shot into and broken up, it stays together and the quail don't mate that year."

"That just proves," she said, "they're fine, moral birds."

I cannot testify as to their morality but I do know they have a diabolical cleverness in outwitting the hunter. Any man who comes home with enough quail for the table has earned his meal. Four miles beyond the Creek there is a mystery covey on Guthrie's land that always outwitted even the Major. There is good quail shooting there, for we were the only hunters allowed on the land. Each fall I swap pecans and oranges for the privilege of hunting there. In consequence of not being much hunted, the quail are as wild as hawks. Birds much hunted will hold for a dog's point. Birds not hunted flush wild far ahead of the dogs. The Guthrie terrain is ideal. Open black jack woods full of partridge peas and sumac and myrtle berries join the cultivated fields of corn and peanuts and chufas. The fields are bordered with blackberry thickets where the quail love to "bunch up" for the night. The woods dip to bay-head swamps where the birds are found in dry weather or in the heat of the day. The shooting in the bay-heads is difficult, but it was to the taste of the Major and his own powerful dog Steve.

We usually had good luck until we fell foul of the mystery covey. It fed from the road back to the bay-head and numbered at least forty birds. After its first mad flushing and our first desperate shots, at too great a distance, it disappeared into thin air. The Major and I came on that covey again and again, knowing about where we should find it at any given time of the day. We never found it that day again. If it flew into the trees, we were unable ever to see the small brown forms that cluster on limbs like pine cones. If it flew farther, it was a greater distance than any covey has been known to fly, for we made wide arcs and circles with the indefatigable Steve and found no trace of it. I spoke of it to old-timers who travel the River Styx road past the Guthrie place. The enormous covey has been known to them for years. Their theory is that one wise old cock has led it all this time, a cock with some special technique for outwitting the hunter.

The Major opened up for me the æsthetic delights of duck-hunting. The sport pleased me particularly because, in the great beauty of the surroundings, there was not a chance that I should ever bring down one of the swift-flying birds. We met on the north side of Orange Lake before dawn and crossed in a small boat to an established duck blind. The lake was gray chiffon, the horizon a gray velvet curtain. Sometimes, on rainy mornings, there was no lifting of the soft mist. Only, in the distance, the palms took shape, the reeds and saw-grass stood out like the lines of an etching, and the water was a silver mirror for the ducks and coots, flying low. On days when the sun rose visibly, the gray was slowly infiltrated with lavender, then with pink, until the sun lifted before us and sky and water blazed with salmon and orange and red, and all the world of lake and shore came to life. The red-winged blackbirds chattered from the tussocks, the coots took off from the water like clumsy sea-planes, the big-mouthed bass leaped and made great whirls and spirals, the ducks gave their harsh vibrant call, white herons winged over, and a fish-eagle screamed, high against the sky. Then we settled quietly in the blind, each listening for the other's "Mark!"

I loved the swift whir of the approaching ducks, the sharp slicing of the air overhead. I lifted my hypocritical gun obediently and fired, usually to hear, "Diana, damn it, the birds almost took your hat off." It was good to be ravenous in early midday, to open the lunch basket and eat the whole length of a Cuban sandwich—eight inches long, four inches thick, stuffed with layers of chicken and ham and roast pork and cheese and chopped sweet pickle—and to digest such a preposterous affair as easily as though it were baby food. A flight of ducks, of course, always came over when one's mouth was full and one's hand was on the beer bottle or the coffee cup instead of the shotgun. That gave me a fine excuse and no alibi was necessary. Then the sun was low and the egrets came in to roost and the ducks were arrows against the sky. Home was good then, with supper of red wine and biscuits and quail from yesterday's hunt, or a roast guinea, and afterward, good talk by the blazing hearth-fire. These are the things my mind holds dear of hunting.

Of my deer hunting I treasure, not a kill, but a hunt deep in the Everglades, when Bob Chancey and I followed two great bucks from dawn to dark, and never once saw the quarry. They were ghost deer, with incredible large tracks running side by side, and they led us through a dream world of gray cypresses and silent Spanish moss and soft knee-deep watery sloughs. The trail once crossed a circular pond and growing on all the cypresses around the pond were orchids, and I stopped and let my companion and his dog go far ahead of me while I stood and stared and could not believe that I held orchids in my hands. In the evening I took up a lone stand deep under a thicket of low growing young cypresses massed with strange exotic flowering vines. Beside the thicket was a clear pool and to this in the rosy sunset hundreds of egrets and great white herons came to drink and roost in the trees around it. They did not see nor hear me and I forgot that the great phantom bucks might pass my way, and sat and drank my fill of white birds and ferns and flowers and crystal pool.

Once upon a time there was snow at Cross Creek. The Chamber of Commerce would insist that this was not a factual item, but the beginning of a fairy tale. Yet oddly, the conditions and the temperature necessary to make snow, are much milder than those prevailing when we have our occasional disastrous and quite snowless freezes. The snow at the Creek came on a cloudy winter evening when the temperature hung at the minutest fraction below thirty-two degrees. It was a fine, dry, powdery snow, like a wandering breath of the north. In its brief falling it sifted through cracks and eaves and lay for a moment like spilled salt. It was surprising that so nebulous a thing should make an entrance anywhere.

"Snow's a searchin' thing," Martha said. "Snow be's like sorrow. It searches people out."

Our periods of cold last for three days at the most, then mildness follows, and even during the bad times the days themselves are bright and sunny. My only concern through the winter is for my young grove. The old section of the grove has taken care of itself since before 1890 and can be trusted to survive if grove anywhere survives. When I came to the Creek, a pecan grove stood across the road from the farmhouse. It was lush and handsome in the summer. It was not profitable, many of the trees being seedlings, many bearing no crop at all. In winter, being deciduous, it was a nightmare; row on row of gaunt gray skeletons. It irked me in a tropical climate to stare day after day at bony, leafless trees, as though there were no escape in all the world from bleakness.

I cut down all but a few of the better trees and used them for fire wood. After them stood a vacant field, fertile and unbred. The lean times came to me, when my reserve money was gone and the grove for two years had not paid its way. I did not know whether the grove and I should be able to weather our difficulties. The field across the road grew high in weeds and was sad for lack of production. It depressed me to look out on those rich acres and know that I was not able to feed them. When things looked the most desperate, my Florida stories found a market. With my first available money I planted the field to orange trees. I chose Valencias, for they are our late orange, maturing in March and April, and I longed to have the bright globes of fruit to look at after the earlier citrus was harvested. But the field proved to be what we call a cold-pocket, lying a little lower than I had realized, and I have been obliged to nurse the young trees year after year. The late maturity for which I chose the Valencias has nearly been my undoing, for they must weather the most severe cold, long after the other oranges have been safely picked.

I invariably put off all the orange picking as long as possible. I have watched the fruit so long, from the first blossoms in February, through the summer growth of the hard green balls, through the sudden swelling on the fall rains, and, with cool nights, the bright color showing. The oranges hang like lighted lanterns through the winter. I use the excuse of waiting for a better market, but I delay in fact only because I cannot bear to see them cut and the globes of light extinguished. Several times I have lost the entire crop in a freeze through my dilatory fondness.

The picking is a colorful process. The Negro pickers arrive on a truck like a cage of birds, huddled together in silence. They hate the early morning cold and mist and cannot be sent up into the trees until the sun is high enough to dry the dew. They build fatwood fires near the barn and crouch close to them. Some have brought their breakfast with them and some are already hungry for their lunch. They open the paper sacks and the tin lard pails and eat, and my chickens have learned to go to them for the crumbs. They eye my dog suspiciously, for a lunch-stealing dog is a catastrophe. They stretch their legs to the fire, and, warmed and fed, the talk and laughter begin, as though a stream had emerged from its winter coat of ice.

The foreman says, "All right, boys. Let's see who's the best man with those ladders. Pick clean as you go. No stem ends. Pick up all dropped fruit from the ground before you leave your tree. Full boxes."

A flock of chattering monkeys is suddenly in the orange trees. There are jests and jibes, the ladders rattle against the boughs, and the sound of the metal orange clippers is like castanets. A powerful young buck begins a song. He is derided and there are calls for "Preacher." Preacher is a wizened little chimpanzee of a Negro, his hands swift as the claws of a hawk among the oranges. He is the best singer of them all. His notes roll out in an old spiritual, low and rich and slowly spaced. One by one the men join in. The orange clippers click in counterpoint against the swell.

My trees are old and tall, and thirty-foot ladders must be used to reach the tops. Only an experienced hand can manage one alone. He runs to his tree with it, balancing it like a juggling acrobat. The tall ladders rest precariously against the frail topmost branches, but the pickers mount quickly and surely. They are reminded of the need for climbing, the age-old set-backs, the burden of their race and their hope. Sooner or later "Jacob's Ladder" sounds mournfully from high in the tallest trees and a great organ seems to roll its notes across the grove. It is the favorite song of the orange pickers and they sing it with a sad fervor.

> Jacob's ladder's steep an' ta-all—
> *When Ah lay mah burden down!*
> If you boun' to climb,
> You boun' to fa-all—
> *When Ah lay mah burden down!*
> Burden down, burden down.
> *When Ah lay mah burden down!*

Sometimes Preacher gives them a sermon, and they chant the responses like a Mass. His strong old voice exhorts them from the top of an orange tree and they cut out in answer.

"Yes, Lord!"

"Preacher right!"

"Ain't it the truth!"

"Lord be praised!"

"Hallelujah!"

Sometimes they sing the songs of the jook-joints, the Saturday night songs, but I have an idea that the day I hear "Shake that thing" ribald from the orange trees, Preacher is not picking that day. He can pick with the best of them, but his strength fails him and he must take a day off now and then.

I acquired an undeserved reputation for ferocity among the pickers. The market price on citrus one season was high, my fruit was unpicked, and word of a freeze impending came in late on a Saturday night. I sent six miles away to Citra early Sunday morning, asking a picking crew to come at once, and offering double the usual pay. The crew came back on my truck, still a little tipsy from Saturday night. They set jovially to work. I sat on the back porch oiling and cleaning my bird gun that had had hard use all the week. Suddenly I became aware that a Sabbath calm lay over the grove, but from the tenant house came sounds of revelry. Black Kate was entertaining the pickers. I dashed toward her quarters, shouting to make myself heard above the gay din. A banjo tinkled, feet beat on the floor, and whoops of laughter lay over Kate's lone female voice.

I called out for the crew to get out and pick oranges or to get out altogether. The pickers did not emerge from the door one by one and sheepishly, as I expected, but amazed me by popping out of every window in the tenant house as though a cage of blackbirds had been liberated. They galloped to their ladders and several fearful souls made a dash for the woods. I looked down. All unconsciously I was toting my gun and flourishing it as I shouted. I had the report later that all records for picking were broken that day. I find that I am still known to the pickers as "the lady who jes' as soon shoot you as look at you."

Twenty boxes a day is a fair average for a picker, but the old hands at it do much better, and in a picking contest this winter, the champion picked more than forty boxes. Pickers are paid by the box and can make much more than at the low hoeing wages. There have been two seasons in which the pickers netted more per box than I did. The orange season is the cash-money season for most of us. The entire village works in season at the orange-packing plant, washing, grading, wrapping and packing the fruit. We pay up our accumulated summer bills and make down payments on cars and radios and set aside money for spring seeds and fertilizer.

Christmas is the height of the orange season. There will be steady shipments for two months more, but in December the citrus has come to full perfection and the oranges are burnished gold, bursting with juice. Christmas is celebrated quietly at the Creek. None of the holidays has the festival air of the north, probably because here we are likely to take a holiday at any moment the fancy strikes us, and live a more liberated life in general. We have no need of the emotional outlet of specified gala occasions. Thanksgiving is only a name. Banks and stores are closed on the Fourth of July, but farm work is likely to go on as usual. A very old black man came to his hoeing in my grove on the Fourth. In late morning he shuffled to the door.

"Please, Missy, I notice de postman don't come this mornin'. Could you tell me, please, be's this Thanksgivin'?"

I undertook to explain the significance of the Fourth of July. In a moment the old Negro and I were beyond our depth. He had heard of George Washington but believed him to be an insignificant contemporary of Lincoln. He had never heard of Europe nor England nor the Declaration of Independence. The United States had no connection with Florida. The only wars he had heard of were "the war jes' a while back" and "the Confed'rit war." "Freedom" meant only one thing, the emancipation. He himself had been born "the year after Freedom." I left him feeling that the Fourth of July most certainly had something to do with emancipation, and wondering vaguely if he should not go home and sit respectfully on his stoop.

There is not much giving of Christmas gifts at the Creek. We give presents to one another at any season according to what we may have in abundance. At Christmas I make up boxes for the Negroes, of frivolities along with needed sweaters and shirts and dresses, candy, fruit cake and pecans, more for my pleasure than theirs. They thank me for the unopened boxes, as a matter of courtesy, and never, with equal politeness, refer to them again, so that I never know whether I have truly pleased them or not. I take boxes of candy and toys to any families of children, migrant or permanent, at the Creek, and while again I never hear of them afterward, I feel more certain of having given pleasure. I have no gifts in return, but sometime during the year there will be a present of wild grapes or blackberries, or a pair of quail, or an especially large bass. One Christmas, Snow gave me a duck-hunt for my present.

He said, "I studied and studied what I could give you that you couldn't buy."

He repaired his outboard motor, borrowed small boats from his frog-hunting friends, located the best duck flights on Orange Lake, set up duck blinds, and on the chosen date, took out my party. A millionaire could not have given a finer present.

Most Christmas days at the Creek have been warm enough to serve Christmas dinner on the veranda. I feel a little cheated on such occasions, for although half the world is warm at Christmas, it is difficult not to think of snow and cold and reindeer and coziness in connection with the day. I have a roaring fire on the hearth no matter what the temperature, and growl a bit at the bright sunshine and the hibiscus blossoms. The holly and the mistletoe that are inseparable from the northern celebration grow in abundance at the Creek, and the poorest families gather a few sprays to hang over the mantel. This mistletoe is a parasite (which the Spanish moss is not) and sucks the substance from my pecan trees. It must be cut out once a year in any case and I have no qualms at breaking immense boughs at Christmas time for furbishing my house and for taking to town friends.

I can never snap off one of the brittle sprays without thinking of Lum. Lum and Ida were my one attempt to have white help on the place. There was a resentment in the village at my using Negro help. A good white man would have been more than acceptable, but it was difficult to explain why I did not want a white woman. It is impossible to make a servant of any southern white, and I rejoice in the fact. But it is irksome enough for me to do my writing on the veranda at the Creek, in the midst of the commotion of grove and stock, with constant interruptions to give advice about broken machinery and escaped cows. I have been obliged to train myself to accept the disturbances as part of the natural background. A white country woman would be much more of a guest than a maid. My aloofness would never be understood if I were reluctant to stop my writing to listen to her personal story and to sit and visit with her when her own work was done. But I was told in the village again and again that it was not fair to the unemployed there to pay my comparatively high wages to Negroes, when white men were hungry. They believed also that my work was all idleness and ease. I tried to tell them that the work was hard and steady, that there was little time for fishing and for long siestas and days and weeks of the complete inertia to which many of them were accustomed.

I think the village backed Lum for a show-down. He demanded the job. He understood, he said, that I needed a woman in the house as well as a man for the grove. He and Ida were the perfect pair and they were coming, whether or no. I protested feebly that Ida was not suitable for the making of a servant, the work too hard—and I needed a servant.

"She waits on me for nothin'," Lum said. "Ain't a reason in the world why she can't wait on you for pay."

They descended on me against my protests. It worked out in exactly opposite fashion from what I had expected. Ida was indeed perfect. She was quiet and very sweet and learned as fast as I could teach her. My habits of cooking were as strange to her as though I had been Chinese, but if by gravy I meant a greaseless, browned and floured affair, instead of a bowl of melted fat, that was the gravy I should have. She was spick and span and I have never lived more immaculately. And miracle of miracles, she had a complete understanding, without my ever having to make mention of it, that one engaged in what she called "composition" needed peace and quiet for the job. In our few weeks together we became deeply attached. We wept and embraced and vowed eternal friendship when Lum tore us apart and took her away.

The job was an appalling blow to Lum. To keep up with the routine winter work meant from eight to ten full hours a day. He could not believe it.

"They ain't no time for a feller jest to set and rest and think," he complained.

I said, "I tried to tell you that my job wasn't play."

The first real rift came over the mistletoe. Whatever man had worked on the place before had brought me at Christmas acceptable boughs without question. I told Lum that I was ready to decorate the farmhouse for Christmas and wanted at least a dozen boughs of mistletoe. He brought me a few small sprays totally without berries.

I said, "These won't do. I want larger ones, and I want the ones with berries. I know there are berries, because I can see them."

"Sure there's berries. But they're high up in the trees."

"Then go higher and get them."

"Listen," he said, "I ain't no damn mockin' bird."

He was indeed no mocking bird. I think he fancied himself as a bird of Paradise. I climbed into the pecan trees myself and broke my mistletoe, thinking to shame the man, but he was unimpressed. The final shock came to him when we fired the young grove on the first freeze. The cold came shortly after Christmas. I rounded up ten hands to help with the firing. Through the afternoon they hauled fat pine from the high stack kept for the purpose, and placed it in the grove, one fire to be laid in the center of each square of four trees. Two four-foot logs of the rich resinous pine are crossed in an X, a little kerosene poured on the center for a quick start when the temperature drops to 28 degrees.

Night came and the temperature dropped steadily. The fatal 28 came at midnight and I gave the word for the lighting of the fires. I put Lum in charge and Ida and I went at the business of preparing food and drink to warm the men through the long bitter night. The work is so cruel that it seems to me the least I can do is take care of the men properly. We had pounds of hamburg, baked beans, bread and butter, jams and relishes, sweet buns and hot coffee, and the men came in relays of two through the night to eat and warm themselves by the roaring wood range in the kitchen. I had also served quarts of gin and whiskey, and I suspect that this heating medium is the source of my success in getting hands for firing. I turned over the liquor to Lum with instructions to parcel it out through the night as the men needed it. Authority and liquor went to Lum's head. He drank the lion's share and toward morning, while the men shivered and went without, Lum was overcome and returned to his bed to sleep in drunken comfort. I was obliged to take over the direction of the firing myself, while Ida fried hamburgers and held the fort in the kitchen.

The cold was so severe, going down to 17 degrees, that we depleted the wood pile. Through the next day, bright and sunny but still icy cold, the helpers took turns at sleeping and hauling more fat wood. We were in for another night of it. Lum appeared groggily to milk the cows and feed the chickens, then went back to bed. When the second night came and all the crew was on hand for the work, Lum calmly announced that he would not be with us. All of us save Lum had worked without sleep for thirty-six hours.

"Hit's too much to ask a feller," he said, "that's used to his comfort."

I asked with what calm I could muster, "How can you expect to keep a job where you won't do what has to be done in an emergency?"

He answered with greater calm, which, unlike mine, was not affected, "Oh, I ain't studyin' on keepin' it. I'm quittin'."

It would have been only a Pyrrhic victory for me to insist that he was not quitting but was fired, so I let it pass.

I said, "Very well. But when you go back to the town, I want you to tell everybody that comes to the post-office that the job out here is a man's job."

"Don't you fret," he said amiably, "I'll tell 'em."

He must have painted a lurid picture of cold nights spent without sleep and days spent gathering mistletoe at dizzy heights. I have not since been asked for my work at the Creek.

There is a healthy challenge in danger and a certain spiritual sustenance comes from fighting it. For all the losses they have cost me, I would not choose to have lived without knowing the nights of firing on a freeze. Nowadays at the Creek we do not have to depend on the wailing of the train whistle for a warning, but have it over the radio. By two o'clock in the afternoon we know for fact that approximate temperatures of the coming night. Mature citrus fruits can stand 28 degrees for four hours, 26 degrees for two hours. The trees themselves, if in good condition, can stand temperatures much lower. The grove itself survived 15 degrees a few winters ago. Some affluent grove owners use smudge pots of the California type, but most of us put our faith in the old-fashioned fatwood fires. The smudge pots cost about seven dollars each, even in large quantities, require from one to two dollars' worth of crude oil a night, and rust to pieces during the two and three year periods in which the cold is not menacing. I am convinced as well that the smudge pots raise the grove temperature by only two or three degrees, while our pine blazes have raised them as much as six degrees. The smudge pots lay a thick smoke, but good fat pine properly handled lays enough of a protective blanket of smoke over the trees against the settling cold.

If we have had warning enough, we place the wood in the afternoon and are ready to touch the pine torches to it at the crucial moment. The weather at such times is always as clear as a bell. A damaging freeze is impossible under cloudy or windy skies. The sun sets magnificently, fiery red, laying lingering fingers across the shining orange trees as though reluctant to withdraw its mercy. The air is so still that voices from far away sound very close at hand, and the champing of the cows on their hay in the lot is audible. It is too cold for the birds to sing an evensong and they go to bed early and uneasily. The first stars are visible while the west is still rosy. They are silver against aquamarine. There is never at any moment complete darkness. The stars take over the sun's work, but with a dispassionate aloof coldness, like a frigid and beautiful stepmother taking over a nursery where once walked warm and true maternity. The earth itself stands like a child, awaiting the injustice and the blow. We have bared our bosoms to the sun, and trusted it, and it has gone and left us to the treachery of the stars.

Yet, as there is mental depression on a low barometer, there is an exhilaration on this high pressure that throws its icy mantle around us. We hurry about in inadequate clothing and are too engaged with fighting to feel the cold. We bring out newspapers and old quilts and sheets and drape them over our favorite shrubs. The poinsettias, as trusting as we, have reached their full brilliant bloom by midwinter and stand with proud heads to be struck down. There will be no saving them, even under the sheets, if the night be bad. The avocados are too tall and brittle to be weighted with covering. The hardy hybrid roses can shift for themselves. The north is in their blood and their sap exults secretly at the touch of cold. We shall have finer roses than ever after the freeze. The plumbago can be saved and perhaps the roots at least of the flame vine. The guavas will survive, and the pomegranate, and the Amaryllis and spider lilies. I pull Spanish moss from the pecan trees to cover the tender plants in the garden. No matter what other help I may have, from wherever she may be Martha comes to help me with this.

"I jes' so feered, Sugar," she says, "evvybody but me be so busy they forget the garden."

We cap each plant with a mound of the soft moss. It will keep safe and warm for as long as needed the delicate gerberas and snapdragons and all the other flowers in bud for the first blossoming. Martha likes to help too with the feeding of the firing crew through the night.

"The mens tells me they looks forward to my coffee," she says. "I makes it double strong and I doesn't stint 'em with the milk and sugar. A night like this be's no time to be scarce with the rations."

Sometimes we wait through most of the night for the temperature to drop low enough to light the fires. Midnight may tell the story. If the temperature has hovered around 32 until that time, then suddenly begins to dip down, slowly but inexorably, we are ready, and watch the thermometer as though the life of a dying man were at stake. The poorest helper, recruited from his clearing in the flatwoods, with not a single orange tree of his own, knows that this is a matter of life and death for something rich and fabulous and beautiful that he longs for as his own, but will fight to save for a more fortunate other. If we have 28 degrees just before daylight and it has not previously dropped to this mark, we are inclined to risk it and to disband, saving the precious fat pine for a worse night. Once I lost the crop through this confidence in the passing by of the enemy. The crew went home and I went to bed and between five and eight in the morning the temperature dropped to 22 degrees and the fruit was lost. If the fatal degree comes, it is usually about two o'clock in the morning. Of late years Snow, like Martha, drops whatever other work he may be doing, to supervise. He comes to me with the word.

"Two o'clock and it's 28. Shall we turn the boys loose, or you want to wait?"

"Turn them loose."

The pine splinter torches flicker in the night. The men have been silent. Now they break into a chattering, like night birds roused from the day's sleeping. Their voices are sharp across the grove. The first fire blazes. There is rivalry to see who will first light his assigned fires and have them burning and smoking to cover his territory with the protective heat and smudge. There has been a great tension, and now, with the grove a pattern of blaze, it cracks. We are like soldiers, taut for the first attack, and sighing deep with relief to have taken over the first front with no casualties. It is important to have all the fires going before the insidious cold has dropped again too sharply.

I have seen no more beautiful thing in my life than my orange grove by night, lighted by the fatwood fires. It is doubly beautiful for the danger and the struggle, like a beloved friend for whose life one battles, drinking in the well known features that may be taken away forever. The fires make a geometric pattern, spaced as regularly as the squares of trees. The pine burns with a bright orange flame and the effect is of countless bivouac fires across a low-wooded plain. The sky is sapphire blue, spangled with stars. The smoke lifts from the fires gray white, melting into gray-blue, drifting like the veils of a dancer under the open skies. Each orange tree is outlined with light. The green leaves shine like jade. The round golden oranges are each lit with a secret inner candle. My heart bursts with the loveliness of the grove and of the night. If only, I think, I could watch such beauty unencumbered by my fears. Then I know that a part of the beauty is the fight to keep it, and that all good things do not come too easily and must perpetually be fought for. Our test is in our recognition of our love and our willingness to do battle for it.

Sometimes the battle is hopeless. We burn all the pine, the great pile accumulated through the summer and enough, I had hoped, for four or five firings. One time it was all gone, and the men and I exhausted, by five o'clock in the morning, and the mercury was still falling. We could only stand and watch the embers die down and the blue smoke fade to tattered wisps, see day come in, gay and gaudy, and the temperature drop and drop, until the sun that had failed us was high in the heavens, shining over a tropical world solid with alien ice.

These mornings after a freeze are unbearably fine. The redbirds take the sun at face value and sing as though they did not know that the very corn in their guest basket were in danger of never being replenished, for their host's sudden catastrophe and poverty. The poinsettias flaunt their redness in the warmth, unaware that they are frozen mausoleums of blossoms, and are doomed within an hour to droop and shrivel on the stalks. The orange leaves are rigid, for they too are frozen, and before the day is done they will curl, then later turn yellow and wither and fall untimely from the trees. Icicles drip from the water tower and there will be no water in the pipes before midday. The oranges themselves are balls of ice, and we make a game of eating them while they are still sweet and frozen, and we offer one another a dish of "orange sherbet." We are sick at heart. But we are relaxed, too, and resigned. We have fought forces stronger than we, and done our best, and lost, and now we may sleep.

There have been many winter battles at the Creek. Most of our deaths come then, and our serious illnesses, as though the lethargy of summer had kept us alive, but with the coming of the enemy cold, we cannot resist any longer.

I remember the winter when Snow and I together saw old Joe to his death. We live close to our animals at the Creek. When I was poor, the death of a cow or mule, even of a brood-hen, came hard, not only for the loss, but because we made our living together. When my mule, old Joe, died in the lean days, I lost a co-laborer.

He was an odd mule—not that all mules are not a little peculiar. The unnatural mating of mare and donkey gives the offspring a touch of the fey. Joe had a quizzical look in his eyes, as though he were in on a joke. Mules in general live in a sterile world of their own, apparently content to pull the plow or harrow, to feed leisurely, and as emotional release to roll gawkily on their backs, snorting at the good scratching of the sand or the cooling touch of the pasture grass. Old Joe had fits of loneliness and in his moods of sociability sought out any company. A human being was preferred, but he had a weakness for cows. I do not know how long it took him to attract the attention of the Glisson milch cows that fed up and down the road, but he made at last fast friends with a pair of young Jerseys. The friendship was a false one, but like all illusions, was as satisfying to Joe as a reality. The contact consisted of his sticking his long nose over the fence of pen or pasture, and of the two cows licking it in what he took for affection. He stood with closed eyes and relaxed ears, drinking in the attention that must last him so long a time. He could not know that the delicious flavor of his salt brick was on his nose. His friends were hypocrites.

When he fell ill, it seemed at first that his eccentricities had for the moment got the better of him. We noticed that he walked in circles. Perhaps his loneliness had touched his queer mule's brain. Then as he paced the lot, he crashed into the side of the barn. It was no ordinary blindness. It was a sightless frenzy, born of pain. The neighbors came and stared and shook their heads and went away. The blind staggers, they agreed. The veterinarian identified the trouble as forage poisoning. It seemed unfair that an old mule could not graze along the marsh edge without meeting so strange an enemy. The poison is like the rust on wheat or corn and grows sometimes on the marsh grass in puffy black balls that give no warning to a creature. Its substance is ergot, killer of human unborn. Purges may be tried but there is seldom recovery.

Old Joe submitted to the drenching, his head tied high to an orange bough. Then the circular walking continued, and the days passed and the nights, and he would not eat nor drink, or could not, and only walked around and around and around like something charmed. We tethered him in the maiden cane until he wore the rope through. He ran so wildly from us, crashing through the orange grove when we pursued him, hurting himself so painfully, that it seemed best to let him go his way. A second drenching had only weakened him and there was nothing more to do, for witch poisons are too much to cope with. The evening came when we knew he would not know another, and somehow Snow and I wanted to keep him company, knowing his spells of loneliness.

I remember the chilly loveliness of the night. The moon was full in December and now and then the ripe pecans dropped sharply in the stillness. We built a bonfire outside the fence to warm us. Snow had not gone home for supper to his shack of the moment and his friend Glenwood came to see about him. Glenwood squatted beside us. It seemed entirely right and natural to him that we should be seeing old Joe out. The mule walked his ceaseless circle through the grove. He sensed our presence and now and then plunged toward us as though for reassurance. Then Snow rose from his heels by the fire and put out his hand to keep him from crashing into the fence and spoke to him.

"Easy, Joe. Easy."

The mule stood a moment, wavering, then made his round again, with death firm at the bridle.

I said, "I hate to keep you up late this way, Snow."

"That's plumb all right. He's likely to have a wild fit at the end and hurt hisself. I reckon the dyin' itself won't hurt. I'd hate to leave him alone. He's been mighty faithful."

Glenwood said, "Shore has been faithful."

Toward midnight I brought the boys ham and bread and coffee, and the occasion in the bright cold moonlight was not at all a sad one. All creatures must die and old Joe had had a good life, as life goes for a mule, and not too hard a one, and now he had companionship at the end. He came to the fence and whinnied and I touched his nose. Then he broke into a gallop and when he was done with that fine burst of living, he was done with it for good.

"We done all we could," Snow said, and walked with Glenwood home in the brightness.

In the early spring there was a circle marked in the maiden cane where he had walked on his tether. There was a different kind of grass that grew there. Even a mule, I thought, might leave his mark a moment on the earth.

It was in a winter that Old Boss came very close to losing Old Miss, and because of it, I knew him suddenly, not as the patriarch of the Creek, venerable and invulnerable, of whom all of us, black and white, stood in awe, but vulnerable, as we, to those intimate, those personal things that make up life for human beings. Old Miss was very ill, Martha told me and I went down to Old Boss' house to inquire of her. He came to the door in answer to my question. His face wore its usual mask, kindly and detached.

"She's not doing well," he said. "I'm afraid—I'll lose her."

I put out my hand to touch him. The next moment he had reached out his arms to me, and Old Boss was crying on my shoulder. I held his small body close to me and was astonished by its frailty. He was not now the giver of laws, but a lonely little old man weeping for his beloved. I knew in that instant how fragile a defense are pride and authority against the common enemies.

I thought, "How can any of us be cruel to one another? How are wars possible, and hate, when we must all face such things? Death is the enemy, and life itself is inimical, for all its bounty. We must hold one another close against the cosmic perils."

For all our battles, winter at the Creek is the cozy time, when fat pine fires crackle on all the hearths. I take my dog for a walk up the road at sunset and the wind blows in our faces. I turn back to walk westward home as the red sun drops behind Orange Lake. The dusk comes quickly and we turn in at the gate and shut the house door behind us and drop down in front of the hearth fire in the living room. A fresh log of fatwood thrown on the slow-burning bed of oak coals catches and blazes and roars up the big chimney. The flames light the old white-walled room so that there is no need even of candles, though one or two over the bookshelves are always pleasant, for candlelight on books is one of the lovely things of this world. The ruby-red velvet sleepy hollow chair glows in the firelight. The dog groans for comfort and turns his belly to the heat and stretches out his paws in the ultimate luxury. Only a hunting dog or a cat can share man's love of the open fire, and if I had a whole kennel full of dogs, on winter nights I should let them all come in to enjoy mine with me.

Sometimes the dog and I go together for our supper to the old-fashioned kitchen where the wood range still glows and is warm and the fire box blinks a red eye in the dusk. Because we like the clean bare snugness of the room, and the bland heat of the range, we often sit beside it when we have finished our bread and Dora's rich milk, and converse together, wordlessly. We drowse and nod and try to decide whether it would be more pleasant to go back to the living-room fire or to go to bed. On the bitter nights the dog is allowed to sleep inside by the fire, and after his day's hunting he knows no greater delight or security.

In the morning the red-birds sing in the crisp air and some one, perhaps Martha, comes to my bedroom and lights a blazing fire on the hearth for me, and when the room is warm I have my tray of coffee, with cream as yellow as buttercups and so thick it must be spooned into the cup, and I lie and watch the aromatic wood burning and think, "What have I done to deserve such munificence?"

22. Hyacinth drift

*O*nce I lost touch with the Creek. I had had hardships that seemed to me more than one could bear alone. I loved the Creek, I loved the grove, I loved the shabby farmhouse. Suddenly they were nothing. The difficulties were greater than the compensations. I talked morosely with my friend Dessie. I do not think she understood my torment, for she is simple and direct and completely adjusted to all living. She knew only that a friend was in trouble.

She said, "We'll take one of those river trips we've talked about. We'll take that eighteen-foot boat of yours with a couple of outboard motors and put in at the head of the St. John's River. We'll go down the river for several hundred miles."

I agreed, for the Creek was torture.

Men protested.

"Two women alone? The river runs through some of the wildest country in Florida. You'll be lost in the false channels. No one ever goes as far as the head of the river." Then, passionately, betraying themselves, "It will be splendid. What if you do get lost? Don't let any one talk you out of it."

The river was a blue smear through the marsh. The marsh was tawny. It sprawled to the four points of the compass; flat; interminable; meaningless.

I thought, "This is fantastic. I am about to deliver myself over to a nightmare."

But life was a nightmare. The river was at least of my own choosing.

The St. John's River flows from south to north and empties into the Atlantic near the Florida-Georgia line. Its great mouth is salt and tidal, and ocean-going vessels steam into it as far as Jacksonville. It rises in a chain of small lakes near the Florida east coast, south of Melbourne. The lakes are linked together by stretches of marsh through which, in times of high water, the indecisive course of the young river is discernible. Two years of drought had shrunken the stream and dried the marshes. The southernmost sources were overgrown with marsh grass. Water hyacinths had filled the channels. The navigable head of the St. John's proved to be near Fort Christmas, where the highway crosses miles of wet prairie and cypress swamp between Orlando and Indian River City.

There is a long high fill across the marsh, with a bridge over the slight blue twisting that is the river. We drove car and trailer down an embankment and unloaded the small boat in the backwaters. The bank was of black muck, smelling of decay. It sucked at our feet as we loaded our supplies. We took our places in the boat and drifted slowly into mid-channel.

Water hyacinths began to pass us, moving with a faint anxiety in their lifted leaves. The river was no more than a path through high grass. We swung under the bridge and the boy at the wheel of the car lifted his hand in parting and shot away. Something alive and potent gripped the flat bottom of the boat. The hyacinths moved more rapidly. The river widened to a few yards and rounded a bend, suddenly decisive. Dess started the outboard motor. I hunched myself together amidships and spread the U. S. Coast and Geodetic Survey river chart on my knees and clicked open my compass. I noticed disconsolately, "Lights, Beacons, Buoys and Dangers Corrected for Information Received to Date of Issue." There would be neither lights, beacons nor buoys for at least a hundred miles. Bridge and highway disappeared, and there was no longer any world but this incredible marsh, this unbelievable amount of sky.

Half a mile beyond the bridge a fisherman's shack leaned over the river. For sociability, we turned in by the low dock. The fisherman and his wife squatted on their haunches and gave us vague directions. We pointed to Bear Island on our chart.

He said, "You won't never see Bear Island. Where they got a channel marked on your map it's plumb full o' hyacinths. Down the river a ways you'll see a big ol' sugar-berry tree stickin' up in the marsh. That's your mark. You keep to the left. The next mark you'll get is a good ways down the river. You go left by a pertickler tall piece o' grass."

The woman said, "You just got to keep tryin' for the main channel. You'll get so you can tell."

The man said, "I ain't never been as far as you-all aim to go. From what I hear, if you oncet get through Puzzle Lake, you got right clare river."

The woman said, "You'll some kind of enjoy yourselves. The river life's the finest kind of life. You couldn't get you no better life than the river."

We pushed away from the dock.

The man said, "I'd be mighty well obliged if you'd send me a postcard when you get where you're goin'. That-a-way I won't have to keep on worryin' about you."

Dess cranked the motor and they waved after us. Dess began to whistle, shrilly and tunelessly. She is an astonishing young woman. She was born and raised in rural Florida and guns and campfires and fishing-rods and creeks are corpuscular in her blood. She lives a sophisticate's life among worldly people. At the slightest excuse she steps out of civilization, naked and relieved, as I should step out of a soiled chemise. She is ten years my junior, but she calls me, with much tenderness, pitying my incapabilities, "Young un."

"Young un," she called, "it's mighty fine to be travelling."

I was prepared for marsh. It was startling to discover that there was in sight literally nothing else. Far to the west, almost out of sight to the east, in a dark line like cloud banks was the distant swamp that edged this fluid prairie. We may have taken the wrong channel for a mile or so, for we never saw the sugar-berry tree; nothing but river grass, brittle and gold, interspersed, where the ground was highest, with butter-yellow flowers like tansy. By standing up in the boat I could see the rest of the universe. And the universe was yellow marsh, with a pitiless blue infinity over it, and we were lost at the bottom.

At five o'clock in the afternoon the river dissolved without warning into a two-mile spread of flat confusion. A mile of open water lay ahead of us, neither lake nor river nor slough. We advanced into the center. When we looked over our shoulders, the marsh had closed in over the channel by which we had come. We were in a labyrinth. The stretch of open water was merely the fluid heart of a maze. Channels extended out of it in a hundred directions—some shallow, obviously no outlets; others as broad as the stream we had left behind us, and tempting. We tried four. Each widened in a deceptive sweep. A circling of the shore-line showed there was no

channel. Each time we returned to the one spot we could again identify—a point of marsh thrust into the water like a swimming moccasin.

Dess said, "That map and compass don't amount to much."

That was my fault. I was totally unable to follow the chart. I
found later, too late for comfort, that my stupidity was not entirely to
blame, for, after the long drought, half the channels charted no
longer existed. The sun had become a prodigious red disc dropping
into a distant slough. Blue herons flew over us to their night's quarters. Somewhere the river must continue neatly out of this desola-
tion. We came back once more to the point of land. It was a foot or
two out of water and a few square yards of the black muck were comparatively dry. We beached the rowboat and made camp.

There was no dry wood. We carried a bag of fat pine splinters
but it occurred to me desperately that I would save them. I laid out a
cold supper while Dess set up our two camp cots side by side on the
open ground. As the sun slid under the marsh to the west, the full
moon surged out of it to the east. The marsh was silver and the water was steel, with ridges of rippled ebony where ducks swam in the
twilight. Mosquitoes sifted against us like a drift of needles. We were
exhausted. We propped our mosquito bar over the cots on crossed
oars, for there was no bush, no tree from which to hang it.

We did not undress, but climbed under the blankets. Three
people had had a hand in loading our cots and the wooden endpieces were missing. The canvas lay limp instead of taut, and our feet
hung over one end and our heads over the other, so that we were dis-
posed like corpses on inadequate stretchers. The crossed oars slid
slowly in the muck, the mosquito bar fluttered down and mosquitoes
were about us in a swarm. Dess reached under her cot for her light
rifle, propped it between us, and balanced the mosquito bar accurately on the end of its barrel.

"You can get more good out of a .22 rifle than any other kind of gun," she informed me earnestly.

I lay on my back in a torment of weariness, but there was no rest. I had never lain in so naked a place, bared so flatly to the sky. The moon swung high over us and there was no sleeping for the brightness. Toward morning dewdrops collected over the netting as though the moonlight had crystallized. I fell asleep under a diamond curtain and wakened with warm full sunlight on my face. Cranes and herons were wading the shore near me and Dess was in the rowboat a few hundred yards away, casting for bass.

Marsh and water glittered iridescent in the sun. The tropical March air was fresh and wind-washed. I was suddenly excited. I made campfire with fatwood splinters and cooked bacon and toast and coffee. Their fragrance eddied across the water and I saw Dess lift her nose and put down her rod and reel. She too was excited.

"Young un," she called, "where's the channel?"

I pointed to the northeast and she nodded vehemently. It had come to both of us like a revelation that the water hyacinths were drifting faintly faster in that direction. From that instant we were never very long lost. Forever after, where the river sprawled in confusion, we might shut off the motor and study the floating hyacinths until we caught, in one direction, a swifter pulsing, as though we put our hands close and closer to the river's heart. It was very simple. Like all simple facts, it was necessary to discover it for oneself.

We had, in a moment, the feel of the river; a wisdom for its vagaries. When the current took us away that morning, we gave ourselves over to it. There was a tremendous exhilaration, an abandoning of fear. The new channel was the correct one, as we knew it should be. The river integrated itself again. The flat golden banks closed in on both sides of us, securing a snug safety. The strangeness of flowing water was gone, for it was all there was of living.

In midmorning, solid land made its way here and there toward us, and then in time withdrew. For a mile we had a low rolling hill for company, with traces of ancient habitation at its peak: a few yards of rotting fence, a crepe myrtle, an orange tree.

We passed a lone fisherman hauling his seine. His legs were planted cranelike in the water. His long arms looped up folds of the gray net with the rhythm of a man swinging a sickle. We told him our origin and our destination. Because we were now a part of the river he offered us a fish. His catch was meager and we refused it. We passed cattle, wild on the marsh. They loomed startlingly above us, their splotched black and brown and red and white luminous against the blue sky, like cattle in Bonheur pictures hung high above the eye-level.

The river dissolved into shallow pools and was interspersed with small islands, palm-crowded and lonely. It was good to see trees, lifting the eyes from so many miles of flatness. The pools gathered themselves together and there was under us again a river, confined between obvious banks. Sometimes the low-lying land was dry for a great distance, specked with soap-berry bushes, and the wild cattle cropped a short grass that grew there.

We had Puzzle Lake and then Lake Harney, we knew, somewhere ahead of us. We came out from a canal-like stretch of river into a body of open water. Dess and I stiffened. She shut off the motor.

Far away across the marsh there was a long white rolling as though all the sheep in the world were being driven through prehistoric dust clouds. The mad thought came to me that we had embarked on the wrong river and had suddenly reached the ocean, that the vast billowing in the distance was surf. But something about the thing was familiar. That distant line was a fill, a forty-foot sand embankment across the marsh between the St. John's River and the east coast town of Mimms, and I had driven its one-rut grade two weeks before. The marsh had been even more desolate from the height of that untravelled, unfinished roadway. The fill ended, I remembered, in a forty-foot drop to a decrepit ferry that crossed the river. The billowing we now saw was loose white sand moving along the embankment ahead of a high wind. I ran my finger along the chart. There was no ferry mapped for the far side of Puzzle Lake. A ferry was indicated, however, on the far side of Lake Harney.

I said, "Dess, we've come through Puzzle Lake and didn't know it. We've reached Lake Harney."

She did not question my surety. She spun the motor.

"All right, young un. Which way across?"

I compared the chart and compass. I pointed. She headed the boat as I directed. I split nautical points to keep our position exactly. I took her across water so shoal we had to pole through it; under overhanging banks and through dense stiff sedge, when often a plainly better channel swung a few feet away in another direction. The extreme low water, I called, had evidently dried Lake Harney to this confused alternating of open lake and maze. Dess whistled dubiously but asked no questions. We struck deep water at last and were at the ferry I had indeed remembered. The old ferryman peered from his hut and came down to meet us, shading his eyes. He seemed to find us very strange indeed. Where had we come from?

"We put in yesterday at Fort Christmas," I answered him, "and I'm glad to say we've just finished navigating Lake Harney."

He stared in earnest.

"Lady," he said, "you haven't even reached Lake Harney. You've just come through Puzzle Lake.

The ferry here simply was not charted, and the episode proves anything one may wish it to prove. I felt contentedly that it proved a harmony with the river so complete that not even the mistaking of whole lakes could lose us. Others of more childish faith were sure it proved the goodness of God in looking after imbeciles. I know only that we were congratulated by fishermen the entire length of the river on navigating Puzzle Lake successfully.

"I brought our boat through Puzzle Lake," I told them with simple dignity, "by the sternest use of chart and compass."

And it was only in Dess' more evil moments that she added, "—in the firm belief that she was crossing Lake Harney."

Lake Harney itself was four miles long, unmistakably broad and open. We crossed in it late afternoon with the westerly sun on our cheeks and a pleasant March wind ruffling the blue water. Passing out of the lake we bought roe shad, fresh and glistening from the seine. The current quickened. The hyacinths plunged forward. The character of the river changed the instant the lake was left behind. It was deep and swift, the color of fine clear coffee that is poured with the sun against it. It was mature. All its young torture was forgotten, and its wanderings in the tawny marsh. The banks had changed. They were high. Tall palms crowded great live oaks and small trees grew humbly in their shadow. Toward sunset we swung under the western bank at one of those spots a traveller recognizes instinctively as, for the moment, home.

If I could have, to hold forever, one brief place and time of beauty, I think I might choose the night on that high lonely bank above the St. John's River. We found there a deserted cabin, gray and smooth as only cypress weathers. There was no door for its doorway, no panes or shutters for its windows, but the roof was whole, with lichens thick across the shingles. Dess built me a fire of red cedar. She sat on the sagging steps and whittled endpieces for our cots, and I broiled shad and shad roe over fragrant coals, and French-fried potatoes, and found I had the ingredients for Tartar sauce.

Dess nailed a board between low rafters in the cabin from which to hang the mosquito bar over our cots, and said, "Young un, Christopher Columbus had nothing on us. He had a whole ocean to fool around in, and a what-do-you-call-it:—a continent, to come out in. Turn that boy loose in the St. John's marsh, and he'd have been lost as a hound puppy."

We had hot baths out of a bucket that night, and sat on the cabin steps in pajamas while the fire died down. Suddenly the soft night turned silver. The moon was rising. We lay on our cots a long time wakeful because of beauty. The moon shone through the doorway and windows and the light was patterned with the shadows of Spanish moss waving from the live oaks. There was a deserted grove somewhere behind the cabin, and the incredible sweetness of orange bloom drifted across us.

A mocking-bird sang from a palm tree at sunrise. We found by daylight that the cabin sat among guava trees higher than the roof. The yard was pink and white with periwinkles. Dess shot a wild duck on the wing with the .22 and I roasted it in the Dutch oven for breakfast. We lay all morning on the bank in the strong sunlight, watching the mullet jumping in the river. At noon we went reluctantly to the water's edge to load the boat and move on. The boat was half filled with water and was resting with an air of permanence on the river bottom.

My first thoughts was of pure delight that it was no longer necessary to leave this place. But Dess was already stepping out of her sailor trousers. I too removed superfluous clothing. We bailed the boat and found two streams of water gushing in steadily under bow and stern seats. We managed to drag the boat on shore and turn it upside down. We found that the caulking had worked loose out of two seams. Dess donated a shirt, and for two hours with pocket knives we stuffed strips of cloth into treacherous cracks. When we put the boat in the river again, the caulking held.

I begged to stay another night, but Dess was restless. We pushed on for the few hours left of daylight. The shore line narrowed to thin strips of sand with tall twisted palms along them. The clear brown river was glassy in the windless evening. The palms were mirrored along both banks, so that when white ibises flew over in a rosy sunset, the river might have been the Nile.

We camped that night in comparative comfort under an upturned tree root. The spot was not tempting from the water, but once we were snugged down, it proved cavelike and cozy. A moccasin slithered from under my feet at the edge of camp and went harmlessly about his business. Dess cut down a young palmetto and we had swamp cabbage for dinner. I cooked it with a piece of white bacon and baked corn sticks in the Dutch oven to go with it.

In the morning we watched the hyacinth drift closely to be sure of taking the cut to Prairie Landing instead of wandering into Lake Jessup. A highway crossed the river here and folk waved down to us. In the cut a woman was running a catfish line. She was gaunt and sun-tanned, ragged and dirty. She pulled in the line, hand over hand, with a quick, desperate accuracy. She lifted a shaggy head when we called "Howdy" and said "Hey," and bent again to her line with a terrifying absorption. Something about her shamed all soft, clean women.

We cut across the south end of Lake Monroe and found that it was Sunday in the city of Sanford. We had reached the outpost of large-vessel traffic on the St. John's, and we put-putted under the bow of an incoming freight steamer. We had meant to bathe and put on clean shirts and slacks that morning, but there had been no landing place among the marshes. Dess strapped around her waist the leather belt that held her bowie knife at one hip and her revolver at the other, and felt better prepared for Sanford than if we had been clean. She landed us neatly at the city dock, in the lee of an immaculate pleasure yacht from Long Island Sound. The owner, trim in double-breasted blue, came to the rail and looked down at us. We had also intended to do a better job of stowing. The bow end of our boat was piled untidily with our supplies, our folded cots, our extra outboard motor and our gasoline tins. Dess stood up in the stern and stretched and shifted her armored belt.

She called up to the yacht owner, "Safe to come into this town?"

"That depends on what you are coming for," he said, and smiled.

"Not a thing but gasoline. Where's the nearest place a fellow can fuel up?"

"All the filling stations near the docks are closed this morning. But I'm having my yacht refuelled, and a station is opening for me. How much do you need?"

Dess checked our tins with her eye.

"Five gallons is about right."

He smiled again.

"I'm sending my car to the station. If you will bring your tins up, I'll be happy to have my man take you along and bring you back."

"Thanks, fellow," Dess said. "You're a white man."

There was a sound inside the yacht. There simmered up the companionway a woman, magnificent in pink spectator sports costume. The crew jumped almost to attention and escorted her down the yacht's gangplank.

The woman snapped over her shoulders, "I must have the car at once. I cannot be late to church for this nonsense."

Our white man turned rosy and made a comradely gesture to us.

He leaned over and whispered, "The car will be back in just a moment. If you don't mind waiting—. Please wait."

"O.K., fellow," Dess said.

The pink spectator sports swept into a limousine. In a few minutes the car had returned. We were driven in style to a filling station and our tins filled with gasoline. We bought the New York Sunday papers. The yacht crew brought the tins down to us and helped us re-stow our duffle. Dess outlined our trip briefly to the owner. She cranked up and we were off again.

"Good luck!" called the yacht owner. "The very best of good luck!"

He waved after us as far as we could see him, as though reluctant to break a mystic thread. His face was wistful.

"The poor b—," Dess said pityingly and indignantly. "I'll bet he'd give his silk shirt to go down the river with us instead of with Pink Petticoats."

We used the gasoline and forgot to read the papers.

Out of Lake Monroe we began to see fishermen pulling seines every few miles along the river. Here and there was a camp. Once a palmetto thatching made a tip-tilted shelter and a startlingly pretty girl in overalls looked out with a placid face. We passed an old fisherman and a little girl in a boat. The child was rowing. We encountered a tall lumber steamer in mid-stream. The book of Pilot Rules on my lap provided that the boat in our position should swing to the starboard, passing to port, and should give two short distinct blasts on the boat's whistle to signify its intention. Two lusty blasts on my dog whistle brought no answering blow from the steamer, but the cook, paring potatoes in the open stern, waved to us as we angled to cross their wake.

We had "right clare river" now, the river life was indeed the finest of lives, and there was no hurry left in the world. We put up a golden-brown deep creek and fished all afternoon. A white egret fished companionably with us a few yards away, and water turkeys flapped their wings lazily from high cypresses. A water moccasin arched his six feet of magnificent mottled hide between a spider lily and a swamp laurel. The laurel was in full bloom and the sunny creek was a wedge of fragrance. We found a white sand bar and had a swim in water clear as amber.

Camp that night was on a pine bluff, very high and dry and decent after the tree root and the moccasin. Storm threatened for the first time and we stretched a tarpaulin between slash pines to make a shelter. We were on the east bank. The moon and sun rose behind us. In the morning we found that small animals had dug holes all about us while we slept.

We pushed the motor that day. The river was deep and narrow. The banks were dense swamp, black with undergrowth. A landing would have been, for the most, impossible. We ate a cold lunch as we travelled. Beyond Deland Landing we called at a houseboat tethered to the bank. Its owner had been captain of the old Clyde River Line, and he received our request for advice on crossing Lake George with the old-school graciousness of large craft meeting small. He took my compass well forward of the houseboat, away from its metal stanchions, to chart our course across the fourteen-mile lake the more precisely. I made the mental note that perhaps I had better move the cast iron Dutch oven from under my seat. He gave us a set of distance cards and a choice of courses. The more sporting course was the main channel used by large steamers. In a boat as small as ours we should be out of sight of land for nearly an hour. The west channel never entirely lost the land, but if it came on to blow, we would do best by taking neither, and hugging the west shore. He bowed us courteously on our way.

We planned to camp as close as possible that night to the Volusia bar. We wanted to cross Lake George in the early morning before the wind rose. Beyond the village of Astor the scrub reared high against the west. Cypress swamp bordered the river. There was scarcely a patch of ground large enough to step out on. We pushed on to a cluster of fishing huts at the junction of lake and river. Hyacinths moved here in vast green flexible sheets. The huts were on stakes over the river and were not inviting.

Only one stood on enough ground to offer camping facilities. We poled through the hyacinths and called from the rickety small dock. A sullen-faced woman spoke curtly from the doorway. We could see the interior of the shack. There were pallets on the floor; a table; a chair or two. A dirty child peered from her skirts. We were not wanted here, it was plain, but she was a squatter, with no right to refuse us. Dess and I debated the matter in low voices. The woman, the place, seemed to me preferable to the dark swamp to which we must return. But the wind was freshening from the west. Even now, hyacinths were piling in behind us.

Dess said, "I'd rather sleep with a moccasin over each shoulder than get caught in a hyacinth block."

We swung about to turn back up the river. As we pushed away, the child dropped to the doorsill and began to pat his hands together. He chanted with shrill delight, "They're going away! They're going away!" I wondered what life had done to this woman and this child, that, among a friendly fisher-folk, they should know such fear and hate of strangers.

When the sun dropped behind the scrub, swamp and river were in darkness. At twilight we had retraced several miles. When we landed at the only promising opening, we found a comfortable square of high ground. As we were making camp three fishermen hailed us excitedly. Were we the women who had put in at Fort Christmas nearly a week before? If so, they must know. Word had been sent down river from other fishermen to watch for us and to report our safety. The three were camped across the river from us.

They had a trail cut into the swamp to a spot of sound dry earth. Their campfire flickered sociably all night.

The course for the main channel was, simply, north by east. But there was fog at daylight, and when the fog lifted a little the wind came freshly from its week-long westerly quarter. Boats twice our size had been in trouble on Lake George. Its squalls were notably dangerous. It seemed needlessly heroic to deny ourselves the comfort of the sight of land. We had no intention of hugging the safe shore, so we compromised on the west channel. We left the great channel markers behind and a gust of wind twisted our stern. There was a half hour when the haze threatened to obscure all visible shore lines. Then Drayton's Island lifted ahead.

Midway, the wind was blowing the whitecaps off the waves, but it was helpfully behind us. With both arms braced against the steering handle of the motor, Dess kept the boat headed when the water that rolled like surf lifted our stern. The propeller churned high out of the water. When it dropped again the boat lunged and turned.

I called, "She's slueing badly!"

Dess shouted, "Young un, if you had this wind under your stern, you'd slue, too!"

The distant shore seemed stationary. We passed the north point of Drayton's Island, where the main channel joined the west, with the lake boiling after us. At the first sheltered dock we stopped to rest and an old Negro gave us fresh drinking water. We had been some two and a half hours in crossing the lake.

The river resumed its broad quiet way as though it had left no tumult behind it. It had the dignity of age, was not now in that dark hurry to reach the sea. At Welaka one afternoon we left the hyacinths swirling leisurely and turned up our home river, the Ocklawaha. I thought in a panic, I shall never be happy on land again. I was afraid once more of all the painful circumstances of living.

But when the dry ground was under us, the world no longer fluid, I found a forgotten loveliness in all the things that have nothing to do with men. Beauty is pervasive, and fills, like perfume, more than the object that contains it. Because I had known intimately a river, the earth pulsed under me. The Creek was home. Oleanders were sweet past bearing, and my own shabby fields, weed-tangled, were newly dear. I knew, for a moment, that the only nightmare is the masochistic human mind.

23. Who owns Cross Creek?

*t*horeau went off to live in the woods alone, to find out what the world was like. Now a man may learn a deal of the general from studying the specific, whereas it is impossible to know the specific by studying the general. For that reason, our philosophers are usually the most unpractical of men, while very simple folk may have a great deal of wisdom. A friend of mine once entertained Einstein on her fishing yacht off Miami. She had ordered the most elegant of lunches put up by the most elegant of hotels. Einstein ate busily on his cold roast squab. He explored the interior and pulled out its stuffing with a finger that had measured the universe. The stuffing was a large French prune, soaked in sherry and stuffed in turn with an almond. The great man eyed it in horror and threw it overboard. He thought plainly that the gizzard had not been removed. All his knowledge of light and space had not fitted him to know that he would not, under any circumstances, find an appended gizzard in a roast squab served him on a yacht off Miami.

We at the Creek draw our conclusions about the world from our intimate knowledge of one small portion of it.

Old Boss said, "The Creek doesn't amount to anything. The people don't amount to anything. But if you're sick and have no money, they'll cook for you and fetch it to you, and they'll doctor you, and if you get past their doctoring, they'll send for a doctor and pay his bill. And if you die, they'll take up a collection and bury you. I figure it's just as close to Heaven here as any other place."

Martha and Old Boss are the best of us, and we trail on down through those of us doing the best we can with whatever we have to work with, to those who make no effort at all, and these lilies of the field are perhaps the most happily if the least profitably adjusted to life of us all. I think we may have more than the average share of tolerance and generosity. This is because life has not been easy for any of us, and because we live so close to one another's difficulties, in spite of our individualistic detachment, that when one of us suffers, the rest of us are outraged and wounded, too.

All of Cross Creek was disturbed when one of the women came close to dying through having "thrown away," as Martha puts it, an unborn child who had no right to enter the world under the handicap of an already over-large family burdened with poverty. Ordinarily Martha does not approve of such a "throwing away."

"I'se always taught my girls," she said, "to mind they manners with the men. But I'se told 'em, too, does you do wrong, now mind, does you, and you gets kotched—be lady enough to bring the child into the world."

In this particular case, she understood its exigencies. I do not know where or how Martha acquired her worldly wisdom, but she knew the woman must have a "remedy" against similar future catastrophes. She knew the best remedy recommended by the medical profession and knew its cost.

"I'se talked to some o' the other ladies at the Creek," she said, "an' times is so hard right now, cain't none of 'em contribute. Hit takes three dollars, and I figured you might like to know."

I gave her the three dollars to take to our neighbor, and the offer of the grove truck to take her to the doctor as soon as she was able. It is perhaps the strangest gift I have ever made.

We step on one another's toes at the Creek, inevitably, but forgiveness follows quickly. Mr. Martin forgave my shooting of his pig because I "talked so honest." We all forgave Henry his shooting of Samson, because after all he was one of us, and we loved the black rascal. Tom Glisson forgave me my injustice against him. Our feud was violent.

One day my beautiful pointer dog, Mandy, struggled home from her morning jaunt down the road and died within a few minutes in convulsions. She had been killed by strychnine poison. I do not know and perhaps shall never know who killed her, or whether the matter was an unaccountable accident. At any rate, I laid the blame on neighbor Tom, for it was reported to me soon after that he had been heard to say he would not have a female dog at Cross Creek. It seemed that backwoods morals were involved. The dog had been in season and I had kept her shut up past the presumably safe two weeks, then had set her loose. The backwoods is prudish, and the mating of animals is not believed to be a salutary thing for the young to observe. It seemed archaic to me to blame the female and not the aggressive males.

I broke off relations with Tom and his friendly family, forbade him to set foot on my land, even to drive out his cows, refused to listen to his explanations, and made dire threats in general. A year passed, a most unpleasant time, for all the Creek was divided. It was necessary for the Glissons to pass my gate with averted head, and when we met in the village grocery store, embarrassment took over the whole shabby building. At the end of the year, my fences were found cut, and the hogs and cattle of all the Creek were at large in my grove. I believe now that vagrant hunters had taken the easiest way to get themselves and their dogs across the property. At the time, nothing would do but Tom was the culprit.

I sent a note to him: "Tom Glisson. I wish to see you. Hurry up about it."

He came, and we laid the cards on the table. I stated my grievances, and one by one he made a fool of me. He had indeed said that he would not have a female dog at the Creek, but he had meant, not that he would take a hand to prevent another from having one, but that he himself would not choose to have one. He reminded me of his own family's love of animals.

"I couldn't lift my hand against a dumb brute," he said, and added, "nor, a speakin' one."

There was an unmistakable integrity in his facing of the facts, going into each situation in detail. His blue eyes were direct and clear. In a revelation, I knew the man's character. Suddenly he burst into tears.

"That note you sent me. I'm as white as you are. You wrote like I was a nigger."

I was sick with shame. I made my apologies, and I was in tears, too. He wiped his away with the back of his calloused hand.

"You abused me once, about the dog, and I forgive you then."

He laid his big hands on my shoulders.

"I'll forgive you again."

We shook hands and agreed to a fresh start.

"All we got to do," he said, "is jest talk things over and stick together."

I asked him then why another neighbor had insidiously tried to lay on him the blame about my dog. He thought deeply.

"All I can figure is, he's jealous. He wanted to make trouble for me. He ain't got anywhere in life. You know how hard me and my wife has worked. You know we want our young uns to get a better chance in life than we've done had. We've got ahead a mite by near about killin' ourselves, workin'. But some folks is jealous of another stridin'."

Tom is one of my best friends today. It makes one very humble to receive forgiveness one does not deserve.

There was mutual forgiveness, too, in a passing triangle at the Creek. Three people lived here for a brief time, a woman, her sweetheart and her husband.

Tom told me, "Luke found the pair of 'em off in the flat woods and he takened a notion to the woman. He washed her bottom and put a clean shift on her and brought 'em both here, all cozy-like."

The husband was much older than the woman and things seemed to go smoothly for a while. Then one day he announced that he was tired of fishing on the lake to make a living, while the newcomer stayed in the house with his wife. He would either stay at home, too, or the intruder could fish with him. The intruder meekly fished with him. While both were absent, their suspicions grew jointly. That strange community of men's reactions linked them together. The sweetheart moved away and the husband moved out.

Martha reported demurely, "Mr. Jackson done left he wife to her devices. I seed him settin' out to move acrost the lake. Him and his bed and his boat."

Soon after, the woman fell ill. Martha nursed her and we all sent her supplies. The doctor reported there was no hope for her. I suspect Martha of having a hand in the general reconciliation. Sweetheart and husband came back to the woman and took turns at taking care of her. The woman died and the two men went away together, and the last I heard were farming and sharing, like good bachelors, the housework.

I suppose there are a hundred other places where I might have found what I found at Cross Creek. George Sand wrote, in "La Mare au Diable":

"Nature possesses the secret of happiness, and no one has been able to steal it from her. The happiest of men would be he who, working intelligently and laboring with his hands, drawing comfort and liberty from the exercise of his intelligent strength, should have time to live through his heart and his brain, to comprehend his own work and that of God. Happiness would be wherever the mind, the heart and the arm should work together beneath the eye of Providence, so that a holy harmony should exist between the munificence of God and the rapture of the human soul."

This holy harmony is the ideal, but it does not take into account the dual nature of man and the dual nature of the universe. All life is a balance, when it is not a battle, between the forces of creation and the forces of destruction, between love and hate, between life and death. Perhaps it is impossible ever to say where one ends and the other begins, for even creation and destruction are relative. This morning I crushed a fuzzy black caterpillar. It was fulfilling its own destiny, trying to complete its own life cycle. Its only sin was that it was feeding on certain green leaves that I wished to look at. In the brief instant after the crushing and before its death, did its minute mind wonder why an unnamable catastrophe had overtaken it? When a human life is snuffed out untimely, can there be invisible forces whose wishes we offend? Can it be that one has eaten green leaves? We should be so happy to cooperate with the unvoiced demands if we were aware of them. The caterpillar would be quite willing to nibble in an adjacent field, if the completion of his life span could be so accomplished.

But in crushing the caterpillar, I have fed the ants. They are hustling to the feast, already tunnelling the body. The ants would applaud the treading of caterpillars. The death of a human feeds, apparently, nothing. Or are there psychic things that are nourished by our annihilation?

We know only that we are impelled to fight on the side of the creative forces. We know only that a sense of well-being sweeps over us when we have assisted life rather than destroyed it. There is often an evil satisfaction in hate, satisfaction in revenge, and satisfaction in killing. Yet when a wave of love takes over a human being, love of another human being, love of nature, love of all mankind, love of the universe, such an exaltation takes him that he knows he has put his finger on the pulse of the great secret and the great answer.

Here at Cross Creek we sense this, sometimes dimly, sometimes strongly. Because we have adapted ourselves, with affection, to a natural background that is congenial to us, we know that the struggle is better done in love than in hate. We feel a great pity for the industrial laborer who toils only for what it will bring him in pay, and will not do his work unless his pay pleases him. If we tillers of the soil sat down in a pet and refused to turn our furrows because our crops had failed us, the world would starve for all its riches. We feel as great a pity for the industrial capitalist who reckons living in terms of profit and loss. Profit and loss are incidental to life, and surely there is enough for us all. We know that work must be an intimate thing, the thing one would choose to do if one had, as Tom said, "gold buried in Georgia." We know above all that work must be beloved.

We know that in our relations with one another, the disagreements are unimportant and the union vital.

The question once arose, "Who owns Cross Creek?" It came to expression when Mr. Marsh Turner was turning his hogs and cattle loose on us and riding drunkenly across the Creek bridge to drive them home. Tom Morrison, who does not own a blade of corn at the Creek, but is yet part and parcel of it, became outraged by Mr. Marsh

Turner's arrogance. Tom stood with uplifted walking stick at the bridge, a Creek Horatio, and turned Mr. Marsh Turner back.

"Who do you think you are?" he demanded. "How come you figure you can turn your stock loose on us, and then ride up and down, whoopin' and hollerin'? You act like you own Cross Creek. You don't. Old Boss owns Cross Creek, and Young Miss owns it, and old Joe Mackay. Why, you don't own six feet of Cross Creek to be buried in."

Soon after this noble gesture was reported to me by Martha, I went across the Creek in April to gather early blackberries. I had not crossed the bridge for some weeks and I looked forward to seeing the magnolias in full bloom. The road is lined with magnolia trees and is like a road passing through a superb park. There were no magnolia blossoms. There were only tall, gray, rose-lichened trunks from which the branches had been cut. The pickers of magnolia leaves had passed through. These paid thieves come and go mysteriously every second or third year. One week the trees stand with broad outstretched branches, glossy of leaf, the creamy buds ready for opening. The next, the boughs have been cut close to the trunks, and it will be three years before there are magnolia blossoms again. After long inquiry, I discovered the use for the stripped leaves. They are used for making funeral wreaths. The destruction seemed to me a symbol of private intrusion on the right of all mankind to enjoy a universal beauty. Surely the loveliness of the long miles of magnolia bloom was more important to the living than the selling of the bronze, waxy leaves for funerals of the dead.

I had a letter from a friend at this time, saying, "I am a firm believer in property rights."

The statement disturbed me. What is "property" and who are the legitimate owners? I looked out from my veranda, across the acres of grove from which I had only recently been able to remove the mortgage. The land was legally mine, and short of long tax delinquency, nothing and nobody could take it from me. Yet if I did not take care of the land lovingly, did not nourish and cultivate it, it would revert to jungle. Was it mine to abuse or to neglect? I did not think so.

I thought of countless generations that had "owned" land. Of what did that ownership consist? I thought of the great earth, whirling in space. It was here ahead of men and could conceivably be here after them. How should one man say that he "owned" any piece or parcel of it? If he worked with it, labored to bring it to fruition, it seemed to me that at most he held it in fief. The individual man is transitory, but the pulse of life and of growth goes on after he is gone, buried under a wreath of magnolia leaves. No man should have proprietary rights over land who does not use that land wisely and lovingly. Steinbeck raised the same question in his *Grapes of Wrath*. Men who had cultivated their land for generations were dispossessed because banks and industrialists believed they could make a greater profit by turning over the soil to mass, mechanized production. But what will happen to that land when the industrialists themselves are gone? The earth will survive bankers and any system of government, capitalistic, fascist or bolshevist. The earth will even survive anarchy.

I looked across my grove, hard fought for, hard maintained, and I thought of other residents there. There are other inhabitants who stir about with the same sense of possession as my own. A covey of quail has lived for as long as I have owned the place in a bramble thicket near the hammock. A pair of blue-jays has raised its young, raucous-voiced and handsome, year after year in the hickory trees. The same pair of red-birds mates and nests in an orange tree behind my house and brings its progeny twice a year to the feed basket in the crepe myrtle in the front yard. The male sings with a *joie de vivre* no greater than my own, but in a voice lovelier than mine, and the female drops bits of corn into the mouths of her fledglings with as much assurance as though she paid the taxes. A black snake has lived under my bedroom as long as I have slept in it.

Who owns Cross Creek? The red-birds, I think, more than I, for they will have their nests even in the face of delinquent mortgages. And after I am dead, who am childless, the human ownership of grove and field and hammock is hypothetical. But a long line of red-birds and whippoorwills and blue-jays and ground doves will descend from the present owners of nests in the orange trees, and their claim will be less subject to dispute than that of any human heirs. Houses are individual and can be owned, like nests, and fought for. But what of the land? It seems to me that the earth may be borrowed but not bought. It may be used, but not owned. It gives itself in response to love and tending, offers its seasonal flowering and fruiting. But we are tenants and not possessors, lovers and not masters. Cross Creek belongs to the wind and the rain, to the sun and the seasons, to the cosmic secrecy of seed, and beyond all, to time.